COMMITMENT TO FULL EMPLOYMENT

COLUMBIA UNIVERSITY SEMINAR SERIES

The University Seminars at Columbia University welcomes this study, *Commitment to Full Employment: The Economics and Social Policy of William S. Vickrey,* edited by Aaron W. Warner, Mathew Forstater, and Sumner M. Rosen, to the Columbia University Seminars Series. The study has benefited from Seminar discussions and reflects the advantages of scholarly exchange provided by the Seminar Movement.

Aaron W. Warner
Director, University Seminars
Columbia University

COMMITMENT TO FULL EMPLOYMENT

The Economics and Social Policy of William S. Vickrey

AARON W. WARNER
MATHEW FORSTATER
SUMNER M. ROSEN
Editors

M.E. Sharpe
Armonk, New York
London, England

Library of Congress Cataloging-in-Publication Data

Commitment to full employment: the economics and social policy of William S. Vickrey /
edited by Aaron W. Warner, Mathew Forstater, and Sumner M. Rosen.
    p. cm. — (Columbia University seminar series)
Includes bibliographical references and index.
 ISBN 0-7656-0632-1 (alk. paper)
 ISBN 0-7656-0633-X
    1. Full employment policies. 2. Employment (Economic theory) I. Warner, Aaron W.,
1908– II. Forstater, Mathew, 1961– III. Rosen, Sumner M. IV. Vickrey, William S.
(William Spencer), 1914- V. Series.

HD5701.5 .C66 2000
339.5—dc21   99-059824

Printed in the United States of America

The paper used in this publication meets the minimum requirements of
American National Standard for Information Sciences
Permanence of Paper for Printed Library Materials,
ANSI Z 39.48-1984.

BM (c)   10   9   8   7   6   5   4   3   2   1
BM (c)   10   9   8   7   6   5   4   3   2   1

Contents

Selected Tables, Figures, and Charts

Tables

Figures

Charts

Robert Heilbroner

Foreword

The Trouble with Capitalism

Recently I have had occasion to reflect on an aspect of capitalism that I would have dearly liked to discuss with Bill Vickrey, a master at perceiving lurking problems in innocent-seeming oddities. It is the curious fact that the name of our economic order is no longer in good repute, at least in America. Pick up any textbook and count the number of times the treacherous term "capitalism" appears. In Gregory Mankiw's highly regarded introductory text, *Principles of Economics*, the word appears but once, in a brief section that compares the success of capitalism with the fate of Soviet communism. In Joseph Stiglitz's equally esteemed and even longer text, *Economics*, Mankiw is outdone: In Stiglitz's tome the word does not appear at all. Last but not least, the merest glance at the last ten years of the *American Economic Review* reveals the same abhorrence. I choose the most "official" of our journals to emphasize that my point is not just a matter of two idiosyncratic authors. Turn at random to issues of the *AER* during the last decade, and you will be able to count the dangerous word on the fingers of one hand—per issue, that is, not per article. By way of contrast, turn the pages of issues from the 1940s and 1950s and the term will be easy to find.

Why this curious abhorrence of a word that seems to me indispensable? How is one to introduce a student to the workings of the socioeconomic formation in which he or she lives without giving it some name to distinguish it from other forms of economic organization? One answer is that textbooks do indeed give it a name, but not a satisfactory one. Capitalism is often called the "Market System" or the "System of Free Enterprise." The trouble is that these names imply that a market system or free enterprise is all there is to capitalism, thereby missing key aspects of the whole, such as the role of government in establishing and protecting both markets and business, or the unique properties and attributes of capital—a word as elusive as it is essential.

What, then, are the elements that must be made explicit to the textbook reader? I shall be brief, insofar as I am only laying the basis for a much more difficult question to come—namely, why we are so reluctant to say the word I shall now quickly spell out.

Capitalism, as it is described, tacitly or explicitly, by every great economist from Adam Smith on, has three clearly differentiated systemic properties. The first is that its energy derives neither from the quiet but powerful pursuit of traditional tasks, nor from obedience to the iron, although vulnerable, hand of command. It is supplied by a drive for capital.

Capital, it cannot be too strongly emphasized, is not wealth. Wealth is static, capital is dynamic. Wealth retains its form and shape for years, even centuries. Capital may assume many forms from one day or even hour to the next—an entry in a book of accounts one minute, a stack of currency the next. Whatever its appearance, we find capital only in societies whose economic energy is derived primarily from the pursuit of money, not as a hoard, but as a means to accumulate still more money. This end is largely achieved by using money to hire labor, including managerial labor, to make goods and services that will be offered for sale at a profit. This is the fundamental source of the capital accumulation whence capitalism derives both its name and its essential identity.

All this is, or certainly should be, elementary to economics students who meet the word "capital" again and again in their texts. It is the "ism" that is lacking, the syllable that converts capital from a mere technical term to a social order in which that term comes to life as the basis on which a social order is built.

After capital come markets—not merely as trading places, but as the institution that normally provides capitalism with its characteristic means of guidance. Indeed, the market system, coupled with the drive for capital, is what most decisively separates capitalism from traditional and command societies. It is the source of the economic enrichment that is undoubtedly the decisive contribution of capitalism to economic history.

There remains to be mentioned only one last identifying feature of capitalism. This is the special place of government, as unique to a system of capitalism as are the quite different structures of government in various command societies. In a word, government in a capitalist society constitutes a "sector," not a stratum, and its function, beyond providing defense and law and order, is to supply the nation with necessary or useful, but nonprofitable, outputs that the society as a whole requires. Among these, policies to minimize the threat to employment from the effects of capitalism's incessant pressures of change rank high, especially in the period since the Great Depression.

All this is preamble, hopefully useful, leading to the question of this essay: Why is the term "capitalism" so sedulously avoided in textbooks, the very place where its presence would appear to be most useful?

One answer that comes to mind is that the word is abhorrent because it evokes the historic derogation of capitalism as a system morally, as well as operationally, inferior to communism or some other form of socialism. Oddly enough, however, during the 1930s, when this evaluation of capitalism was widespread, the term "capitalism" was freely used in basic texts. Hence, that hardly seems a convincing reason for its present-day disappearance.

A second explanation might be that economists forget or ignore the interdependence of the three main institutional features of capitalism, which causes them to forget or ignore that "markets" or "business" are not sufficient to identify the complex reality of the social order in question. I can only say that this seems to me a plausible reason for students to make this error, but hardly for professors.

That leaves one further rationale, which, to my mind, appears the most likely. It is the increasingly explicit desire of economists to consider their task as related to that of science; as a consequence, to avoid words, such as capitalism, that unmistakably announce their political nature and the conflicts over the role of government that follow. From a kindlier perspective, there is also a more respectable reason for this search for scientific status. It is that causal sequences abound in the workings of capitalism, strongly suggesting the cause–effect relationships characteristic of scientific inquiry. I know of no other field of social activity in which such stimulus–response effects exist, whence comes a highly understandable tendency to interpret economic behavior as displaying scientific attributes.

Would it be wisest, then, to acquiesce in the avoidance of the term "capitalism"? Here I find it necessary to proceed directly to what I see as a curious central issue. It is the fatal confusion posed by the use of the *same word* to hide *different attributes* in true scientific work and the work of economic inquiry.

The crucial word is "behavior." When used by scientists, it refers to changes or movements in the objects that come under its scrutiny—the behavior of electrons and protons, for example. In the work of social explanation, such as economics, behavior also describes movements or changes, such as the behavior of buyers and sellers, or employers and workers. What, then, is the passable divide? It is the absence, to the best of our knowledge or imagination, of any element of *intent* in the "behavior" of objects studied by scientific inquiry, compared with its unmistakable presence in the behavior to which social inquiry directs its attention. More important yet, without the element of intent, social behavior becomes meaningless in the only terms we can apply to it, whereas in quite the opposite manner, the introduction of intent makes scientific behavior quite incomprehensible.

I can now conclude very briefly. If capitalism, like hunting and gathering or feudal or socialist or other forms of social order, is a *scientific* entity, it is extra-existential in nature, a prison, not an abode. I suggest that we avoid this moral and intellectual incarceration by using, whenever needed, the ten-letter word that is at the center of this short essay. It will serve to concentrate our attention where it belongs—utilizing the marvelous capacities of science better to understand the workings of the larger world within which we exist, wherein we can utilize our existential as well as functional economic knowledge both to understand and to seek to better capitalism; perhaps one day even to supersede it.

Acknowledgments

This book grew out of a symposium held at Columbia University in November of 1998 in commemoration of the 1996 Nobel Laureate William S. Vickrey. We would like to thank the University Seminars of Columbia University, the Jerome Levy Economics Institute of Bard College, the Graduate Faculty of Political and Social Science of the New School for Social Research, the National Jobs for All Coalition, and the Center for Full Employment and Price Stability for supporting the conference. We are grateful for the funds and technical support provided by University Seminars at Columbia that made publication of this book possible.

We owe a special debt of gratitude to the staff of University Seminars and especially to Janet Cavallero whose valuable assistance in organizing the symposium and bringing this volume into print is deeply appreciated.

Aaron W. Warner
Mathew Forstater
Sumner M. Rosen

Aaron W. Warner

Introduction

The Commitment to Full Employment: Macroeconomics and Social Policy in Memory of William S. Vickrey

Essays in this volume were contributed by participants in a symposium in honor of William Vickrey that took place in November 1998.

Vickrey, who received the 1996 Nobel Prize in economic science, was McVickar Professor of Political Economy at Columbia University in New York City. Among many distinctions, he had served as president of the American Economic Association, from 1992 to 1993, and was designated a Distinguished Fellow in 1978. He was a Fellow of the Econometric Society and of the American Academy of Arts and Sciences.

A distinguished contributor in many fields of micro- and macroeconomics and social policy, Vickrey wrote and lectured extensively in the last years of his life, expressing his commitment to full employment as a prerequisite for a decent standard of living for all. He died tragically in 1996, just a few days after the announcement of his Nobel Prize. His friend and long-time colleague, C. Lowell Harriss, a contributor to this volume, accepted the prize in Stockholm on behalf of Vickrey.

Although acknowledged by the economics profession as a brilliant theorist, Vickrey was impatient with theorizing for the sake of theorizing. His interest in theory was always related to its relevance to policy issues. Theory was a way to understand the economy so that he could design policies and new institutions to make the economy operate more efficiently and fairly. One commentator has correctly observed that Vickrey possessed a unique combination of mastery of economic analysis and passionate concern for human beings. A deeply religious and moral person, Vickrey had become increasingly articulate in his later years in condemning the toleration of un-employment, which he regarded as an unnecessary evil. In particular, he assailed the view that unemployment was necessary to hold down inflation. It was his contention that an appropriate policy to deal with inflation was to adjust the institutions of the economy so that lower unemployment was con-sistent with the control of inflation. In his judgment, economists have a moral obligation to reduce unemployment. The goal, in Vickrey's view, was to achieve what he described as "chock-full employment."

The contributions in this volume expand and elaborate issues relevant to Vickrey's focus on full employment, taking Vickrey's work as a point of departure. Topics addressed divide between full-employment theory and policy and those focusing on related social policy issues. The volume con-cludes with two previously unpublished papers by Vickrey that deal with many of the issues discussed in these papers.

As one of the basic economic and social issues of our time, full-employment policy has appeared in many contexts. Several of the contributors to this volume begin their papers with quotations or references to Sir William Beveridge's 1945 dictum in England that full employment exists when there are as many unfilled job openings as there are individuals seeking work. In this country, there have been a number of legislative measures dealing with employment policy, beginning with the Employment Act of 1946 and in-cluding, among others, the Manpower and Training Act of 1962, the Com-prehensive Employment and Training Act (CETA) of 1973, which established the National Commission for Manpower Policy as a statutory body, and the Humphrey–Hawkins Employment and Balanced Growth Act of 1978. In addition to legislative measures, employment policy has been a concern of the Council of Economic Advisors under a succession of presidential admin-istrations. In spite of the many attempts to formulate a national employment policy, the challenge still exists. As set forth in the Preamble of the Employ-ment Act of 1946, "The Congress declares that it is the continuing policy and responsibility of the Federal government to use all practicable means consis-tent with its needs and obligations and other considerations of national policy . . . to promote maximum employment, production and purchasing power." The question of the meaning of "maximum employment" remains of critical concern to those involved with macroeconomic policy.

It is well recognized that the fear of inflation stands as a barrier to achiev-ing a macroeconomic government policy that would achieve full employ-ment in the Beveridge sense. As exemplified during the 1960s by the Phillips curve, it was believed by many that a fairly stable relationship could be main-tained between a specified unemployment level and a reasonable level of inflation. When the economy later experienced the simultaneous increase in rates of unemployment and inflation, the relationship posited by the Phillips curve became untenable, and a new approach became necessary. Basically, the question raised takes the following form: When is the unemployment rate too low to cause a spiraling inflation or too high to cause a deflationary trend? Many believe that between the two, there is an employment rate at which some sort of steady state is possible. This is usually called the "natural rate of unemployment." It suggests, although evidence is weak, that something around 5.5 or 6 percent unemployment is the "natural rate" in the United States.

The strong economy of the 1990s has apparently undermined the theory of a "natural rate of unemployment," a notion Vickrey had attacked vigorously from its inception. In David Colander's speech given at the American Economics Association luncheon honoring Vickrey after his death ("Was Vickrey 10 Years Ahead of the Profession in Micro?"), Colander stated:

> For most of us interested in the spread of ideas, the introduction of the natural rate as the fulcrum for economic policy is an interesting case study. It caught on because it fit in the data of the 1970s better than did the standard Phillips curve. It has, however, never provided an especially good statistical fit in the data, and in the 1990s, it has failed miserably. . . . Given recent experience it is clear that the natural rate theory has provided a false certainty about policy prescriptions. It should . . . be declared dead, and given a proper burial, just as the false certainty of fine tuning was declared dead some thirty years ago.

Colander, who has also contributed a significant paper to this volume, had more to say about the "natural rate theory" in his AEA talk. He asks: "What theory are we going to replace it with?" He suggests a theory that might be called a "natural range of unemployment theory," which he explains at some length in the current volume as having a "complexity foundation."

Several contributors to this volume have discussed theories relating to full employment and their implications for policy. The paper by Mathew Forstater, "Savings-Recycling Public Employment: Vickrey's Assets-Based Approach to Full Employment and Price Stability," presents an analysis of Vickrey's approach to macroeconomic processes as evidenced in his writings. Forstater reviews Vickrey's commitment to full employment as indicated in a series of papers written in the last years of his life.

Forstater, in his review of Vickrey's full-employment policy, determines that for Vickrey, the key policy instrument for achieving full employment is the necessary recycling of net nominal savings to achieve full-employment levels of output and income. Essential to the achievement of this result is the government budget. For Vickrey, the main task for economists is to devise means for the necessary recycling of net nominal savings without there being unexpected changes in the rate of inflation or deflation. Vickrey questioned the widely held view that there is a non-accelerating inflation rate of unemployment (NAIRU) and the belief that there is a trade-off between unemployment and inflation. In his view, unemployment is not needed to control inflation. Following an analysis of savings and investment theory, Vickrey argues that the inadequate recycling of the full employment level of savings through investment by private enterprise necessitates government spending (that is, deficit spending) in order to achieve the desired full employment level. Vickrey also concluded that a new tool would be needed to complement conventional fiscal and monetary measures to accomplish the macroeconomic goals of promoting full employment, stable prices, and economic growth.

Forstater sets forth Vickrey's proposals in considerable detail and formulates a comprehensive view of their theoretical underpinnings. Many of the findings are relevant to current problems and policy debates. The need for deficit spending is explained. The national debt, it is asserted, is not a burden on future generations. Assertions that deficits cause inflation, high interest rates, or the crowding out of private investment are refuted. In regard to current international problems, Vickrey expressed considerable concern. In his view, countries are increasingly unable to rely on conventional approaches to counter recessions and depressions. He warned against growing calls for budget balancing, decreasing the deficit, and running budget surpluses to pay off the national debt. With particular reference to the United States, he concluded that we are woefully ill-prepared for the next economic downturn. Conventional fiscal and monetary policy, Vickrey asserted, is not sufficient to deal with a significant reduction in output and income and with rising unemployment. What is needed to deal with the macroeconomic challenges of modern society, he concluded, is a Savings-Recycling Public Employment Plan that can provide the automatic stabilizer the system requires.

Of necessity, the foregoing depiction of Vickrey's views is drastically curtailed in this introductory statement. They are considered in greater relevant detail, however, in other contexts. Dimitri Papadimitriou ("[Full] Employment Policy: Theory and Practice") explores the extent to which conventional measurements of unemployment rates, even when, as now, they indicate a full employment level with low and stable inflation, do not represent the true unemployment level. Apart from the importance of "disguised" unemployment, there are perhaps millions of potential workers who could work if jobs were made available. Papadimitriou turns his attention to earlier attempts to address unemployment through the intervention of government. After exploring the inadequacies of previous efforts to achieve lasting positive results, two questions are posed: (1) Is this the best we can do in terms of prosperity? (2) Are we prepared to meet the challenges of the next downturn? Setting forth criteria for a suitable policy to meet these challenges, Papadimitriou then examines a number of proposed measures that have received substantial currency. The preferred measure, in his judgment and based on his analysis and the detailed study by a group of researchers at the Levy Institute, is a proposal for government as the employer of last resort (ELR). The underlying theory of the proposal is examined in some detail. Papadimitriou evaluates a number of measures currently proposed to secure full employment, including reduction of the workweek and employment subsidies, such as the Earned Income Tax Credit (EITC) and the negative income tax. He concludes that a preferable method is to have government become the employer of last resort. Under this plan, he suggests, government would provide a job guarantee and could promote full employment without inflationary pressures and structural rigidities.

Pursuing a similar theme from another perspective, Philip Harvey ("Direct Job Creation") notes that policy debates during the twentieth century have been dominated by the different views of the causes of joblessness. He classifies these as the behaviorist, structuralist, and job shortage views. Emphasizing his support of the job shortage approach, Harvey argues that, according to empirical evidence, job shortage exists not only during recession, but during all phases of the business cycle. To remedy aggregate job shortages, Harvey proposes a strategy of direct job creation. He notes that in previous writing, he had indicated that direct public service job creation programs had taken their inspiration from New Deal initiatives, namely, the Civilian Conservation Corps (CCC) and the Works Progress Administration (WPA), and that such programs can provide an efficient and cost-effective way of achieving the functional equivalent of full employment. In the present paper, he explores the question of why the direct job creation strategy only occasionally attracts significant support.

In describing the advantages of a program of direct job creation, Harvey stresses issues of program cost and the impact of the program on inflation. Selecting the ten-year period from 1967 to 1976, a period of exceptionally high unemployment, he estimates, using a variety of relevant assumptions, that the cost of a direct job creation program could have averaged $213 billion per year. This, he contends, would not have been an unprecedented expenditure for a major social insurance benefit. He also calculates offsetting savings and revenues, which would have covered a substantial portion of the total program cost. Since direct job creation would lower the rate of unemployment, the impact on inflation would naturally be of concern. Interestingly, he contends, direct job creation may be the least inflationary way to achieve full employment.

The Keynesian underpinning of Vickrey's approach to full employment is brought out by David Colander in his paper, "Vickrey, Macro Policy, and Chock-Full Employment." A former Vickrey student and later a consultant on many of Vickrey's macroeconomic proposals, Colander informs us that Vickrey was an Old Keynesian supporter of functional finance. As such, he advocated a greater expansiveness of monetary and fiscal policy than was the current vogue. Although an early convert to the Walrasian general equilibrium theory that postulated a single equilibrium state, Vickrey came to see the economy as capable of achieving a variety of unemployment equilibriums and to regard the economy as a multiple-equilibrium economy. According to Colander, the macro policy question for Vickrey concerned what policies should be used to get the economy to a desirable equilibrium. His support of substantial deficits can be understood in this light.

Expanding on Vickrey, Colander states his own view that there is no one model of the economy that is appropriate for all times. The job of the policy-oriented economist, he contends, is to select the right model for the time, not to provide a single model for all time. The model selected by Colander, as indicated earlier, is "complexity foundation." It deals explicitly with the possibility of multiple equilibriums. It incorporates an explanation of how and why markets develop. Colander recognizes that his proposal cannot use existing formal analytic theory. He shies away from deductive theorizing for complex systems such as the macroeconomy. In its place, he offers an inductive approach. His direction is toward building real-world institutions into working models. As applied to Vickrey's chock-full employment, the policy analysis is directed to specifying alternative institutions that lead to preferable results. He also proposes a "real" theory of inflation, not centered on monetary policy but on institutional processes. Colander does not hold that there is no relationship between unemployment and inflation, only that within the economy's normal range, the connection is weak. Seeing inflation and unemployment as the results of separable real processes leads to thinking of macro policy in quite different ways. We are also reminded of Vickrey's reaction to fear of deficits based on false arguments and unproven allegations. We are informed that, in Vickrey's view, if deficit spending to increase employment does not cause inflation, that is great. If it does cause inflation, then it is time to get going with building institutions that stop inflation. Colander writes in this spirit.

Edward Nell, in his detailed exposition, "The Simple Theory of Unemployment," takes exception to the need for new and complicated theories to deal with macroeconomic issues. He regards Colander's approach, for example, as unnecessarily complex. Nell provides a theoretical model for investigating macroeconomic problems, including questions relating to

Vickrey's proposals for achieving full employment. Not satisfied with general statements of principles, he provides an approach to solving technical issues using conventional Keynesian methods of analysis. In this respect, his contribution to this volume is unique.

With the aid of multiple diagrams, Nell demonstrates that adequate tools exist in the classical repertory to study the economy as an evolving system. From a few basic assumptions of market forces, the model is shown to cover major topics of policy concern—growth, profits and wages, unemployment, and the government budget. He then extends the model to include money and interest. The theory of unemployment is described at length.

The scarcity theory of value, in Nell's view, leads to unnecessary complexity in explaining the existence of unemployment. He proposes rejection of the scarcity theory in favor of a reproduction theory that reveals the economy as an evolving system from one period of development to another, as in the decline of a craft economy to the rise of mass production. He states that the economy transforms itself as it grows and that the process is one of *transformational growth*. The paper concludes with the application of the reproduction theory to the proposal for government as an employer of last resort. The lost advantage of a built-in automatic stabilizer in the flexible prices and wages of the craft era can be restored in the less flexible market industries of the mass production era by "a policy-designed large-scale counter-cyclical government program." This analysis of such a program, Nell states, can be taken as an example of sensible thinking about unemployment. The essay concludes with a reaffirmation of the advantages of a simple approach.

C. Lowell Harriss, in his provocative essay, "Fuller Employment: William Vickrey's Challenge to Economists," prods macroeconomists to undertake additional study in pursuing Vickrey's challenge to do more to reduce the losses to the economy resulting from unemployment. While agreeing that such losses exist and should be addressed, he cautions that the results of government measures such as those proposed by Vickrey, even when well intentioned, may have a less than desirable impact on individual freedoms. This would apply to proposals for pumping more money into the economic system, as in Vickrey's views on the recycling of savings and on the spending of the deficit. Questions are raised regarding many aspects and implications of the Vickrey approach to full employment, such as the relation of wage rates to the price level, and Vickrey's proposed programs for preventing inflation. In considering the problem of disposing of otherwise unused funds, that is, budget surpluses, Harriss comments wisely that new realities may call for policies "whose justification rests on unfamiliar economic analysis."

In many respects, Harriss's comments may be considered by economists as a call to action to validate Vickrey's concerns. The intent is to expand the range of inquiry and to reconcile differences in views and approaches. Although he does not project a theory of his own, he clearly reminds his readers of the concerns of orthodox theorists as they confront new challenges. As pointed out by David Colander in his paper, Vickrey had no hesitation about confronting orthodox theorists with what for them were novel propositions. Harriss describes in some detail the range of issues deserving of study.

The many areas for potential study are beyond the scope of the current volume, but significant areas deserving of analysis and research are included. The views expressed by Harriss reflect thoughtful consideration of a vast array of issues, many controversial, that have challenged the profession he has served for many years. As he was a long-time colleague and close friend of Vickrey, we may assume that he has engaged Vickrey in discussion of many of these issues.

Although Vickrey did not theorize specifically about the welfare state, the linkage between full employment and welfare considerations is clearly evident. Gertrude Schaffner Goldberg, in her paper, "Full Employment and the Future of the Welfare State," builds on the theme that Sir William Beveridge treated full employment not only as a means of financing income security, but also as an important social welfare goal. This theme is supported to some extent by reference to the Swedish model, that is, Sweden's postwar comprehensive social welfare policy, which for a time implemented ideas akin to those of Beveridge. The key factor was the integration of progressive economic and social policies. Unfortunately, in Sweden's current economic phase, full employment is less a goal, leaving the social welfare program, such as it is, burdened with the high cost of unemployment. The paper makes a case for restoring full employment as a primary objective goal of public policy and as a necessary ingredient in a program of social welfare. At the same time, it is asserted that full employment by itself does not obviate the need of social welfare, even in economies with adequate wages. When properly integrated, for example, full employment and social welfare in the United States could afford advantages far beyond alleviating the poverty of vulnerable populations, such as introducing programs of universal health insurance, family allowances, subsidized child care, and support for single-parent families.

In describing the current widespread retreat from full employment and the consequent loss of confidence in the affordability and effectiveness of the welfare state, Goldberg indicates some of the contributing factors to this decline. As in the Swedish example, these include the power of business interests, the pressures of globalization, the implementation of nonliberal policies, and the abandonment of the historic commitment to full employment.

These issues are given further emphasis and are expanded in the paper of Helen Lachs Ginsburg, "A Humanistic Concept of Full Employment Transcends the Welfare State." The main concepts are set forth in sections labeled "How a Humanistic Concept of Full Employment Transcends the Welfare State"; "Why Real Full Employment Means Decent Wages"; "How Full Employment Enhances Human Welfare by Making It Easier to Transform Workplaces"; and "How Unemployment Can Lead to Negative Ideological Shifts, While Full Employment Makes It Easier to Maintain Social and Intergenerational Solidarity." The paper is less focused on the Swedish experience and is much more a generalized discussion with frequent references to relevant sources, including proposals by Vickrey. It is a useful companion piece to the antecedent paper by Goldberg.

Sumner Rosen's paper ("Economics and the Welfare State") concludes the section on issues relating to the welfare state. The Swedish economy is again the central focus for an analytic study of the interrelationship of economic policy and social welfare, which are said to be "interactive and interdependent in theory and practice." This idea has particular relevance to the "social democratic regimes that held power in most of the postwar period." As populations age and become more susceptible to chronic illnesses and debilitating infirmities, social welfare provisions become increasingly vital. Families and communities, Rosen asserts, "cannot be held hostage to economic policy makers and large private economic entities that exert disproportional influence on labor market dynamics and national political deliberations." Full employment economies, he continues, cannot flourish without providing services to meet the needs "of not only the young, the old, and the poor, but the working-age population as well."

Rosen explores at some length the origin, successful implementation, and reasons for the eventual decline of the Swedish model. He concludes that "Sweden's record over decades tells us that full employment, comprehensive social welfare protection, national prosperity, and steadily rising living standards could be achieved and sustained for a long time."

Statistical studies have consistently shown a wide range of unemployment rates for different demographic groups. Heather Boushey, in her innovative study of discrimination, "Rethinking Full Employment: Unemployment, Wages, and Race," selects gender and race discrimination in employment as subjects for intensive investigation. Although usually treated as a microeconomic subject for analysis, Boushey believes the dynamics of discrimination are macroeconomic in nature. We are also shown that aggregate unemployment data, as often relied upon in dealing with studies of discriminatory behavior, do not reveal the whole story, and that there is a need to look at disaggregated numbers to get the full picture. Her findings lead to the conclusion that we cannot commit to full employment without simultaneously committing to ending discrimination in the labor market, and that seeing discrimination and full employment as linked requires rethinking of our models of the labor market.

Boushey presents a model for the labor market based on the dynamic between unemployment and wages. In her assessment, a theory that accounts for the role of discrimination in regulating wages is better equipped to lead to a full-employment economy. This conviction in turn leads to her consideration of the "social structures of insulation," that is, that workers have different degrees of insulation from unemployment or underemployment. In the United States, gender and race serve as allocative mechanisms for determining the degree of insulation. Boushey presents voluminous data showing how gender and race discrimination permeate the labor market. The forms taken by discriminatory tactics, as dealt with in her studies, are wage inequality, employment inequality, and occupational segregation. She concludes that an understanding of the macroeconomic mechanisms that engender discrimination resulting from inequality leads to taking a different approach to the achievement of full employment.

Paul Davidson ("Commitment to Full Employment in a Global Economy") turns our attention to global problems that would have concerned Vickrey. He pays homage to Vickrey as a spokesperson who would have attracted attention to Keynesian verities regarding the role of government in exercising a "guiding influence" in support of the maintenance of effective demand at a full employment level. He refers to Vickrey's "Trans-Keynesian Manifesto" that goes beyond Keynes to deal with the economic environment of the twenty-first century. The manifesto sets forth a number of Vickrey's proposals, but Davidson focuses in his paper on only one: Vickrey's proposition, namely, that full employment in open economies requires floating exchange rates. In supporting this position, Vickrey recognized the danger of generating speculative gyrations in foreign exchange markets, but expressed his belief that the costs of such an occurrence would be of little moment. Davidson, on the other hand, asserts that current experience casts doubts on Vickrey's claims. It appears, he states, that speculative gyrations in international capital markets can inflict long-run and serious damage.

Davidson reinforces his argument by referring to stability and growth in the United States during the Bretton Woods period 1950–1973, a period of the gold standard and rigidly controlled exchange rates. Since 1973, he states, enterprise has slowly become enmeshed in an ever-increasing whirlpool of speculation. Instead of the utopian benefits that were to follow, he continues, the post–Bretton Woods system of flexible exchange rates combined with financial and labor market deregulation generated a growing international monetary crisis as well as global unemployment on a grand scale.

Utilizing the innovative principles recommended by Keynes for the postwar international monetary system, Davidson believes a system can be designed that would prevent currency fires while promoting global prosperity. Going beyond the question of the advantages and disadvantages of fixed versus flexible exchange rates, he depicts in some detail the foreign exchange difficulties emerging after World War II that, in his analysis, resulted in the loss of the last vestiges of Keynes's enlightened international monetary approach, with adverse consequences for the global economy. This is followed by a proposal for a post-Keynesian international payments system.

It is not possible in a short space to do justice to the elaborate arrangements proposed by Davidson for the international payments system. He does not propose a global supranational central bank, but rather a more modest undertaking to obtain an international agreement that does not require participating countries to forgo control of their banking systems or their independent national fiscal policies. What is proposed is a clearing union, that is, a bookkeeping clearing institution to keep track of trends and payments among the various trading regions and to have some mutually agreed-upon rules "to create and reflux liquidity" while maintaining the international purchasing power of the international currency. This is followed by a number of provisions to meet criteria that had been laid down by Keynes. The proposed system is complex, carefully crafted, and innovative, and deserves careful study. The author recognizes that his proposal is in an exploratory stage and invites comparison with other proposed innovations. He proclaims that the health of the world economic system will not permit us to muddle through! Because of its relation to the purpose of this volume, namely to explore issues relevant to Vickrey, it seems pertinent to quote Davidson's concluding paragraph:

> Once we have reformed the international monetary payments system so that nations do not have to fear balance-of-payments problems, then the leaders of the major nations of the world can take steps to stimulate domestic aggregate demand in line with Vickrey's trans-Keynesian manifesto without having to fear adverse economic consequences for their own nation. Then, and only then, we may restore a golden age of economic development to our planet.

Not surprisingly, Davidson's far-reaching innovative proposals reach a critical audience. Thomas Palley ("Why a Global Clearing Union Based on Fixed Exchange Rates Won't Work") has made a formidable reply. Starting with Davidson's attack on flexible exchange rates as the cause of financial instability in international trade, Palley states that, in reality, the alleged damage has been caused not by flexible exchange rates but by excessive capital mobility. It is not at all clear, according to Palley, that fixed exchange rates had much to do with the prosperity of the 1950s and 1960s, as Davidson claims. Other factors, he contends, were of greater importance, including strict capital controls and, most importantly, rising production capacity. In short, the prosperity of the period was the result of Keynesian macroeconomic policy combined with the right structural conditions. In fact, Palley continues, fixed exchange rates not only failed to be of help, but may actually have hindered in ways he describes.

In regard to Davidson's proposed international clearing union, Palley concedes that the motivation is right, but he finds many problems with the scheme. Although Davidson describes his proposals as constituting a clearinghouse, it is in fact a de facto global central bank. Moreover, while redesigning the international financial structure to eliminate instability and deflationary tendencies is surely necessary, Palley argues, it is only part of the solution. To restore the equitable pro-growth environment that prevailed in the period 1950–1973, according to Palley, would require not only restoration of expansionary domestic monetary and fiscal policies but, most importantly, the restoration of a balance of power between capital and labor.

A second response to Davidson's proposal comes from John Langmore ("Employment and International Financial Markets"). Langmore agrees that anarchic international financial markets can cause massive destruction and be a major impediment to economic and social development. He is favorably inclined to Davidson's proposal, which he regards as one of a number of suggestions that should be seriously evaluated. It has become clear, he states, that strengthening the international financial institutional structure is essential. An open, accountable process is needed, but does not exist at present. Referring to the hegemonic superpower management of global affairs, he concludes that there may be an opportunity at the United Nations in 2001 for a global conference on finance.

James K. Galbraith ("The Keynesian Economics of Unemployment and Inequality"), in his remarks at the conclusion of the Vickrey symposium, offers some spirited and incisive comments on a number of issues relevant to Vickrey's quest for full employment. In keeping with Vickrey's belief that full employment is not just a political matter and that the laws of economics do not preclude its achievement, Galbraith both supports this view and argues for a practical approach to its attainment. In the course of his discussion, he reminds us importantly that "economics is unitary; it cannot be divided effectively in some grand ideological compromise into separate domains of micro and macro."

Galbraith's treatment of the demise of NAIRU is unique. Although it is clear, he states, that NAIRU has lost its value as a policy tool, its practical influence remains because people act in the belief that policymakers continue to act in the spirit of NAIRU. He cites as an example the adverse reaction of the stock market to any progress against unemployment, regardless of economic conditions. On the other hand, he points out that the termination of any ostensible linkage between low unemployment and expectations of rising inflation is consistent with Keynesian theory and, by implication, with the views of Vickrey and himself. It is also, he comments, a practical triumph for Keynesian economics.

The essay continues with challenging questions and insights on significant issues of contemporary importance, such as the United States' ability to adjust to global challenges rapidly enough to regain control of the world economy, the need to bring proposals dealing with employment problems into useful and effective contact with the policy-making process, and reconsideration of the structure of the economy in the light of technological and other significant developments. Galbraith concludes with a discussion of his own current research involvements.

Vickrey, in receiving the Nobel Prize, had hoped that the award would afford him a bully pulpit to expound on his views to the economics profession and to the makers of economic policy. The symposium on the commitment to full employment was conceived as a means of honoring Vickrey and exploring his views as he might have wished. It is anticipated that many lectures and symposiums will follow, and that scholars will find this an appropriate vehicle for expressing their interest and concern for developing macroeconomic theorizing for bettering the condition of mankind.

The two articles appended to the volume were proposed and circulated by Vickrey before his death. They remind us of the range of Vickrey's interests, and the tremendous impact of his contribution to the long-standing controversies regarding employment policies. The diversity of the articles contributed to this volume exemplify the importance of Vickrey's proposals and the value of his impact on the understanding of the economic system. That the importance of his ideas will be long-lasting is a fitting tribute to an exceptionally gifted scholar.

William S. Vickrey

William Spencer Vickrey was awarded the Nobel Prize in economics in October 1996; he was a joint winner with James A. Mirrlees of Cambridge University.

Vickrey was born in Victoria, British Columbia in 1914, where his maternal grandfather had established the Spencer's department stores. His father, a Congregational minister, raised money after World War I for the relief of Greeks and Armenians forcibly displaced from Turkey. Vickrey received his elementary and secondary education in Europe and the United States, graduating from Phillips Andover Academy in 1931. He received a B.S. in mathematics from Yale University in 1935, followed by graduate work in economics at Columbia University where he received the M.A. degree in 1937. He then worked for the National Resources Planning Board in Washington, D.C. and the Division of Tax Research in the U.S. Treasury Department.

As a conscientious objector during World War II, part of his alternate service was spent in designing a new inheritance tax for Puerto Rico. Columbia University awarded him the Ph.D. in economics in 1948. His doctoral dissertation, *Agenda for Progressive Taxation*, was reprinted as an "economic classic" in 1972.

In 1946 he began his teaching career at Columbia University as a lecturer in economics. He became a full professor in 1958 and was named McVickar Professor of Political Economy in 1971. He was chairman of the Department of Economics from 1964 to 1967 and retired as McVickar Professor Emeritus in 1982.

Vickrey's long research career covered a wide range of subjects. The first of many involving efficient pricing of public utilities was done in 1939 and 1940 for the Twentieth Century Fund and dealt with electric power. In 1951, he studied transit fares in New York City for The Mayor's Committee on Management Survey. He was a member of the 1950 Shoup mission that developed a comprehensive program for revising the tax system of Japan. He lectured widely and served as a consultant in the United States and overseas and to the United Nations.

He was elected to the National Academy of Science and in 1992 served as president of the American Economic Association. Vickrey received an honorary degree from the University of Chicago in 1979, and was a Fellow of the Econometric Society.

He was a founding member of Taxation, Resources, and Economic Development (TRED) and was a member of many professional and civic organizations and an active supporter of organizations promoting world peace. He belonged to The Religious Society of Friends.

A 1994 volume, *Public Economics* (Cambridge University Press), contains a complete bibliography of Vickrey's work, listing 8 books, 139 articles, 27 reviews, and 61 unpublished articles and notes.

Vickrey was married to Cecile Thompson in 1951. They lived in Hastings-on-Hudson in New York. He died in October 1996.

Vickrey spoke and wrote with passion about unemployment and the waste of life in undesired idleness. He is remembered to have characterized unemployment as analogous to vandalism and inflation analogous to embezzlement. Vickrey believed that employment conditions could be greatly improved and considered that it was the obligation of economists to marshal their abilities and efforts toward the goal of achieving truly full employment.

COMMITMENT
TO FULL
EMPLOYMENT

1

Mathew Forstater

Savings-Recycling Public Employment

Vickrey's Assets-Based Approach to Full Employment and Price Stability

William Vickrey's single-minded commitment to full employment is evident in a series of papers written in the last years of his life (Vickrey 1992a, 1992b, 1993a, 1993b, 1993c, 1994, 1996, 1997). In this work, Vickrey formulated an assets-based approach to macroeconomic analysis with definite implications for budgetary and employment policy. In Vickrey's approach, the difference between desired and actual holdings of net financial assets—or net nominal savings—is the crucial relation in understanding macroeconomic processes, and the government budget is the key policy instrument in the necessary recycling of net nominal savings to bring the desired and actual levels into equality at the full-employment level of output and income. Vickrey believed that the major task for economists and policymakers was to devise the means whereby the necessary recycling of net nominal savings can take place without unexpected changes in the rate of either inflation or deflation. This paper explores Vickrey's proposal for government deficit-financed guaranteed public employment as an automatic stabilizing policy instrument capable of serving as just such a means.

Vickrey's Commitment to Full Employment

For Vickrey, 1926 was the last time there was an acceptable level of employment during peacetime in the United States (Vickrey 1994, 39). He embraced the William Beveridge definition that full employment holds when "there are at least as many unfilled job openings as there are unemployed individuals seeking work" (Vickrey 1993a, 1). Elsewhere, he describes full employment— what he called "chock-full employment" (Vickrey 1992b, 1994)—as the situation in which individuals "can find work at a living wage within 48 hours"

(Vickrey 1994, 40). Vickrey recognized that there are huge social and economic costs to unemployment, and that the promotion of full employment must be a top priority. Among these costs is the direct and real loss of potential output and income, as well as the nominal costs of lower tax revenues because of the smaller tax base and higher rates of government expenditure in unemployment compensation and various forms of "welfare" assistance. But Vickrey also consistently emphasized the social and economic costs linked to unemployment in the form of poverty, crime, drug addiction, homelessness, malnutrition, poor prenatal care, ethnic antagonism, school dropouts, broken families, and other social problems (Vickrey 1992a, 310; 1992b, 341; 1993a, 2; 1993c, 16; 1997, 504–505). He also recognized that unemployment differentially impacts certain sectors of the population, so that an overall official unemployment rate of 5 percent can mean rates of "10, 20, and 40 percent among disadvantaged groups" (Vickrey 1994, 39). The benefits of full employment thus include improved security for society's most downtrodden, alleviation of a variety of social ills, and expanded output and income. In addition, full employment stabilizes business expectations and impacts positively the wages and status of unskilled workers (Vickrey 1993a, 9; 1997, 505).

Given these views, it is not surprising that Vickrey vehemently rejected the notion of the non-accelerating inflation rate of unemployment (NAIRU), and any kind of "natural" rate of unemployment, calling the latter "one of the most vicious euphemisms ever coined" (Vickrey 1992b, 341). At the heart of the NAIRU and the natural rate of unemployment are the beliefs that a trade-off can exist between unemployment and inflation and that, inflation being the greater evil of the two, some unemployment is necessary to guarantee price stability.

For Vickrey, "unemployment is not needed to control inflation" (Vickrey 1997, 507). Adherence to the view that price stability requires maintaining a reserve army of the unemployed, a view Vickrey believed to be "especially strong in influential financial circles and among monetary authorities," means that fiscal and monetary brakes must be slammed down every time economic growth causes unemployment to drop below a certain level (Vickrey 1992b, 341). One implication of such a belief is that efforts at such things as worker retraining become "a cruel game of musical chairs" with the "keepers of austerity" making sure the total number of chairs stays fixed (Vickrey 1997, 504; 1993b, 3). This is a high price to pay for a view that "lacks historical or analytical basis" (Vickrey 1997, 504).

While he believed the dangers of inflation to be overstated, Vickrey recognized that unexpected changes in the rate of inflation, whether up or down, can have undesirable effects. Therefore, developing a means to chock-full employment without unstable prices is a priority. But it does not follow from this necessity that inflation is a greater evil than unemployment. In Vickrey's view, while inflation is a "redistribution of the given total output . . . unemployment involves a reduction in the total product to be distributed" and therefore clearly does greater social harm (Vickrey 1992b, 341). In fact, the greatest dangers of inflation for Vickrey turn out to be the measures taken to control it, that is, enforced unemployment: "[Political maintenance] of unemployment as [a] prophylactic measure against a highly problematic threat of mismanaged inflation is a cure far worse than the disease" (Vickrey 1997, 505).

Vickrey scolded the economics profession and policymakers for what he saw as time wasted in arguing "over which foot is the better to shoot ourselves in" (Vickrey 1993b, 3). Extolling the benefits of full employment, he urged his colleagues, and anyone willing to listen, to immediately focus their "concentrated attention to working out the practical details and bringing the concept to realization" (Vickrey 1992b, 345). Vickrey himself led by example, racking his brains throughout his life to lay bare the fundamental causes of unemployment and devise the means of its elimination. These untiring efforts yielded his assets-based approach to macroeconomics, with its implications for the government deficit-financed recycling of net nominal savings, and it is to this work that I now turn.

Savings and Investment: Toward an Assets-Based Approach to Macroeconomics

Vickrey's assets-based approach to macroeconomics is rooted in the analysis of savings and investment. In orthodox neoclassical theory, savings determines investment through variations in the rate of interest. Thus, income not consumed is transformed into investment expenditure in the market for loanable funds. It is this mechanism that, under perfect competitive conditions, ensures that all output will be purchased at the full-employment level of output and income. Vickrey rejected such a view, which he identified as the heart of "Say's Law," and targeted for rebuttal the implication that economic growth is achieved by promoting an increase in savings (Vickrey 1993c, 6).

Vickrey casts doubt on the conventional view of the interest-elastic nature of both savings and investment:

> On the one hand, the demand for asset accumulation and the supply of savings have become relatively insensitive to interest rates and may even have developed an inverse relationship as lowered interest rates increase the amount of assets required to provide a given level of old-age security. On the other hand, high risk, obsolescence, maintenance, and other user costs

have diminished the long-run responsiveness to interest rates of investment in productive assets. The implicit assumption of the neoclassical paradigm that the potential for profit-seeking capital investment would expand without limit as real interest rates fell, so that there would always be an interest rate that would close the gap, fails in the face of the reality of uncertainty concerning conditions that will obtain in the remote future. (Vickrey 1997, 498)

Thus, both the positively sloped neoclassical saving function and the downward-sloping interest-elastic demand curve for investment are brought into question in Vickrey's analysis.

Key to understanding the savings-investment relation is comprehension of the two-sided nature of saving and spending:

[M]ost economic transactions have at least two aspects, and much of our present plight is the result of looking at only one aspect and failing to follow through on the obverse aspects and their consequences. Nowhere is this more apparent than in the popular discussions of the levels of saving and capital formation and their impact on the health and growth of our economy. (Vickrey 1993c, 5)

Savings is income not spent. It is, in Vickrey's word, "nonspending" (Vickrey 1993b; 1993c, 5; 1994). Increased savings is therefore an increase in nonspending, most often in the form of a reduction of consumption, and this causes the income of others to fall. This in turn leads those experiencing falling incomes to reduce their own savings. Vickrey liked to demonstrate this principle with his now well-known story of abstaining from an $8 haircut:

Savings are not like a sack of potatoes which if not sold at the current price will stay on hand and put a downward pressure on the price until sold. Savings not immediately taken up to create capital simply vanish in reduced income, without even exerting a downward pressure on interest rates. If I yield to the allurements of tax concessions to IRAs to the point of not having my hair cut, this puts $8 more in my bank account, but $8 less in the barber's account; there is nothing that makes it any easier for anyone to obtain funds with which to create capital, nor anything that makes the prospect more attractive. . . . If the barber reacts by curtailing his consumption, this further reduces national income and saving. I may succeed in my attempt to save, but only by reducing the saving of others by even more. Savings are an extremely perishable entity. Say's law fails as soon as part of the income generated in the process of producing the supply is shunted off into new savings that fail to get converted into new capital goods. (Vickrey 1993a, 6)

Not only has the increased saving not been translated into investment, but the decline in aggregate demand that results may further impact investor expectation so that investment may actually be discouraged (Vickrey 1993b, 2).

For Vickrey, the causality runs in the opposite direction, from investment to savings:

> [I]f some genius invents a new product or process and obtains a credit or borrows the funds needed to finance the capital involved in its production, this added real wealth is, *ipso facto*, someone's savings. Instead of Say's law, we have "Capital formation creates its own saving." (Vickrey 1993a, 6)

Thus, investment determines savings and the mechanism that brings them into equality is not variations in the interest rate but, rather, changes in the level of income:

> Attempted saving, with corresponding reduction in spending, does nothing to enhance the willingness of banks and other lenders to finance adequately promising investment projects. With unemployed resources available, saving is neither a prerequisite nor a stimulus to, but a consequence of capital formation, as the income generated by capital formation provides a source of additional savings. (Vickrey 1996, 5)

Vickrey's analysis of the investment-saving relation leads him to view private-sector investment as a means whereby savings is recycled back into the income stream. (Of course, the savings would not exist without some initial investment.) It is a means whereby nonspending is turned into spending. If the entirety of the full-employment level of savings is not recycled into spending by private investment, some of the full-employment level of output fails to be justified by actual sales, and disappointed businesses cut back production, laying off workers. Incomes of the unemployed fall, and saving declines until it is brought into equality with the below-full-employment level of private investment. In other words, Vickrey's analysis of the savings-investment relation leads him to focus on the crucial issue of the recycling of net nominal savings.

Net Nominal Savings and the Savings-Recycling Government Budget

Another way of stating the problem is to focus on the relation between the desired and the actual levels of holdings of net financial assets, or net nominal savings. If, at the full-employment level of output, "the total asset supply held by individuals falls short of what they desire to hold, the curtailing of expenditures by individuals in an attempt to bring their net worth up to a desired level will reduce sales, production, employment, and GNP until the corresponding demand for assets has been reduced to the available supply" (Vickrey 1997, 497–498). Vickrey believed that there are social, institutional, and technological reasons for a growing gap between the private demand and private supply of assets, and that private investment cannot be relied upon to recycle the full-employment level of savings. Unemployment is the real, material evidence of a discrepancy between desired and actual levels of net nominal savings, for if the desired level was lower, individuals would be spending more, sales would be higher, and firms would be hiring more workers.

For Vickrey, there is only one solution to closing the gap between desired and actual levels of net nominal savings: government deficits. If we consider the problem from an assets-based approach, it is clear why this is in fact the case: There is no other source of change in the private sector's total holdings of net financial assets (in dollars). One private-sector individual's desire to increase his holdings of net financial assets can only be realized if another individual is willing to decrease her holdings by the corresponding amount. The private sector is incapable of creating net nominal assets. Thus, Vickrey concludes, there is "no adequate solution without long-term and continued increases in government debt" (Vickrey 1997, 499): "The 'deficit' is not an economic sin but an economic necessity" (Vickrey 1993b, 1).

While many have promoted the use of a capital budget by the federal government, for Vickrey, this is beside the point, even though he considered that there might be political or ideological reasons why capital budgeting might make deficits more palatable:

> The savings-recycling budget is possibly the most important of budgetary concepts from the standpoint of day-to-day policy. This budget would reflect the effect of government outlays . . . in recycling savings, in excess of those absorbed by private investment, into the stream of demand for output. It is the crucial element in curbing the business cycle and bringing employment of resources up to a satisfactory level. From this standpoint, it matters relatively little whether outlays are for current or for capital-account items. (Vickrey 1992a, 307)

In fact, if government investment replaced private investment, the net effect desired might be offset, while the income-recycling function itself would be served just as well from projects with no other justification (Vickrey 1993a, 6). Despite the crucial importance of grasping this point, Vickrey did note that government investment that spurs further private investment, or otherwise benefits the public, refutes the argument that the national debt is a burden on future generations. He argues instead that much of the activity undertaken for the purpose of recycling savings "will form part of the real heritage left to the future" (Vickrey 1996, 4). Because savings-recycling through government deficits permits chock-full employment economic growth, "[t]his means an increased heritage of real capital plant and equipment, to say nothing of the human capital induced by fuller employment" (Vickrey 1997, 509).

Neither is the savings-recycling deficit something that can be "balanced over the cycle" (ibid. 499): "The supply of government securities will need to grow *pari passu* with the gross domestic product, to correspond to the gap between the demand of the population for assets and the provision of assets by the private sector" (Vickrey 1993b, 1). It must be emphasized that this is not a "closed economy" argument, the foreign sector—including foreign government, firms, and individuals—is included in the private demand for assets. As Vickrey recognized, exporting unemployment through "export surpluses . . . is essentially a beggar-my-neighbor policy not available as a general policy" (Vickrey 1997, 499). While Americans could indeed save net dollar assets with a trade surplus, this would only be temporary, as the resulting worldwide dollar squeeze would cause the government deficit to rise.

In promoting the need for savings-recycling government deficits and a growing national debt, Vickrey rejected many of the common myths and misconceptions concerning deficits and the debt held by the economics profession and politicians, and repeated *ad nauseam* by the press (Vickrey 1994; 1996). These include the assertions, unsupported by either careful analysis or the historical record, that deficits cause inflation or high interest rates, or crowd out private investment. Vickrey points out that not only have deficits and the national debt not resulted in these harmful effects, but that the "existence of large government debt may be one reason we have not had a recurrence of a depression of the severity of the 1930s" (Vickrey 1997, 508–509):

> To assure against such a disaster and start on the road to real prosperity it is necessary to relinquish our unreasoned ideological obsession with reducing government deficits, recognize that it is the economy and not the government budget that needs balancing in terms of the demand for and the supply of assets, and proceed to recycle attempted savings into the income stream at an adequate rate, so that they will not simply vanish in reduced income, sales, output and employment. There is too a free lunch out there, indeed a very substantial one. But it will require getting free from the dogmas of the apostles of austerity, most of whom would not share in the sacrifices they recommend for others. Failing this, we will all be skating on very thin ice. (Vickrey 1996, 32)

Vickrey's assets-based approach to macroeconomic analysis elucidates the fundamental relation between desired and actual net nominal savings and offers it as the key to understanding the problems of persistent unemployment. Furthermore, it leads straight to the conclusion that the savings-recycling deficit is the only way to close the gap and bring the desired and actual levels of net holding of financial assets into equality at the full-employment level of output and income. "An economy with ten percent inflation and two percent unemployment would be far healthier in human terms than one with one percent inflation and eight percent unemployment." But fortunately, such a trade-off is not necessary, as unemployment is not needed to keep prices stable (Vickrey 1997, 505). Vickrey did feel, however, that a "new tool is needed" to complement fiscal and monetary measures if we are to accomplish the three macroeconomic goals of promoting full employment, stable prices, and economic growth (Vickrey 1993a, 7). A number of proposals have been made for government to promote full employment through direct job creation (Minsky 1986; Lowe 1988; Harvey 1989; Collins et al. 1994; Gordon 1997). Recently, several proposals have explicitly highlighted the ways in which such guaranteed public employment can serve as an effective automatic stabilizer by recycling savings through government budget deficits in just the manner proposed by Vickrey (Mosler 1997–1998; Mitchell 1998; Wray 1997; 1999).

Savings-Recycling Public Employment

We have seen that Vickrey's chock-full employment means more vacancies than individuals seeking work, and a situation in which workers can find a decent job at a living wage within forty-eight hours. We have also seen that Vickrey considered a means to full employment without inflation a top priority for economists and policymakers. In addition, Vickrey felt that pursuing three macroeconomic goals with only two policy instruments is like "trying to fly an airplane without ailerons, . . . the third dimension of control that was the key to the success of the Wright brothers." In his view, a new tool is needed (Vickrey 1993a, 7). We must devise a means of promoting chock-full employment without unexpected changes in the rate of inflation or deflation and must "fill the gap between the asset aspirations of individuals at this level of income and the ability of the private sector to provide assets" through savings-recycling deficits (Vickrey 1993b, 1). "There is no reason inherent in the real resources available to us why we cannot move rapidly . . . to a state of genuinely full employment and then continue indefinitely at that level" (Vickrey 1993a, 10).

Vickrey rejected the draconian "workfare" that is not combined with increases in aggregate demand:

[A]ttempts to move selected unemployed individuals or groups into jobs by training, instruction in job search techniques, threats of benefit withdrawal or denial and the like, merely move the selected individuals to the head of the queue without reducing the length of the queue. Merely because any one traveler can secure a seat on a flight by getting to the airport sufficiently early does not mean that if everyone gets to the airport sufficiently early, 200 passengers can get on a flight with seats for 150. (Vickrey 1996, 27)

But when financed by deficit spending, public employment "can indeed" result in net job creation (Vickrey 1996, 28). The key, then, is to combine guaranteed public-sector employment with the savings-recycling government budget in what we here call "savings-recycling public employment," but which has elsewhere been termed "buffer-stock employment" by Mitchell and "government as employer of last resort" (ELR) by Mosler, Wray, and others (Mitchell 1998; Mosler 1997–1998; Wray 1997; 1999).

In this approach, the government pledges to hire anyone ready and willing to work at a basic public-sector (living) wage, and the wage bill is paid for by deficit expenditure. Since unemployment is the physical evidence of desired levels greater than actual levels of net holdings of financial assets, deficit spending fills the gap by employing the unemployed. This eliminates the problem of estimating the needed level of government deficit spending, as it is reflected in the number of unemployed showing up for government guaranteed jobs. As long as the desired holdings of net financial assets is greater than the actual holdings, there will be unemployed. As the unemployed show up for public employment, the deficit will expand to pay the public employment wage bill, recycling the excess of savings over private-asset supply, and closing the gap between the desired and actual levels of net nominal savings at chock-full employment. An ELR scheme that is deficit-financed thus serves as a powerful automatic stabilizer, simultaneously guaranteeing an infinitely elastic demand for labor and the recycling of excess savings.

As Vickrey emphasized, savings-recycling public employment must not replace either private-sector or other public-sector employment. Under such a program, all the benefits of full employment outlined by Vickrey are obtained, and the social and economic costs of unemployment substantially eliminated. To the extent that savings-recycling public employment involves the enhancement of worker skills, the benefits of the program as a means of job training are actualized. While the retraining effect may prove "essential in abating structural mismatch between job requirements and individual qualifications," net job creation means the program is not simply a cruel game of musical chairs (Vickrey 1993c, 9). Considering these factors, Vickrey also predicted an increase in "the wages and status levels" of the lowest skilled and least well paid (ibid.).

Savings-recycling public employment will not generate deficits that will be inflationary, since the deficit will only be permitted to expand up to the point where the gap between desired and actual holdings of net financial assets is filled at zero involuntary unemployment, which corresponds to the degree to which aggregate demand falls short of the level corresponding to chock-full employment. While increasing deficits beyond that point might be inflationary, there will be at that point no more unemployed workers showing up for savings-recycling jobs, and so the scheme includes a built-in feature preventing the deficit from becoming too large. At the same time, although Vickrey recognized that, depending on the value of the initial savings-recycling public employment wage-benefits package set, "a small one-time increase in the overall price level" might be expected at the start of the program, this is in no way the same thing as "an inflationary spiral" (Vickrey 1997, 505). Other features of the program additionally guarantee against unexpected changes in the rate of inflation—which, as Vickrey emphasized again and again, is what we should have as an actual concern, as opposed to a fear of some vague notion of inflation.

First, savings-recycling public employment may be directed toward public works such as infrastructure revitalization that may promote private-sector productivity growth. Second, productivity will also be enhanced by virtue of the fact that, while unemployment is associated with the depreciation of human capital, savings-recycling public employees will experience an appreciation of skills and knowledge. Third, in addition to the decrease in the social and economic costs of unemployment, savings-recycling public employees may be engaged in activities that help reduce other social costs, such as environmental protection and cleanup. Fourth, the increase in expenditure on savings-recycling public employment will be at least partially offset by decreases in other forms of expenditure on the unemployed. Thus, expenditures on unemployment insurance and other forms of general assistance should be expected to decline. Fifth, public works tend to be less inflationary than "the dole" because the former increases both supply and demand, while the latter increases only demand. Sixth, inflationary bottlenecks and structural rigidities associated with high levels of employment can be avoided with the savings-recycling approach. Workers employed in savings-recycling public employment are still available to the private sector should the demand for labor rise, maintaining numerical flexibility without the social and economic costs of unemployment. In addition, flexibility in terms of capital goods and natural resources is maintained, as government can strategically choose to utilize methods of production and types of resources that will avoid bottlenecks and even enhance system flexibility (Forstater 1998; 1999). Seventh, firms may still be expected to maintain planned reserve capacity to meet both peak and unexpected increases in demand, so that full employment of labor will be consistent with a "normal level of capacity utilization." Eighth, since government is willing to hire as few or as many people who want to work at the savings-recycling public employment wage, it is free to set that wage exogenously rather than paying a market-determined wage. Being fixed, the program's wage is perfectly stable and sets a benchmark price for labor. It is obviously unlikely that unexpected changes in the rate of inflation will be due to wage-related factors under such a system. In fact, the exogenous pricing component of the savings-recycling public employment approach may be seen as a means of defining the national currency in terms of fairly homogeneous low- or semi-skilled labor. The program wage thus serves as an anchor to which the currency is tied. Because labor is a basic commodity, employed directly and indirectly into the production of every other commodity, the savings-recycling public employment program offers a mechanism for regulating the value of the currency and thus controlling the price level. In this sense, the savings-recycling public employment approach resembles a commodity buffer-stock scheme; only here it is labor that is being used as the buffer-stock to stabilize the currency.

Savings-recycling public employment is an automatic stabilizing policy instrument that can ensure chock-full employment, generating the savings-recycling deficit necessary to equate the desired and actual levels of net holdings of financial assets as prescribed by Vickrey's assets-based approach to macroeconomic analysis without the danger of unexpected changes in the rate of inflation. Guaranteed public employment establishes the infinitely elastic demand for labor required to meet the Vickrey-Beveridge definition of chock-full employment, and financing such employment through deficit spending guarantees the recycling of excess savings necessary to bring the desired and actual levels of holdings of net financial assets into equality at the zero-involuntary-unemployment level of economic activity. A number of features of the approach establish it as not only a viable means to true full employment, but a tool for price stability as well.

Vickrey's analysis was heavily influenced by the state of affairs existing around the time of the recession of the early 1990s. What are the implications of this work for more recent developments in the United States—and the global economy generally—as we prepare to enter the next millennium?

Vickrey's Macroeconomics and the Current Situation

In retrospect, Vickrey's articles from the early and mid-1990s seem incredibly prescient, as relevant to the situation in the late 1990s as they were when they were written. We have seen that this work emphasizes the increasing inability of governments to rely on conventional monetary policy to counter recessions and depressions, due in no small part to the insensitivity of investment to lower interest rates. One need only cite the recent experience of Japan, where interest rates near zero did nothing to budge the economy out of its deep downturn. Vickrey's further related observation, also cited above, concerning the association of lower interest rates with higher rates of saving, also appears to be supported by the Japanese experience.

Vickrey was skeptical of the conditions of the European Monetary Union (EMU), and utilized that case to express a more general concern about the desirability of fixed versus flexible exchange rate policies:

> Freely floating exchange rates are the means whereby adaptations are made to disparate price level trends in different countries and trade imbalances are brought into line with capital flows appropriate to increasing the overall productivity of capital. Fixed exchange rates or rates confined to a narrow band can be maintained only by coordinated fiscal policies among the countries involved, by imposing efficiency-impairing tariffs or other restraints on trade, or by imposing costly disciplines involving needlessly high rates of unemployment as is implied by the Maastricht agreements. (Vickrey 1996, 15)

As Vickrey recognized, a successful domestic full-employment policy requires flexible exchange rates: "Restraints on exchange rates, such as are involved in the Maastricht agreements, would make it virtually impossible for a small open economy, such as Denmark, to pursue an effective full-employment policy on its own" (ibid. 16).

Vickrey's articles were written in the context of government budget deficits, private-sector surpluses, and trade deficits in the United States, and it has been noted that he believed institutional, historical, and social factors supported the view that private-sector surpluses were likely to continue and even grow. He thus warned against the growing calls for budget balancing, decreasing the deficit, and even running budget surpluses to pay down the national debt. In the late 1990s, the tightening fiscal stance has come to pass, coupled with a deterioration in the position on foreign trade, with the result that the private sector has actually gone into deficit.

The private sector may be divided into firms and households and, since firms have been able to maintain a surplus, it is households that have gone into deficit, with household savings exceeding incomes at record rates (Godley and Wray 1999). This has been due to credit-financed spending by households, supported by sharp rises in stock market prices. Vickrey noted the possibility of such a scenario and warned against this means of closing the gap between desired and actual levels of net holdings of financial assets: "Meeting the demand for assets by a speculative boom in stock market and other assets prices is a temporary bubble solution that is bound to burst with catastrophic consequences" (Vickrey 1997, 499). Vickrey further warns that this is particularly dangerous when combined with budget balancing, a condition that the current scene shares with the Great Depression:

> There is a serious danger that the bidding up of asset prices could create a bubble of unsustainable values that is likely to collapse disastrously, as occurred in 1929 after the budget surpluses of the preceding years. Sooner or later a reduction in production and national income will set in until the reduction in income reduces the demand for assets to conform to the supply. (Vickrey 1993b, 2)

Whether precipitated by a "correction" in the stock market, a drying up of easy credit for American consumers, further instability in Asia, Latin America, or Russia, or problems related to the EMU, the United States is woefully ill-prepared for the next economic downturn. As Vickrey's analysis makes clear, conventional fiscal and monetary policy is not sufficient to deal with a significant reduction in output and income and rising unemployment. Fortunately, Vickrey's analysis demonstrates that a savings-recycling public employment plan could provide the automatic stabilizer that the system requires to deal with the macroeconomic challenges of modern society. We can have chock-full employment *with* price stability if our economic experts and political leaders can exhibit clearheaded, common-sense thinking and the courage of their convictions. They need look no further than Bill Vickrey for an outstanding example in both these regards.

References

Collins, Sheila D., Helen Lachs Ginsburg, and Gertrude Schaffner Goldberg. 1994. *Jobs for All: A Plan for the Revitalization of America.* New York: Apex Press.
Forstater, Mathew. 1998. "Flexible Full Employment: Structural Implications of Discretionary Public Sector Employment." *Journal of Economic Issues* 32, no. 2: 557–563.
———. 1999. "Public Employment and Economic Flexibility: The Job Opportunity Approach to Full Employment." Public policy brief no. 50, Jerome Levy Economics Institute, Annandale-on-Hudson, NY.
Godley, Wynne, and L. Randall Wray. 1999. "Can Goldilocks Survive?" Policy Note 1999/4, Jerome Levy Economics Institute, Annandale-on-Hudson, NY.
Gordon, Wendell. 1997. "Job Assurance—The Job Guarantee Revisited." *Journal of Economic Issues* 31, no. 3 (September).

Harvey, Philip. 1989. *Securing the Right to Employment*. Princeton: Princeton University Press.

Lowe, Adolph. 1988. *Has Freedom a Future?* New York: Praeger.

Minsky, Hyman P. 1986. *Stabilizing an Unstable Economy*. New Haven: Yale University Press.

Mitchell, William F. 1998. "The Buffer Stock Employment Model and the NAIRU: The Path to Full Employment." *Journal of Economic Issues* 32, no. 2: 547–555.

Mosler, Warren. 1997–1998. "Full Employment and Price Stability." *Journal of Post Keynesian Economics* 20, no. 2: 167–182.

Vickrey, William. 1992a. "Meaningfully Defining Deficits and Debt." *American Economic Review* 82, no. 2 (May): 305–310.

———. 1992b. "Chock-Full Employment Without Increased Inflation." *American Economic Review* 82, no. 2 (May): 341–345.

———. 1993a. "Today's Task for Economists." *American Economic Review* 83, no. 1 (March): 1–10.

———. 1993b. "We Need a Bigger 'Deficit,'" manuscript.

———. 1993c. "The Other Side of the Coin." *American Economist* 37, no. 2: 5–16.

———. 1994. "Why Not Chock-Full Employment?" *Atlantic Economic Journal* 25, no. 1: 39–45.

———. 1996. "Fifteen Fatal Fallacies of Financial Fundamentalism." Working paper, Columbia University.

———. 1997. "A Trans-Keynesian Manifesto (Thoughts about an Assets-Based Macroeconomics)." *Journal of Post Keynesian Economics* 19, no. 4: 495–510.

Wray, L. Randall. 1997. "Government as Employer of Last Resort: Full Employment Without Inflation." Working paper no. 213, Jerome Levy Economics Institute, Annandale-on-Hudson, NY.

———. 1999. *Understanding Modern Money: The Key to Full Employment and Price Stability*. Cheltenham, UK: Edward Elgar.

2

DIMITRI B. PAPADIMITRIOU

(Full) Employment Policy

Theory and Practice

Unemployment cannot be conquered by a democracy until it is understood. Full productive employment in a free society is possible but it is not possible without taking pains. It cannot be won by waving a financial wand; it is a goal that can be reached only by conscious continuous organization of all our productive resources under democratic control. To win full employment and keep it, we must will the end and must understand and will the means

(Beveridge)

Introduction

Writing in the 1940s, William Beveridge defined full employment as a labor market in which the number of job vacancies would be higher than the number of jobless (Beveridge 1945), a condition that would guarantee no long-term unemployment. What Beveridge envisaged was achieved in the immediate postwar years, but, alas, was not sustained during the past two or even three decades. Differing from the past three decades, however, the United States economy *appears* currently to have reached *full employment* with low and stable inflation. Low unemployment rates, however, as conventionally measured, cannot tell the entire unemployment story. The Bureau of Labor Statistics regularly reports that the flows among the categories "officially unemployed," "employed," and "out-of-the-labor-force" are very large. In August 1999, for example, of those unemployed, 44.6 percent were job-losers, 13.9 percent were job-leavers, and 41.5 percent came from out of the labor force. Those who find jobs typically come from the out-of-the-labor-force category. Of the 68 million people in this category, 4.74 million wanted a job and only 1.1 million indicated a marginal attachment to the labor force and were not currently working; the rest had no attachment to the labor force. As Lester Thurow notes (1996), there are a few more million "missing" males who used to be in the workforce who are not in school, are not old enough to have retired, and are neither employed nor unemployed. They have either been dropped from, or have dropped themselves out of, the U.S. Gross National Product machine. Thus, the 4.2 percent unemployment rate reported for August 1999 does not represent the true unemployment level for the United States. The unemployment landscape would not look as rosy if adjustments were made for the large number of the "employed" who are involuntarily working part-time (almost 3.3 million in August 1999) and who, for statistical purposes, are not differentiated from those working on a full-time, year-round basis. While it is not possible to calculate how many more individuals could work if jobs were made available, there undoubtedly exist millions of potential workers. Finally, to make matters worse, the unemployment rate is underestimated if the concept of "disguised" unemployment (defined as low productivity employment as compared to manufacturing productivity) is to be applied, since by and large, employment growth is not in the manufacturing sectors, but in services whose productivity lags that of manufacturing (Robinson 1937; Eatwell 1995).

This state of affairs coincides not only with the rush to deficit reduction embraced by the American, European, and Asian economies, but also with the implementation of a "welfare reform" in the United States that seeks to force recipients off assistance through setting time (and other) limits on eligibility. This policy leaves it to individual states to try to find jobs for former beneficiaries, a task that they are unable—even if they are willing—to shoulder. A recent survey in New York State, for example, showed that cutting off aid will not necessarily put people to work. Imprecise as the survey may be, it still showed that a large proportion (two-thirds) of the individuals leaving the rolls of the Aid to Families with Dependent Children (AFDC) and Home Relief programs failed to get jobs (*New York Times*, March 23, 1998, 1, B6). These individuals were left without the means to provide for themselves and for their families, and were thereby driven deeper into poverty rather than to self-sufficiency. This has occurred in concert with the strategy enforced by the current political infrastructure that aims to progressively dismantle the public-sector social safety net that had traditionally protected the most vulnerable segments of the population against economic and other hardships.

A similar employment situation prevails in Europe, where central banks continue a policy of tight money even while many countries—within and outside the European Union (EU)—experience double-digit official unemployment rates. Belgium, France, Germany, Italy, and Spain have all had unemployment rates over 10 percent (Germany's July 1999 rate was over 10 percent, France's was over 12 percent, while Spain's has averaged closer to 20 percent for over two years), and are projecting similar rates through the year 2002. At the same time, EU member states are preparing to give up their sovereignty to conduct coordinated fiscal and monetary policy by accepting the rules of a flawed European Monetary Union (EMU). The Maastricht accord sets ceilings for inflation and government deficits and debt, but not for unemployment, which, as of the end of July 1999, stood at approximately 15.6 million individuals for the fifteen member states. When asked about remedies to ameliorate high unemployment rates, EU economics ministers respond with descriptions of a type of progress identified as "[a] change in trend but not yet [a] breakthrough" (*Financial Times*, March 12, 1998).

During the Great Depression, unemployment was addressed through interventionist government. The government-instituted programs were temporary, however, and they were discontinued with the economic recovery that accompanied the United States' entry into World War II. In the postwar era, promotion of "full" or "maximum" employment meant macroeconomic policies designed to manage aggregate demand, supplemented by selective programs, such as job training and limited income maintenance. With the onset of 1970s stagflation, however, even the moderate approach of demand management faltered and led to a consensus among economists and policymakers that a "natural rate" of unemployment, or Non-Accelerating Inflation Rate of Unemployment (NAIRU), of 5 percent in the United States and as high as 10 percent in France, for example, would be too inflationary. This received wisdom continues to this day with the result that, to ensure price stability, millions of individuals who are ready, willing, and able to work remain idle, thereby serving as a "reserve" or "forgotten army" of labor. Two important questions, then, may be posed regarding unemployment. First, is this the best we can do at times of prosperity? Second, are we prepared to meet the challenges of the next downturn? (Worrisome signs have already appeared: equity and bond markets' volatility in the United States and overseas, the Asian and Russian crises, unprecedented rates of household and business indebtedness in the United States, and an obsession for meeting government budget deficit reduction targets everywhere.)

The challenge confronting policymakers is the crafting of employment policies that (1) uphold the basic human right to a job while neither interfering with microdecisions of individual firms nor relying on the failed approach of "fine-tuning" aggregate demand; and (2) are not inflationary. The policy (in order to be implemented) should be consistent with the fundamental premise that, to the extent possible, socially productive work is preferable to income maintenance. Thus, the structure within which the policy options are to be framed, as has been recognized by academics and policymakers across the theoretical and political spectrum, would necessarily call for bold initiatives. Many measures have been suggested. This essay examines those that, as of late, have received substantial currency and are presently proposed as viable options to achieving higher employment. These include: reduction of the workweek, employment subsidies, and public service employment or the government becoming the employer of last resort (ELR). The essay first analyzes each of the three already instituted or proposed policy options, and then determines the preferred policy option that best meets the criteria of (1) not causing inflationary pressures, and (2) not interfering with the microdecisions of the entrepreneur.

Employment Policy Options

Reduction of the Workweek

Reducing the workweek or sharing available work has been introduced many times by governments and trade unions alike as a mechanism to, first, ameliorate high unemployment and, second, to provide flexibility and power sharing in the workplace. Work-sharing arrangements are not strictly limited to reducing the normal workweek, but also include other schemes, that is, job sharing or job splitting, elimination of overtime, phased-in retirement, phased entry-through-extended education and training, and part-time work in general. Working part-time was promoted in the Organization for Economic Cooperation and Development (OECD) *Jobs Study* (1995, 23) as a measure to increase flexibility that "could enhance job creation and employment prospects."

The principal argument made for implementing work-sharing arrangements is that they "redistribute work over people so as to reduce the extent of involuntary unemployment" (Drèze 1986, 1). Similarly, the Commission of the European Communities (CEC) endorsed the measure twenty years ago, stating:

> [T]he aim of work-sharing is to redistribute the total volume of work in the economy in order to increase employment opportunities for all those wishing to work. This does not mean that the volume of work remains constant. Rather, it is based on the observation that this volume is at present inadequate and that we must try to redistribute it. (CEC)

The EU renewed its endorsement of this employment strategy by incorporating it in the Working Time Directive issued in 1993 (*European Industrial Relations Review*, 1993). The trading of hours for jobs scheme that results from the reduction of the normal workweek has been desirable to both employers and employees for different reasons. Employees' desires are based on what may be called the "sovereignty of time," while the employers' desires reflect changes in production schedules and product demand, and the implementation of new technology.

As Europe's unemployment rates have remained at record levels, the strategy of trading hours for jobs has reappeared as a viable employment policy. This approach to employment has been favored by trade unions. In Germany, however, reductions in the normal workweek implemented in the 1950s and 1960s, while causing no apparent increase in employment, did establish a new normal workweek (Hinrichs 1991). Germany's economics minister, Gunter Rexrodt, has suggested that saving jobs will require shorter hours and longer holidays. Volkswagen has pushed hard for the trade-off of a four-day workweek for a 20 percent wage cut or massive layoffs (Gow 1993; *Economist*, November 13, 1993). This kind of employment policy resembles the "shock therapy" applied to Russia and the former Warsaw Pact economies during transition, the abysmal results of which have been documented (Papadimitriou 1991).

Other examples of implementing such policies abound. During the 1970s and 1980s, the Netherlands experienced high unemployment along with an increase in the labor force, which led in 1982 to experiments with a reduced workweek and forfeiture of pay increases. Research studies that attempted to quantify the impact of the experiment on employment growth showed that no significant changes occurred, and thus indicated that reducing the workweek was "a relatively ineffective policy for reducing unemployment" (Roche, Fynes, and Morrissey 1996, 136). The empirical evidence from reduced working hours schemes implemented in Belgium in the 1980s, and in Australia in the 1970s and 1980s (where unemployment rose), further supports the argument that reduced working hours produce no growth in employment (ibid., 137–139). To the contrary, in the case of Australia it has been shown that reduction in working hours may lead to increased overtime costs that result in a decrease of employment (Dixon 1987).

In the United States, reduction in working hours has not been used as a strategy to increase employment. In *The Overworked American* (1991), Juliet Schor reported that Americans worked 1,924 hours in 1989 compared with 1,786 hours two decades earlier, an increase of 7.7 percent. She suggests that reducing the forty-hour workweek would lead to less absenteeism, less turnover, less personal business on company time, lower costs, and, perhaps, increased employment. As unemployment rose in the 1970s and 1980s, some labor economists and others advocated shorter workweeks to "spread the work," arguing that reducing the standard workweek would put millions of individuals to work (Levitan and Belous 1977; Morand and Macoy 1984; McGaughey 1981). In the United States, what has been seen instead is that many employers and consenting employees have increased the workweek through overtime as a means to decrease costs (employers do not pay benefits on overtime work) and to increase employees' income in an environment of job insecurity. This phenomenon has generated considerable debate involving so many aspects of employment and work hours that many question the official statistics on unemployment rates (Bluestone and Rose 1998), since voluntary overtime of the employed does not reduce the number of the involuntarily unemployed.

During the last two recoveries—1982 to 1989 and 1992 to 1995—average weekly hours increased significantly without a pronounced change in the number of prime age workers, which indicates a reduction in the labor supply, and provides reasons for the low unemployment and low inflation experienced in the United States in the 1980s and 1990s. In simple arithmetic terms, if the employed labor force was about 100 million in 1982, the increase in hours is calculated to be the equivalent of 3.7 million additional workers, or a decrease of the official unemployment rate by 3.7 percent (ibid., 35).

The Japanese experience with shorter working hours has been slight. Until recently, Japan's official unemployment rates have been significantly low, thus negating any interest in full employment policy. As Deutschmann (1991) put it, Japanese human resource practices are associated with a larger number of normal work hours, a lot of overtime, and fewer paid holidays than other industrial countries; moreover, there is no clear separation between time devoted to leisure and to work. During the 1990s, some significant reductions in working time have been implemented. The likely employment effects of shorter working hours have been simulated by using a simple model (Brunello 1989). The econometric results of this model indicated that the outcome of a reduction of the workweek would be associated with an increase in overtime and a reduction in employment.

Finally, the experience in France is perhaps the most interesting since there is a national belief derived from opinion polls and shared across the political spectrum that shortening the workweek will lead to employment creation (*International Labor Review* 1993). The working time policies in France have been detailed in Jallade (1991), who, contrary to the sentiment of the general public, argued that no significant employment effects were discernible from reductions in the workweek in the 1980s, and, if there were any, they were most likely offset by the decline in the French economy's competitiveness resulting from increased wage costs. Furthermore, he suggests that advocating the spreading of work by means of reducing work hours may not lead to additional jobs but, rather, to faster-paced work and higher productivity. The latest attempt of Prime Minister Jospin to reduce the workweek to thirty-five hours as a macroeconomic policy for job creation met strong criticism by economists and trade unions alike. Objections and criticisms notwithstanding, France has gone ahead and instituted the thirty-five-hour workweek. Early reports indicate not only insignificant reductions in the ranks of unemployed, but projections of higher unit costs.

The work-leisure allocation is important in our lives and economy, and it could be argued that reducing the workweek will solve a number of social problems and alleviate many personal concerns. From the European experience, reducing work hours to generate employment has been shown, however, not only to have failed to enlarge the pool of employed workers, but also to have resulted in a number of negative side effects, that is, loss of output, inflation, and imbalance of trade. Moreover, working-time reductions instituted during periods of persistently high unemployment may become permanent, adversely affecting individual preferences for more income over more leisure (Owen 1989, 141). Even though some share of unemployment is due to the business cycle, a significant number of individuals are chronically unemployed. In Europe and the United States, reported statistics on unemployment mask the true story. As mentioned earlier, jobless rates do not distinguish between those who are involuntarily employed part-time; year-round, full-time workers; discouraged workers; and those who are not part of the official labor force. All individuals who are able and willing to work cannot be employed by spreading the work of those already employed. This would be, to use a musical analogy, as if a string quartet had five players. Instead, to deal adequately with the level of structural unemployment and its enormous social and economic costs requires not a rationing of work, but a radical change in the institutional arrangements that presently guide economic and political thinking. These changes include active government fostering of increases in the demand for labor that can lead to further employment from increases in effective demand. It is to these options that we now turn.

Employment Subsidies

In a series of articles culminating in a recent highly acclaimed book, Edmund Phelps of Columbia University has proposed subsidizing the employment of low-wage, lower-skilled workers (1994a; 1994b; 1997). Aside from ethical considerations that a wage be fair, an employment subsidy may become, he contends, the impetus for higher levels of employment from the ranks of unemployed and those not presently in the labor force. Wage subsidies were first proposed by Pigou (1933), Kaldor (1936), Jackman and Layard (1986), and Snower (1993), all in Britain, and in the United States by Hammermesh (1978), Haveman and Palmer (1982), Phelps, and many others.

Employment subsidy schemes, which require that the cost to firms of employing additional workers be partially offset by public purse payments to the employer, have gained considerable currency as a means of countering economic contraction and high unemployment (that is, in the 1930s and 1970s), and for lifting or "rewarding" low-wage workers. However, as Phelps points out, when the Keynesian notion of insufficient effective demand caused by monetary and fiscal policies won the argument of how to deal with unemployment, "wage subsidies fell out of fashion, if not into disrepute. Then, when economists concluded that the usual monetary maladjustment works itself out—that unemployment tends toward its current 'natural' level through wage adjustments or the traditional behavior of the central bank—the way was clear for a return of the idea of employment subsidies" (Phelps 1997, 144). The case has also been made that wage subsidies to employers impact not only those directly affected, but also their dependents, as well as the wider community; that is, disadvantaged workers or those involuntarily not in the labor force are susceptible to opportunities for criminal and illegal activity (Phelps 1994b, 57). Furthermore, low wages in general are a disincentive for the unskilled to seek employment, encouraging them to rely instead on benefits and entitlements afforded by the safety net (ibid.).

To be sure, subsidies for rewarding work exist. The evidence of their success is mixed. The Earned Income Tax Credit (EITC), for example, has been criticized for many reasons: (1) it is vulnerable to abuse since it does not take into account nonwage income; (2) it is directed mainly to heads of households and neglects many poor, single workers; (3) it intervenes in labor markets by depressing wages; and (4) it provides the least incentive to work to those whose job commitment is the weakest, since potential benefits are very low (Phelps 1997). These criticisms notwithstanding, many commentators have urged that the EITC be expanded to boost poorly paid work (Bluestone and Ghilarducci 1996). Another form of subsidy is the "negative income tax," which benefits every individual regardless of employment. Such a tax works more to alleviate the problem of redistribution than to maximize employment (Tobin 1966; Tobin et al. 1967). There is, by and large, a general agreement that neither the EITC nor the negative income tax provide inducements for employment growth or incentives to hold onto a job to the same extent that a wage subsidy would pull workers from the ranks of the unemployed, nonemployed, or welfare rolls. Phelps estimates that the initial cost of his proposed plan of a "graduating" employment subsidy (the subsidy decreases as the wage increases) would be about $98 billion, if it were to be in place in 1990 as indicated in Table 2.1 (Phelps 1997, 175).

Table 2.1

Cost of the Model Wage Subsidy Plan

Hourly wage	Hourly subsidy	Annual wage	Annual subsidy	Number of Employees (%)	Number of Employees (millions)	Subsidy outlay ($billions)
$1 or less	$0.00	—	—	1.0	0.061	—
2 to 1.01	0.00	—	—	0.2	0.122	—
3 to 2.01	0.00	—	—	0.8	0.488	—
4 to 3.01	3.00	$7,000	$6,000	5.9	3.599	$21.594
5 to 4.01	2.29	9,000	4,580	10.4	6.344	29.056
6 to 5.01	1.65	11,000	3,300	9.4	5.734	18.922
7 to 6.01	1.12	13,000	2,240	9.6	5.856	13.117
8 to 7.01	0.71	15,000	1,420	9.1	5.551	7.882
9 to 8.01	0.43	17,000	860	7.0	4.270	3.672
10 to 9.01	0.24	19,000	480	8.1	4.941	2.372
11 to 10.01	0.13	21,000	260	4.2	2.562	0.666
12 to 11.01	0.06	23,000	120	5.3	3.233	0.388
13 to 12.01	0.00	25,000	0	4.6	2.806	0
14 to 13.01	0.00	27,000	0	3.4	2.074	0
15 to 14.01	0.00	29,000	0	3.7	2.257	0
20 to 15.01	0.00	35,000	0	10.4	6.344	0
25 to 20.01	0.00	45,000	0	4.3	2.623	0
More than 25	0.00	—	0	3.5	2.135	0
Total				100.0	61.000	$97.669

Source: From *Rewarding Work* by Edmund S. Phelps. Copyright © 1997 by the President and Fellows of Harvard College. Reprinted by permission of Harvard University Press.

Notes: Percentage distribution from the Current Population Survey, March 1990. Number of employees from the U.S. Census 1990. Table covers full-time employees in the private sector (full-time employees taken to work 2,000 hours per year).

The estimate for 1997 goes up to $125 billion, reflecting inflationary increases in money wages and the resulting increased employment over the 1990–1997 period (ibid., 116). Phelps is not concerned with the cost of his proposal, however, since a small increase in the payroll tax, which he calculates at 2.5 percent, can finance it.

Phelps's plan has had a fair number of criticisms that have focused on the general issue of the effectiveness of subsidies, since it is possible that employers will seek to substitute subsidized workers for those currently employed. If the plan is successful in promoting higher levels of private-sector employment, as assumed, it is also likely to result in upward pressure on money wages, which would lead to inflation and add to rigidities in the economic system that hinder expansion. Furthermore, even though Phelps refers to his scheme as a "market-based approach," the plan entails significant interference with employer decisions, thereby distorting the market mechanism. There is a question whether a firm's behavior will become directed toward obtaining the subsidy rather than toward the market to obtain profits. Phelps argues these criticisms away by distinguishing "private" from "social" productivity, and thus, the "free-market" from "social" prices of labor, this difference giving rise to the distinction of private versus social costs. Economists have recognized since the early 1900s that, even in competitive markets, there are many instances in which a "free market" price diverges from the "right" price (Pigou 1933). Phelps insists his plan is based "on the view that judicious subsidies are acceptable . . . as long as the system of free enterprise is kept firmly in place," and that "if low-wage workers become better rewarded, a more adventurous and less bridled capitalism might well be justified" (Phelps 1997, 123). In the end, what can be said is that subsidized low-wage labor schemes, despite their high price tag, may not guarantee full employment.

Government as Employer of Last Resort

Hyman P. Minsky (1986) was skeptical of employment policies based on subsidies because he believed such policies were liable to lead to inflation, financial crisis, and serious instability. Minsky proposed an alternative employment strategy, which he called an "employer of last resort" (ELR) policy, in which government provides a job guarantee. He felt such a plan would promote full employment without the inflationary pressures and structural rigidities usually associated with economies operating at full employment. Minsky's proposal has been developed in considerable detail by a group of researchers at the Levy Institute (Wray 1997; Forstater 1997) who have provided even greater theoretical support for a government-guaranteed job assurance.

The first component of the proposal would be relatively simple. The government as employer of last resort would announce the wage at which it will offer employment to anyone who wants to work in the public sector, and then would employ all who want to work at that wage. Normal public sector employment will not be affected by this job-guaranteed plan, but will remain a vital and separate component of public employment. Under this program, the government would become in a sense "a market maker for labor" by establishing a "buffer stock of labor" as it would stand ready to "buy" all unemployed labor at a fixed price (wage), or to "sell," that is, provide it to the private sector at a higher price (wage). As is the case in all buffer stock schemes, the commodity used as a buffer stock is always fully employed. It always has a very stable price, which cannot deviate much from the range established by the government's announced "buy" and "sell" price. This feature of the proposal ensures full employment with stable prices. The buffer stock aspects of this job-guaranteed program generate "loose" labor markets even as they ensure full employment. This stands in stark contrast with Keynesian demand management policies that were designed to "prime the pump" with government spending that would increase private demand sufficiently to lower unemployment to the full employment level. The danger was that the Keynesian policies would lead to tight labor markets and that inflation would be generated long before reaching full employment. The program entailing a "public service employment" strategy would operate through increases or decreases to the buffer stock of labor, rather than causing unemployment. (If the buffer stock of labor shrinks in an expansion causing pressures on inflation, government raises taxes or reduces spending to replenish the buffer stock.)

This program can eliminate all involuntary unemployment by providing jobs for every person ready, willing, and able to work. There will still exist many individuals—even those in the labor force—who will be voluntarily unemployed, unwilling to work for the government, unwilling to work for the government's predetermined wage, unable to meet the minimum standards for such employment, or choosing to look for a better job while unemployed. But any person willing and able to work—*able* defined very broadly as virtually all Americans who can contribute to the economy and society, irrespective of the size of the contribution—will have the opportunity to do so.

The implication of the program is that much social spending that is currently targeted to the unemployed can be discontinued or eliminated altogether. Unemployment compensation is one example that provides some income for some of the unemployed. Guaranteed "public service employment" will render unemployment compensation unnecessary since coverage would be conceivably universal; no one would be paid for not working, and pay would be equalized. Moreover, some other forms of social spending, that is, Temporary Assistance to Needy Families (TANF), Aid to Families with Dependent Children, and food stamps, could be substantially reduced. A public-service guarantee program cannot substitute all social support since many individuals currently receiving such assistance are not, and probably could not, be in the labor force. Precisely who would be forced out of these current programs and into the "public service employment" plan outlined here cannot be easily determined. However, unlike welfare-to-work schemes, this employment program is voluntary, ensures a job is available, and has no lifetime limit.

Taking the current number of unemployed, as well as the cost of various programs that would be either reduced or eliminated, and projecting the cost of the job guaranteed policy and potential savings, it has been calculated that the net cost to the government could be as high as $50 billion (Wray 1997). Obviously, the budgetary effects of such a policy are quite small relative to the size of the federal budget, to the size of the U.S. GDP machine, and to the size of [1999's] actual federal budget surplus (and those projected well into the future). Moreover, this estimate does not include any indirect benefits likely to redound from this policy, such as those resulting from decreases in the social costs of unemployment (decreases in criminal activity and physical and mental health problems), and the benefits of some public-sector projects, such as those relating to environmental protection and improvements in the physical condition of the cities and the country as a whole.

A proposal for a "public service employment" program raises many questions. Is full employment going to increase aggregate demand to the level that accelerating demand-pull inflation would follow? Can aggregate demand increase to the level at which additional federal budget spending will not generate inflation? The answers to these questions seem clear. If in the absence of a guaranteed public service employment policy, public- and private-sector spending provides a level of employment at which more than 6 million workers are unemployed and more than 3 million underemployed, then aggregate demand is too low. For if it were higher, the population would be spending more and creating more jobs for the unemployed. Indeed, existence of involuntarily unemployed workers is de facto evidence that aggregate demand is below the level required for full employment. Thus, additional government spending that increases employment is indicative of aggregate demand being below the full employment level. The "public service employment program" can be designed to ensure that additional federal spending will rise only to the point at which all involuntary employment is eliminated. Once no workers are willing to accept a guaranteed job, spending will not be increased further. The program therefore ensures that spending does not become "excessive," that is, it will not cause aggregate demand to increase beyond the full employment level. Fine-tuning of aggregate demand is still possible with the adoption of this policy, since increases in demand will cause the guaranteed job pool to shrink, while decreases will result in its expansion. This policy limits spending to the level that will guarantee true full employment, thereby alleviating concern about demand-pull inflation.

What about cost-push inflation resulting from the pressure on wages and, in turn, costs and prices? The wage paid by the government for the public-service employment program is exogenously set, stable, and establishes a benchmark price for labor. Although some jobs might still pay a wage below the program's wage—for example, for work that is more pleasurable—once the program is put in place, most of the low-wage jobs will experience a one-time increase in wages or may disappear altogether. Employers will be forced to cover these higher costs through a combination of higher product prices, greater labor productivity, and lower realized profits. Some product prices, therefore, would experience a one-time increase, but this phenomenon is not inflation, nor does it accelerate inflation as normally defined by economists.

Recent literature attributes a high rate of depreciation to idle human capital and, in turn, a high resultant cost: Labor productivity falls quickly when labor is unemployed and, beyond some point, labor probably becomes unemployable because of loss of "work habit." With a "public service employment" policy, those who are not employed in the private sector continue to work, with the result that skills do not so quickly depreciate. Indeed, social policy could be geared toward enhancing the human capital of the guaranteed job pool, which, in turn, would reduce the productivity-adjusted cost of hiring out of this pool relative to unemployed workers, and thereby diminish inflationary pressures.

It is, therefore, not clear that this type of full employment policy will be inflationary in terms of generating continuous pressure on wages and prices. Wages might experience a one-time increase because of the approximately $12,500–plus markup to annual labor costs (calculated at $6.00 per work hour for 2,080 hours per year) required to hire unemployed workers. And workers of higher productivity might become more obstinate in their wage demands, causing other wages to also ratchet upward. However, against this tendency is the likelihood that the public-service employment program will reduce the erosion of human capital, and possibly will develop or maintain the human capital of workers who are temporarily unneeded in the private sector. When demand for private output rises sufficiently for these workers to be hired in the private sector, the somewhat higher cost of workers in the program relative to the cost of unemployed workers in the absence of the program is offset by higher productivity, thereby reducing any pressure on prices. Moreover, because unemployment compensation may no longer be needed, there would be no need for experience-rated unemployment insurance taxes on firms and workers. That is, those firms that typically have volatile (seasonal or cyclical) demand for labor would experience a reduction in overall labor costs, which, again, would tend to offset higher wage costs. By and large, even the one-time upward adjustment in wages and prices might be quite small.

It is difficult to see why true full employment under a public service job opportunity program could be more inflationary than the current system, which pays people for not working, allows their human capital to depreciate, and results in high economic and social costs associated with unemployment. In addition, income maintenance programs increase aggregate demand without increasing aggregate supply, while this employment program increases both aggregate supply and aggregate demand, putting less pressure on prices.

Even if successful at substantially increasing employment, programs calling either for a wage subsidy or reductions in the workweek could result in the inflation and sluggish growth associated with tight labor markets and structural rigidities. In contrast, a public-service employment solution could provide a full employment policy that retains price stability and labor market flexibility. Such an approach will also be relatively inexpensive and is likely to pay for itself. Public-sector employment will preserve and could even enhance the productivity of the "reserve pool" of guaranteed job holders, and potentially could provide valuable public services, including many reducing social and environmental costs. As Minsky put it, "only an infinitely elastic demand for labor can guarantee full employment without setting off a wage-price spiral, and only government can create an infinitely elastic demand for labor" (Minsky 1986). At the same time, as long as those holding a guaranteed job are available when private-sector demand increases, such a program would not result in inflationary pressures or structural rigidities.

There will surely be many objections to a program of public-service guaranteed jobs. These will undoubtedly include the following: Will this public-service job opportunity program be another make-work New Deal Works Projects Administration (WPA)? If such a program is instituted, can it be efficiently administered? States are already implementing welfare-to-work programs, why is this program needed? Will not participation in such a program lead to stigmatization? And finally, why worry now, when unemployment is at its lowest level in a generation?

Proponents of the public-service guaranteed-jobs program can easily respond to these objections. First, they would cite the numerous WPA achievements that enhanced the country's physical infrastructure and its artistic and educational accomplishments; and, most importantly, the opportunity the WPA gave to millions of people to productively contribute to the American economy and society (Minsky 1986). Second, they would enumerate the plethora of needed, but unfilled jobs—that is, teachers' assistants; library and day care assistants; companions to senior citizens, the bedridden, and the mentally and physically impaired; neighborhood and highway cleanup; environmental safety monitors; and many more jobs that this program can help fill. Third, given the abuses of some public programs, the concern about efficient administration of a public-service guaranteed-jobs program is legitimate, but there are some existing programs that can serve as models. VISTA, the Peace Corps, or Americorps could be modified to administer an ELR program with minimum costs. Fourth, state after state, with only a few exceptions, has indicated that it will not offer permanent work to prior welfare recipients, leaving them to fend for themselves. Fifth, given the experience and the enthusiasm of participants in the Peace Corps, VISTA, and Americorps, a public-service work assignment may be a good resumé entry. Finally, as I argued earlier, a closer look at the official unemployment measurements does not show a "worker heaven."

What Is to Be Done?

The costs of unemployment are significant and many of them can be quantified, especially those associated with the loss of output that unemployed workers could have produced. Furthermore, those who are working (and their employers) are burdened with financing unemployment insurance and other maintenance support that the unemployed receive. Alas, the "damages" of unemployment do not stop with these. There are many other negative effects that inflict the unemployed (Sen 1997), including loss of freedom and social exclusion, poor health and mortality, discouragement and loss of motivation for future work, weakening of family structure, racial and gender intolerance, cynicism and ultimate loss of social values and self-reliance, psychological suffering, mental agony, and even suicide. Unemployment also breeds resistance to organizational flexibility and promotes technical conservatism from those currently employed who fear downsizing and joblessness.

The realized costs and negative effects of unemployment are undoubtedly much higher in Europe than in America, although it is difficult to discern if this is so from official statistics. Yet, the absence in the Maastricht Treaty (which implements a single European currency and includes specific resolutions to reduce inflation and budget deficits) of any requirement for an all-round unemployment rate is disturbing. Even in the United States, an articulated commitment of employment targets enumerated in the Employment Act of 1946 and the Humphrey-Hawkins Act of 1978 has been affirmed by each successive political establishment. But the real issue is not to discover each continent's or country's skeletons in the closet, rather, it is whether policymakers are willing to learn the lessons of successful (and failed) policies of the past, amend them to reflect current economic conditions, and finally marshal the resources needed to implement them.

Vickrey ended his American Economic Association Presidential Address in 1993 with these words:

> There is no reason inherent in the real resources available to us why we cannot move rapidly within the next two or three years to a state of genuinely full employment and then continue indefinitely at that level. We should

then enjoy a major reduction in the ills of poverty, homelessness, sickness and crime that this would entail. We might also see less resistance to reductions of military expenditure, to liberalization of trade and migration policy, and to conservation and environmental protection programs.

Should this be "Today's Task for Economists?" I think so and I hope so.

References

Bean, C. 1994. "European Unemployment: A Survey." *Journal of Economic Literature* 32, no. 2.

Beveridge, William. 1945. *Full Employment in a Free Society.* New York: W.W. Norton.

Blaug, Mark. 1993. "Public Enemy No. 1: Unemployment Not Inflation." *Economic Notes by Monte dei Paschi di Siena* 22, no. 3: 387–401.

Bluestone, Barry, and Teresa Ghilarducci. 1996. "Wage Insurance for the Working Poor." Public policy brief no. 28, Jerome Levy Economics Institute, Annandale-on-Hudson, NY.

Bluestone, Barry, and Stephen Rose. 1998. "The Unmeasured Labor Force: The Growth in Work Hours." Public policy brief no. 39, Jerome Levy Economics Institute, Annandale-on-Hudson, NY.

Brunello, Giorgio. 1989. "The Employment Effects of Shorter Working Hours: An Application to Japanese Data." *Economica* 56 (November): 473–486.

Bureau of Labor Statistics. 1998. "The Employment Situation: October 1998," Washington, DC: U.S. Government Printing Office (May).

Calmfors, Lars. 1985. "Work Sharing, Employment and Wages." *European Economic Review* 27, no. 3: 293–309.

Commission of the European Communities (CEC). 1978. "Work Sharing: Objectives and Effects." Commission staff paper, Annex to SEC, 78 (740).

DeRong, Annik, and Michel Molitor. 1991. "The Reduction of Working Hours in Belgium: Stakes and Confrontations." In *Working Time in Transition: The Political Economy of Working Hours in Industrial Nations*, ed. K. Hinrichs, W. Roche, and C. Sirianni. Philadelphia: Temple University Press, 149–169.

Deutschmann, Christoph. 1991. "The Worker-Bee Syndrome in Japan: An Analysis of Working-Time Practices." In *Working Time in Transition: The Political Economy of Working Hours in Industrial Nations*, ed. K. Hinrichs, W. Roche, and C. Sirianni, 189–202.

Dixon, Peter B. 1987. "The Effects on the Australian Economy of Shorter Standard Working Hours in Construction and Related Industries." *Australian Bulletin of Labour* 13, no. 4 (September): 264–89.

Drèze, Jacques H. 1986. "Work-Sharing: Why? How? How Not . . ." *Centre for European Policy Studies Papers*, 27.

Drèze, J., and C. Bean, eds. 1990. *Europe's Unemployment Problem.* Cambridge: MIT Press.

Eatwell, John. 1995. "Disguised Unemployment: The G7 Experience." Discussion paper, United Nations Conference on Trade and Development, no. 106.

Economist. 1993. "Sharing the Burden." November 13.

European Industrial Relations Review. 1993. "Working Time Directive: Common Position." 235 (August): 15–18.

Forstater, Mathew. 1997. "Selective Use of Discretionary Public Employment and Economic Flexibility." Working paper no. 218, Jerome Levy Economics Institute, Annandale-on-Hudson, NY.

Garfinkel, Irwin. 1973. "A Skeptical Note on 'The Optimality' of Wage Subsidy Programs." *American Economic Review* 63, no. 2 (June): 447–453.

Gow, David. 1993. "More Time Off Could Save German Jobs." *Guardian*, London, November 4.

Hammermesh, Daniel S. 1978. "Subsidies for Jobs in the Private Sector." In *Creating Jobs*, ed. J. Palmer. Washington, DC: Brookings Institution.

Haveman, Robert H., and John L. Palmer, eds. 1982. *Jobs for Disadvantaged Workers*. Washington, DC: Brookings Institution.

Hernandez, Raymond. 1998. "Most Dropped from Welfare Don't Get Jobs." *New York Times*, March 23, B6.

Hinrichs, Karl. 1991. "Working-Time Development in West Germany: Departure to a New Stage." In *Working Time in Transition: The Political Economy of Working Hours in Industrial Nations*, pp. 27–59, ed. K. Hinrichs, W. Roche, and C. Sirianni.

Hinrichs, Karl, William Roche, and Carmen Sirianni, eds. 1991. *Working Time in Transition: The Political Economy of Working Hours in Industrial Nations*. Philadelphia: Temple University Press.

International Labour Review. 1993. "France: Company Work-Sharing Agreements." 132, no. 2: 293–298.

Jackman, R., and Richard Layard. 1986. "A Wage-Tax, Worker-Subsidy Policy for Reducing the 'Natural Rate of Unemployment.' " In *Wage Rigidity*, ed. Wilfred Beckermann. Baltimore: Johns Hopkins University Press.

Jallade, Jean-Pierre. 1991. "Working-Time Policies in France." In *Working Time in Transition: The Political Economy of Working Hours in Industrial Nations*, pp. 61–85, ed. K. Hinrichs, W. Roche, and C. Sirianni.

Kaldor, N. 1936. "Wage Subsidies as a Remedy for Unemployment." *Journal of Political Economy* 44 (December).

Layard, Richard, Stephen Nickell, and Richard Jackman. 1991. *Unemployment: Macroeconomic Performance and the Labour Market*. New York: Oxford University Press.

Levitan, Sar A., and Richard S. Belous. 1977. *Shorter Hours, Shorter Weeks: Spreading the Work to Reduce Unemployment*. Baltimore: Johns Hopkins University Press.

McGaughey, William Jr. 1981. *A Shorter Workweek in the 1980s*. White Bear Lake, MN: Thistlerose.

Minsky, Hyman P. 1986. *Stabilizing an Unstable Economy*. New Haven: Yale University Press.

Morand, Martin J., and Ramelle Macoy, eds. 1984. *Short-Time Compensation: A Formula for Work Sharing*. New York: Pergamon Press.

Norman, Peter. 1998. "Rexrodt Hails Change in Jobless Trend." *Financial Times*, March 12.

Organization for Economic Cooperation and Development. 1995. *The OECD Jobs Study: Implementing the Strategy*. Paris: OECD.

Owen, John D. 1989. *Reduced Working Hours: Cure for Unemployment or Economic Burden?* Baltimore: Johns Hopkins University Press.

Papadimitriou, Dimitri B. 1991. "Western Approaches for Restructuring the Central and Eastern European Economies." *Working Papers of the World Economy Research Institute, Warsaw School of Economics* 49 (October).

Phelps, Edmund S. 1994a. "Economic Justice to the Working Poor Through Wage Subsidy." In *Aspects of Distribution of Wealth and Income*, ed. Dimitri B. Papadimitriou. New York: St. Martin's Press: 151–164.

———. 1994b. "Raising the Employment and Pay of the Working Poor: Low-Wage Employment Subsidies Versus the Welfare State." *AEA Papers and Proceedings* 84, no. 2 (May): 54–58.

———. 1997. *Rewarding Work*. Cambridge: Harvard University Press.

Pigou, A.C. 1933. *The Theory of Unemployment*. London: Macmillan Press.

Robinson, J.V. 1937. *"Disguised Unemployment": Essays in the Theory of Employment*. London: Macmillan.

Roche, William K., Brian Fynes, and Terri Morrissey. 1996. "Working Time and Employment: A Review of International Evidence." *International Labour Review* 135, no. 2: 136–139.

Schor, Juliet B. 1991. *The Overworked American: The Unexpected Decline of Leisure*. New York: Basic Books.

Sen, Amartya. 1997. "Inequality, Unemployment and Contemporary Europe." *International Labour Review* 136, no. 2 (summer).

Snower, Dennis J. 1993. "Getting the Benefit Out of a Job." *Financial Times*, February 23.

Solow, Robert. 1998. "Guess Who Pays for Workfare?" *New York Review of Books*, November 5.

Thurow, Lester. 1996. *The Future of Capitalism*. New York: W. Morrow.

Tobin, James. 1966. "The Case for an Income Guarantee." *Public Interest* 4 (summer).

Tobin, James, et al. 1967. "Is Negative Income Tax Practical?" *Yale Law Journal* 77 (November).

Wray, L. Randall. 1997. "Government as Employer of Last Resort: Full Employment Without Inflation." Working paper no. 213, Jerome Levy Economics Institute, Annandale-on-Hudson, NY.

3

PHILIP HARVEY

Direct Job Creation

In a 1989 book (Harvey 1989), I argued that direct public-sector job creation in programs taking their inspiration from New Deal initiatives, such as the Civilian Conservation Corps (CCC) and Works Progress Administration (WPA), could provide an effective and cost-efficient way of achieving the functional equivalent of full employment. In this paper, I explore the question of why, despite its advantages, the direct job creation strategy only occasionally attracts significant support in public policy debate concerning possible responses to the problem of joblessness in the United States.

I argue that policy debates in this area during the twentieth century have been dominated by three distinct views of the causes of joblessness. I call these three perspectives the "behavioralist," "structuralist," and "job shortage" views of the problem. According to the behavioralist view, joblessness is caused by the behavior of jobless individuals themselves. According to the structuralist view, joblessness is caused by barriers to equal employment opportunity. According to the job shortage view, joblessness is caused by an aggregate shortage of jobs. The behavioralist perspective tends to be favored by conservatives, while the structuralist and job shortage perspectives are favored by liberals (as those designations are used in ordinary political discourse in the United States today).

Direct job creation tends to attract significant interest as a policy response to the problem of joblessness only when the problem is perceived to flow from the existence of an aggregate job shortage. Since this view of the problem tends to attract broad support only during recessions, direct job creation tends to gain significant advocacy only during such periods. During nonrecessionary periods, joblessness is more likely to be attributed to structuralist or behavioralist factors, and support for direct job creation dissipates, except as a form of targeted job training.

Moreover, even during recessions, other policy options compete with direct job creation for support among liberals. Since the late 1930s, Keynesian macroeconomic policies have provided the strongest competition, promising a remedy for cyclically induced job shortages that is easier to implement and less controversial politically. The result over the past several decades has been diminished support for direct job creation even during recessions.

These tendencies provide a good explanation for the limited interest displayed in direct job creation as a policy response to the problem of joblessness since World War II. Nevertheless, I criticize these trends to the extent that they are based on a misperception of actual labor market conditions. I argue that empirical evidence suggests that aggregate job shortages exist not only during recessions, but across all phases of the business cycle, and that the amount of joblessness experienced in the economy is just as much a product of these conditions during periods of prosperity as it is during periods of recession. What behavioralist and structuralist factors explain, I suggest, is not the dimensions of the joblessness problem (how many people are jobless) but rather, its distribution among population groups (why some people experience more joblessness than others).

Based on this analysis, I argue that direct job creation warrants renewed attention in discussions of the problem of joblessness. Moreover, it is owed this attention not only during recessions, but also during periods of relative prosperity when macroeconomic policies are less likely to provide a satisfactory alternative means of closing the economy's aggregate job gap.

The Advantages of Direct Job Creation

Because readers of this article may be unfamiliar with the attractions of direct job creation as a policy response to the problem of joblessness, I shall begin with a brief review of my earlier work on the subject (Harvey 1989; 1993; 1995), focusing on the issues of program cost and inflation.

Program Cost

My interest in the cost of direct job creation arose out of a desire to determine whether it would be feasible to impose on governments an obligation to secure the right to employment proclaimed in international human rights agreements such as the Universal Declaration of Human Rights (United Nations 1948). To address that question I estimated what it would have cost to achieve full employment by means of direct job creation during a ten-year period of exceptionally high unemployment in the United States (Harvey 1989). The period I selected was 1977 through 1986. The national unemployment rate averaged 7 percent during that period, the third highest ten-year average in over a century. If all able-bodied recipients of Aid for Dependent Children (AFDC) had been counted as unemployed, the unem-

Figure 3.1 **Estimated Number of Jobs Needed to Achieve Full Employment, 1977–1986** (thousands)

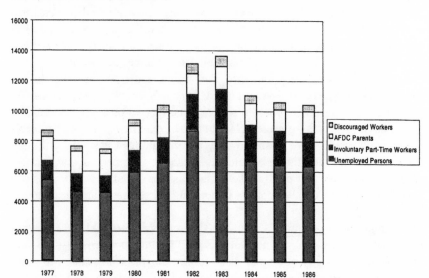

ployment rate would have averaged about 9.5 percent for the ten-year period. The cost of a job-creation program capable of achieving full employment in such a period seems a good test of the fiscal feasibility of such an undertaking in general.

The hypothetical program whose cost I estimated would have created enough jobs to eliminate involuntary part-time employment while reducing official unemployment to the 2 percent level for an enlarged labor force that I assumed would include able-bodied AFDC recipients and discouraged workers as well as officially unemployed workers. I estimated that such a program would have needed to create an average of 8.2 million jobs per year over the ten-year estimation period, ranging from a low of 7.4 million in 1979 to a high of 13.6 million in 1983. Figure 3.1 shows the distribution of those jobs among assumed program participants. About three-fifths of the jobs would have gone to officially unemployed workers. The rest would have been divided among involuntary part-time workers, AFDC recipients not already counted as unemployed, and discouraged workers.

I assumed the program would have paid market wages, which I defined as the wage that unsuccessful job seekers reasonably could expect to receive if enough additional jobs became available at existing wage rates to employ them all. For officially unemployed persons, I assumed this would average 79 percent of the average hourly wage earned by nonsupervisory and production workers in the United States as a whole. This estimate was based on a 1976 survey of unemployed persons that found this to be the average last wage they actually had earned prior to becoming unemployed. For other program participants (involuntary part-time workers, AFDC parents, and discouraged workers), I assumed that average program wages would equal the average hourly earnings of part-time workers in the United States as a whole.

Based on these assumptions, program wages expressed in 1998 dollars would have averaged $10.16 per hour for officially unemployed persons and $6.81 per hour for other program participants. Not all program participants would have earned these wages. Based on their experience and skills, many participants would have qualified only for minimum-wage jobs. I merely assumed that the cited figures would have been the arithmetic average wages paid by a program that paid market wages as I have defined that standard. This assumption, along with others underlying my estimate, are summarized in Chart 3.1.

As indicated in Chart 3.1, I assumed the program would have offered forty-hour-per-week jobs to participants who wanted to work full-time, and jobs averaging twenty hours per week to participants who wanted to work part-time. I assumed that all participants would have been paid for a full fifty-two weeks per year (therefore allowing for the payment of holiday, vacation, and sick leave at whatever levels were deemed appropriate).

I further assumed that an amount equal to one-third of the program's direct wage costs would have been spent on facilities, equipment, materials, and supplies required to carry out the program's work projects. This was the approximate ratio of nonlabor to labor costs in New Deal work programs. It also was the approximate ratio of nonlabor to labor costs in child day care programs operated in the United States during the 1980s—one of the services I assumed the program would produce.

I assumed that program wages would have been treated like any other wage income for tax purposes (which means the employer share of FICA taxes would have been an additional program cost), and that program participants would have been provided the same health insurance benefits as regular federal employees (and on the same terms).

I also assumed that free child care would have been provided to all program participants in child care centers operated as one of the work activities of the program. Interestingly, this means the cost of providing child care to program participants would not have added anything to the program's total cost. The same would have been true of a range of other employee services—such as paid job training, substance abuse counseling, and sheltered-workshop employment for program participants who needed such services.

The estimated year-to-year cost of the program based on these assump-

Chart 3.1

Assumptions Underlying Cost Estimate for Direct Job Creation Program Capable of Achieving Full Employment

Wages: Program Participants paid "market wages" averaging $10.16 per hour in 1998 dollars for officially unemployed persons and $6.81 per hour in 1998 dollars for other program participants.

Hours: Forty hours per week for persons seeking full-time jobs and twenty hours per week for persons seeking part-time jobs.

Taxes: Program wages fully taxable. Program employment also covered by Social Security, with program participants (and the government as employer) liable for FICA taxes at same rates as other covered employees (and employers).

Insurance: Federal employee health insurance benefits provided on same terms as for regular federal employees.

Paid Leave: Medical leave, holidays, and vacation time provided to program participants at whatever level is deemed appropriate, with cost or benefit covered by assumption that wages would be paid for a full work year (2,080 hours/year for full-time workers and 1,040 hours/ year for part-time workers).

Child Care: Free to all program participants (provided in child care centers operated as employment projects by the program).

Services: Free job training and other support services (for example, substance abuse counseling or sheltered workshop assignments) provided to all program participants (with services provided through programs operated as employment projects by the program).

Materials: Spending on nonlabor costs (facilities, tools, materials, and supplies) assumed to equal one-third of program's direct wage bill.

tions is shown in Figure 3.2. Expressed in 1998 dollars, these costs would have averaged $213 billion per year. While high, this level of spending is not unprecedented for a major social insurance benefit. In 1986, for example, the jobs program would have cost $146 billion in current dollars compared to $194 billion actually spent for Social Security pension benefits.

Figure 3.2 also includes estimates of certain offsetting savings and revenues that such a program would have generated. The offsetting savings shown in Figure 3.2 consist of reduced spending on cash and in-kind transfer benefits actually provided to able-bodied persons of working age and their dependents during the ten-year period. I estimated that these savings would have covered about 60 percent of total program costs over the ten-year pe-

Figure 3.2 **Estimated Cost of Achieving Full Employment through Direct Job Creation, 1977–1986** (billions of dollars)

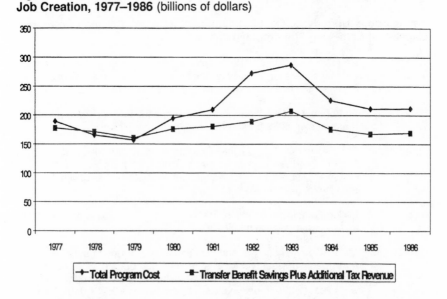

riod. The offsetting revenue shown in Figure 3.2 consists of additional income and payroll tax payments by program participants. I estimated that this revenue would have covered another 20 percent of the program's total costs during the ten-year period.

As Figure 3.2 illustrates, the program's remaining funding deficit (about 20 percent of total program costs) would not have been spread evenly across the ten-year period, but would have been concentrated in 1982 and 1983 when the nation's unemployment rate was elevated by the worst American recession since the Great Depression.

This calls attention to a third source of savings such a program would have generated. A jobs program such as I have described would be a powerful automatic stabilizer—functioning in that respect like the nation's Unemployment Compensation program—but with a much stronger countercyclical impact because of its greater size. If the program I have described had been in place during the 1977–1986 period, the deep recession of the early 1980s almost surely would have been less severe. This, in turn, would have resulted in lower program costs and a smaller program deficit. It also would have resulted in substantial increases in government tax receipts during the period—additional revenues that reasonably could have been attributed to the jobs program. I did not try to estimate what the program's likely countercyclical effect would have been. Nor did I try to estimate the savings and revenues likely to have resulted from that effect, but they could have been substantial. It is significant to note in this regard that, prior to the recession of the early 1980s, the program would have had virtually no budget deficit after taking into consideration transfer benefit savings and additional income tax revenues attributable to it.

A fourth source of savings attributable to the program would have consisted of reductions in government spending for items other than transfer benefits. Joblessness has been shown to contribute to a range of social and medical problems that impose significant costs on governments other than the payment of transfer benefits. These problems range from increased criminal activity to increased heart disease. A jobs program that reduced unemployment to genuinely voluntary levels almost surely would have produced savings in budget areas not included in the estimate of transfer program savings shown in Figure 3.2.

Finally, my cost estimate for the program was based on the assumption that everything the program produced would have been given away for free. Such a policy is certainly not required, and there is no reason to believe it is even desirable. If the program sold some of its output, even at deeply discounted prices, the program's funding deficit would have been reduced. In deciding what, if anything, to charge for the goods and services produced by such a program, fiscal policy considerations could play a role. For example, if it were considered desirable that the program be fiscally neutral compared to current levels of taxation and government spending, prices for program outputs could be set at a level calculated to achieve that goal. Given the relatively small size of such a program's likely funding deficit (after taking into account other sources of savings and revenue), that particular goal should be easy to achieve. In fact, my analysis suggests that such a program is more likely to save governments money than to require additional outlays, in which case fiscal neutrality would require either additional government spending for other purposes or a tax cut.

Other fiscal policy goals could be pursued, of course. My point is that support for the use of direct job creation as a means of achieving full employment is not necessarily linked to support for deficit spending or an expansionary fiscal policy. Operation of such a program could be combined with increased deficit spending, the maintenance of balanced government budgets, or a deflationary policy devoted to generating government budget surpluses.

Inflationary Pressures

Because inflationary pressures tend to increase as unemployment rates fall, it is natural to worry about the possible inflationary effects of using direct job creation to achieve full employment. Interestingly, direct job creation may be the least inflationary way to achieve full employment.

When full employment is approached as a result of growing aggregate demand, both demand-pull and cost-push factors contribute to the build-up of inflationary pressures. Growing aggregate demand puts pressure on prices (the demand-pull factor) while tightening labor markets place upward pressure on wages (the cost-push factor).

Consider what would happen, however, if unemployment rates were to fall with little or no increase in aggregate demand. My analysis of program costs suggests that even a very generous direct job creation program could be financed in a way that was fiscally neutral. In other words, such a program could achieve the functional equivalent of full employment without increasing demand for the economy's existing output of goods and services. The increased income of program participants (and increased purchases of supplies and materials used in the program) could be exactly offset by (1) increased income tax payments by program participants and by vendors selling goods and services to the program; (2) reductions in government transfer payments; and (3) increased payments to government for a portion of the goods and services produced by the jobs program. The result would be a somewhat larger public sector, but no net increase in demand for privately produced goods and services and, therefore, no demand-pull effect on product prices.

Consider, too, that the increased demand for labor produced by the hypothetical program I have described would emanate not from private-sector employers competing for workers in bottle-necked industries, but from a government program that offers work (1) at fixed wage rates no higher than those prevailing in the market for similarly qualified labor, and (2) only to persons unable to find employment in the regular labor market. Such a program should not generate cost-push pressures in the labor market. In fact, the program's labor force could function as a "buffer stock" tending to stabilize wage rates at the level paid by the program (Wray 1998).

Some temporary inflation could be expected as *relative* wage rates adjusted to the increased relative bargaining power of low-wage workers, but there is no reason to believe such adjustments would cause a permanent inflationary spiral. The likely end result should be a somewhat flatter wage distribution with no increase in basic inflationary tendencies (see Harvey 1989, 75–78).

Alternative Strategies for Combating Joblessness

The surprising conclusion that flows from my analysis of program cost is that a generous direct job creation program could achieve full employment without (1) requiring increased taxes or deficit spending; or (2) significantly increasing inflationary pressures in the economy. This raises the question of why the idea has had such a low profile in policy battles since World War II. There was a flurry of interest in the idea in the 1970s—as reflected in the enactment of the Comprehensive Employment and Training Act (CETA)—but except for that period, the idea has been conspicuous for the lack of attention it has received from scholars and politicians alike.

This puzzling omission is symbolized in my mind by the response of liberals to the civil rights movement and the rediscovery of poverty in the early 1960s. It was widely recognized at the time that poor people and disadvantaged minority groups wanted more and better jobs. The official slogan of the 1963 March on Washington was "Jobs and Justice," and, lest the message be misinterpreted, the demonstration's official list of demands included the adoption of a massive direct job creation initiative by the federal government (Hamilton and Hamilton 1997, 123–128). Instead of direct job creation, however, the liberal response to the demonstration and to the political movement it represented focused exclusively on structuralist remedies for the problem of joblessness—initiatives designed to attack employment discrimination, to remedy educational and training deficits among jobless individuals, and to move a larger share of the nation's jobs into economically depressed communities. No significant direct job creation initiatives were undertaken during the decade. As one commentator has noted,

> The poverty policies of the 1960s incorporated two decisions about the proper focus of labor market policies: such policies should be remedial measures targeted on the lowest end of the labor market, and they should aim to alter the supply of labor by modifying workers' characteristics rather than seeking to change the demand for labor. (Weir 1992, 64)

Another commentator described this policy even more succinctly: "The Johnson administration's aim was 'not more jobs, but a more equitable distribution of the nation's 3.5 percent unemployment.'" (Mucciaroni 1990, 71).

Why didn't liberals embrace direct job creation as a primary element in their response to the problem of joblessness in the 1960s? Direct job creation had constituted the heart and soul of the New Deal's response to the problem of joblessness (Harvey 1989, 18–20; Committee on Economic Security 1985, 23–24, 27–30; Burns and Williams 1941; National Resources Planning Board 1943; Rose 1994). When liberals regained effective political power in the 1960s, why didn't they resurrect the New Deal's policy agenda in this area, and why has direct job creation continued to receive so little attention from liberals (except during the CETA period) since then? I believe the key to this puzzle resides in the different way liberals thought about the problem of joblessness in the 1960s compared to the 1930s.

The strategy for combating joblessness preferred by conservatives has never varied in its fundamentals. This strategy can be termed "behavioralist" because it is based on the view that joblessness is caused by the failure of jobless individuals to seek work with adequate determination and to accept it on terms the market sets. According to this view, the goal of public policy should be to avoid rewarding jobless individuals for their nonoptimal behavior. Humanitarian considerations may dictate that public assistance be offered to jobless individuals, or at least to their minor dependents, but the amount of aid offered should be as small as possible and be accompanied by measures designed to discourage jobless individuals from accepting it. This strategy dominated public policy responses to joblessness in the United States prior to the 1930s (Harvey 1999b), and it is currently experiencing a resurgence of popularity (see, for example, Mead 1992).

Liberals have pursued two different policy responses to the problem of joblessness during the twentieth century. The first of these strategies—which I call the "job shortage" approach—is based on the view that joblessness is caused by the economy's failure to provide enough jobs for everyone who wants to work. According to this view, public policy should focus on efforts to reduce the economy's job gap while providing jobless individuals with reasonably generous and nonstigmatizing forms of public assistance. This strategy dominated American public policy responses to joblessness during the 1930s (National Resources Planning Board 1943; Burns and Williams 1941), and it has been periodically resurgent since then for short periods of time during recessions (Levitan and Gallo 1991).

The second liberal response to the problem of joblessness can be called the "structuralist" strategy because it is based on the view that joblessness is caused by structural barriers to equal employment opportunity embedded in the economy. These barriers are of three general types. The first are skill barriers that prevent jobless individuals from qualifying for available jobs. The second are geographic barriers that limit the accessibility of available jobs. The third barrier is employment discrimination that causes employers not to hire members of disfavored groups.

According to the structuralist view of the causes of joblessness, public policy to combat the problem should focus on removing barriers to equal employment opportunity. General education and special training programs should be provided to jobless individuals; employers should be provided incentives to locate businesses in depressed communities or regions; and employment discrimination should be outlawed. This is the liberal strategy that dominated public policy responses to joblessness in the 1960s, and it is the strategy that has continued to dominate liberal thinking about the problem since then (Sundquist 1968, 57–110; Mucciaroni 1990, 32–42).

These two liberal strategies are not inconsistent with one another and could be pursued simultaneously, but, generally, that has not happened (Harvey 1999a). As indicated above, the job shortage approach dominated the liberal policy agenda in the 1930s, while the structuralist approach has dominated liberal thinking since the 1960s. Why? The most obvious answer is to be found in the contrast between general economic conditions in the 1930s and the 1960s. When the economy is suffering a recession or depression—especially one as severe as that of the 1930s—it is obvious to almost all observers that there aren't enough jobs to go around. Disadvantaged population groups are likely to suffer disproportionate joblessness during such periods, but solutions to their special problems are likely to be perceived as contingent on a solution first being found for the aggregate shortage of jobs dragging down the entire economy.

In contrast, when the economy as a whole is prospering, as it was during the 1960s, the special problems of disadvantaged population groups stand out as exceptional rather than as similar to the problems suffered by workers in general. The elevated unemployment rates suffered by minority populations and the persistent joblessness suffered by the able-bodied poor appear to reflect problems unique to them. The liberal response is not to absolve the economy of blame, but to look for a solution to the special problems suffered by disadvantaged population groups. This results in policies designed to end or compensate for the disadvantages suffered by members of these population groups rather than a reduction in aggregate levels of joblessness.

The pattern is understandable. During recessions, when the existence of job shortages are taken for granted, liberals tend to advocate policies designed to close the economy's job gap. During nonrecessionary periods, when aggregate job shortages seem less important as a source of social stress than the special disadvantages that handicap certain population groups, liberals tend to advocate structuralist policies designed to attack those disadvantages.

It is only during recessions, then, that liberals are likely to attach a high priority to reducing aggregate levels of joblessness, and direct job creation may not be the most attractive policy option for pursuing that goal. Since the late 1930s, Keynesian macroeconomic theory has provided a powerful and attractive alternative strategy for combating joblessness in periods of recession. Liberals gravitated to the Keynesian strategy in the late 1930s and, following the practical demonstration of its success during World War II, direct job creation seemed no longer necessary (Weir 1992, 27–61; Mucciaroni 1990, 17–45). The demotion of direct job creation in the liberal policy arsenal was symbolized by the terms of the full-employment legislation proposed by liberals in Congress in 1944. It would have obligated the federal government to maintain full employment—but not by direct job creation. Instead, the proposed legislation relied upon an automatic appropriation of sufficient funds to maintain full employment by Keynesian means (Bailey 1950).

Since then, Keynesian measures almost always have seemed more attractive to liberals than direct job creation as a means of closing the economy's job gap during recessions. The exception that proves this rule was liberal support for direct job creation during the 1970s when the problem of "stagflation" undermined confidence in the Keynesian policy alternative. Direct job creation—in the form of the CETA program—attracted surprisingly broad support as a less inflationary response than Keynesian measures to unacceptably high unemployment rates during the recession of 1973–75 (Mucciaroni 1990, 83–90).

Reassessing the Strategies

To assess the relative strengths and weaknesses of behavioralist, structuralist, and job shortage strategies for combating joblessness, it is helpful to distinguish between the aggregate level of unemployment in society and its distribution among population groups. The role of this distinction is illustrated by the following parable.

There once was an island with a population of 100 dogs. Every day a plane flew overhead and dropped ninety-five bones onto the island. Every day the dogs fought over these bones. Every day ninety-five dogs ended up with bones, while five went hungry. Hearing that there was a problem of bonelessness on the island, a group of social scientists was sent to assess the problem and to recommend remedies.

The social scientists ran a series of regressions and determined that bonelessness was associated with a lack of motivation on the part of boneless dogs and that boneless dogs also lacked important skills in fighting for bones. As a remedy for the problem, some of the social scientists proposed that boneless dogs needed motivational training (or possibly just a good kick in the side) to get them moving when the bones began to fall each day. Others proposed that boneless dogs be provided special training in bone-fighting skills.

A bitter controversy ensued over which of these two strategies ought to be pursued. Over time, both strategies were tried, and both reported limited success in helping individual dogs overcome their bonelessness—but despite this success, the bonelessness problem on the island never lessened in the aggregate. Every day, there were still five dogs that went hungry.

Figure 3.3 **Estimated Number of Officially Unemployed Persons Per Job Vacancy, Scattered Surveys 1964–1994** (average contemporaneous unemployment rate in parentheses)

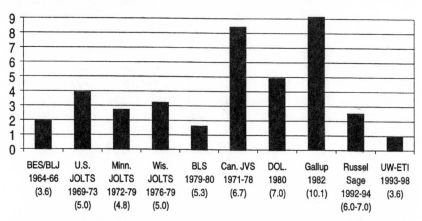

The point of this parable is not to suggest that the social scientists were mistaken in assessing the causes of bonelessness on the island. In one sense, they were right. A lack of motivation or a lack of skill in fighting for bones did cause the dogs that suffered these deficits to go without bones. The problem with their analysis was that, in concentrating their total attention on factors that determined the distribution of bonelessness among the dog population, they ignored the process that actually determined how many dogs went without bones. They discovered why some dogs suffered more bonelessness than others; but they could neither explain nor suggest policies to remedy the fact that there always were five hungry dogs on the island.

Like the bonelessness problem in this parable, there is strong evidence that the level of joblessness in the United States economy is determined by the aggregate number of jobs that employers are willing to fill at any point in time compared to the number of persons who want employment. The best evidence of this relationship is found in job vacancy surveys that occasionally have been conducted in the United States since the mid-1960s (Abraham 1983; Holzer 1989, 1996; Employment and Training Institute 1993).

Figure 3.3 shows the ratio of officially unemployed persons to job vacancies found in these surveys. The data suggests that substantial and continuing job shortages are not just a fact of economic life during recessions. The shortages are most severe during recessions, but they persist at a lower level of severity during periods of relative prosperity as well.

The surveys conducted in the mid-1960s are particularly intriguing because liberals were politically dominant at the time, yet chose to pursue an exclusively structuralist strategy in combating the problem of joblessness. Aggregate unemployment rates were very low by historic standards, averaging only 3.6 percent in the surveyed labor markets, yet the surveys suggest there still were almost twice as many active job seekers as there were available jobs.

Moreover, these surveys probably understate the extent of the job shortages that actually existed. First, the data do not take into consideration categories of job needers other than officially unemployed workers. If we counted involuntary part-time workers, discouraged workers, and able-bodied welfare recipients as unemployed, the job gaps shown in Figure 3.3 would be substantially larger.

Second, there is some evidence that the proportion of all job vacancies that are for part-time jobs is higher than the proportion of all job seekers who desire part-time work (Employment and Training Institute 1993). A comparison of full-time equivalent job vacancies to full-time equivalent job seekers most likely would enlarge the job shortages reported here.

Finally, since workers can (and frequently do) occupy more than one job, while job vacancies normally cannot employ more than one worker, the number of job vacancies needed to provide employment for everyone who wants work is greater than the number of unemployed persons seeking (or needing) work.

It is possible, of course, that aggregate unemployment rates are elevated by structural and/or behavioral factors as well. This would mean that the level of unemployment is partly determined by the size of the economy's aggregate job gap and partly by structural or behavioral factors. This almost certainly is true. There always are some jobs that go begging in the economy. The question is how many.

The job vacancy rates reported in these surveys generally varied in accord with the so-called Beveridge curve—with vacancy rates rising as unemployment rates fell (Holzer 1989, 27–29). This phenomenon is consistent with the conclusion that structuralist and behavioralist factors do affect the vacancy rate and thereby also affect the aggregate level of unemployment. Still, average vacancy rates over time tended to be in the 1.5–2.5 percent range. If the economy's unavoidable frictional unemployment floor is somewhere in this range, this survey data suggests that structural and behavioral problems probably haven't contributed very much to aggregate levels of unemployment in the United States during the past several decades.

What, then, do behavioralist and structuralist accounts of joblessness explain? Are they simply mistaken? I do not think so. What they explain is the distribution of joblessness—not how many people are without work, but who those people are likely to be.

While job vacancy rates appear to be significantly lower than unemployment rates in the U.S. economy, job turnover rates appear to be significantly higher. Job turnover data is also scarce, but what little exists suggests that gross hiring rates are very high. In the study reported in the next-to-last bar of Figure 3.3, job turnover data was collected in addition to job vacancy data. The average job vacancy rate was only 2.7 percent, but the annual gross hiring rate—the proportion of all jobs filled by persons newly hired in the preceding twelve months—was 25.7 percent (Holzer 1996, 143). If this were the average figure over time for the entire economy, it would mean that over 30 million jobs become available every year.

Because job turnover rates are high, each unemployed person can be viewed as having multiple opportunities to secure a job over the course of a year, even if there is a shortage of jobs relative to job seekers at any point in time. Stated differently, there may not be enough jobs to go around, but enough jobs become available over time that unemployed persons would not have to wait very long for a job if all job seekers had an equal chance of being hired as positions became available.

This suggests the image of a hiring queue. Unemployed workers are waiting their turn to move to the head of the line and get a job. If particular groups of workers lose jobs more frequently than other groups of workers, or if they do not move through the hiring queue as quickly as others, they will experience more unemployment. It is the causes of these differential rates of unemployment that behavioralist and structuralist explanations of joblessness help us to understand, even if they tell us nothing at all about how much unemployment there is in the economy.

If I am correct in this assessment—that the level of unemployment is determined by the size of the economy's job shortage, while the distribution of that unemployment is determined by structuralist and behavioralist factors—then the goals of behavioralist and structuralist policies for combating joblessness also require reassessment. The goals of these policies should not be seen as the reduction of unemployment, but rather as the equalization of its social burdens.

There is nothing to be said against this policy goal in principle. If 5 percent unemployment were equally shared by the entire labor force, it would mean, in effect, that everyone would have to take a two-week unpaid vacation each year. Episodes of unemployment as short as that seem unlikely to cause major social problems. The question that must be asked, however, is whether structuralist and behavioralist policies reasonably can be expected to achieve this goal under job-shortage conditions. Their actual performance in this regard has not been stellar. There are a number of factors that likely contribute to the disappointing success rates of these policies.

The first reason is the peculiar way in which labor market queues work. Labor markets tend to reward success with more success and punish failure with more failure. Under conditions of full employment, this tends to sort workers among jobs, but under conditions of less than full employment, it creates special disadvantages for jobless individuals who are seeking work, even in the absence of structuralist impediments to their employment.

Unemployed job seekers are sometimes described as queuing for jobs, but hiring queues function differently from most waiting lines. The distinguishing characteristic of most queues is that people move forward from the back to the front of the line as they wait. Hiring queues tend to move in the opposite direction. The longer a job seeker remains jobless, the less attractive she is likely to become to potential employers. The most attractive candidates are likely to be those who haven't even joined the hiring queue—currently employed persons who are looking for a new or second job. And available data suggests there may be as many of them as there are unemployed job seekers (Bureau of Labor Statistics 1997).

This does not mean that structurally disadvantaged job seekers cannot find work, but it makes it harder for them. Nor does this mean that efforts to help jobless individuals overcome structural barriers to equal employment opportunity will fail, but that such efforts must overcome the natural tendency of labor markets to favor the already advantaged with more success. The larger the economy's aggregate job shortage, the longer hiring queues will be, and the farther back in line unemployed job seekers, especially disadvantaged job seekers, are likely to find themselves.

Second, to the extent that special efforts to help disadvantaged job seekers do succeed, the population most likely to sacrifice jobs to the newly employed comprises workers who are only marginally better situated and who probably have personal characteristics very similar to those of the assisted population. A redistribution of the burdens of joblessness among the lowest strata of the labor force isn't likely to reduce the social harms caused by the problem. The severity of this problem is linked to the size of the economy's job gap, because that is what determines the intensity of the competition for available jobs among unemployed and marginally employed workers.

Third, if jobs are scarce, efforts to increase the employment of disadvantaged individuals are likely to elicit nullifying counterresponses from more privileged workers. The counterresponse may take benign forms, such as increased investment in education, but they also may take less benign forms, such as growing resentment directed at disadvantaged groups and increased opposition to access-broadening initiatives. Opposition by white male workers to the use of hiring preferences to increase the employment of minority and women job seekers illustrates this kind of reaction. Whether it takes benign or destructive forms, the efforts by more privileged workers to keep ahead in the competition for available jobs is likely to frustrate efforts to increase the job security of less advantaged workers.

Finally, to the extent that the distribution of joblessness is a product of discriminatory hiring practices, the existence of a significant job gap makes it much harder to alter employer practices. Surplus labor supply provides both a cover for discriminatory hiring practices and an economic cushion that allows employers to indulge their biases. Proving discriminatory treatment is very difficult when large numbers of workers apply for a small number of jobs and are evaluated according to multiple, incommensurable hiring criteria. This may be one reason for the prevalence of discriminatory firing cases over discriminatory hiring cases in employment discrimination litigation (Donohue and Siegelman 1991). The existence of labor surpluses also permits employers greater latitude in deciding where to locate their businesses, avoiding minority populations if they want, without fear of not being able to recruit adequate numbers of workers (Holzer 1996, 131). As the economy's job gap shrinks, the economic pressure on employers not to discriminate increases, and the deterrent effect of antidiscrimination law probably becomes more effective.

These factors do not mean that structuralist and behavioralist strategies cannot succeed under job-shortage conditions, but they do suggest that the limited success these strategies have enjoyed may be based on the failure to link them to an effective policy for reducing the economy's job gap. We implicitly accept this fact, for example, when we acknowledge that current welfare reform initiatives are not likely to work if the economy goes into recession. Why? Jobs turn over, even during a recession. Why shouldn't we expect welfare recipients to grab those openings? What we implicitly acknowledge in recognizing the limitations of welfare reform in those circumstances is that the existence of a large job gap reduces the likelihood that welfare recipients will be able to find work.

The same can be said, however, of the smaller but still significant job gaps that exist in periods of relative prosperity. Structuralist and behavioralist policies work better during periods of relatively low unemployment, but the continued existence of a significant aggregate job shortage, even in periods of relative prosperity, tends to limit the effectiveness of such policies.

In light of these considerations, a strong argument can be made that an effective strategy for combating joblessness cannot be founded on behavioralist and structuralist policies alone. It has to include an effective strategy for reducing or eliminating the economy's job gap—not only in periods of recession but in periods of relative prosperity as well.

Resurrecting the Direct Job Creation Option

Given the strong commitment of American liberals to direct job creation in the 1930s, it seems surprising at first that the policy option has attracted so little interest since World War II. The neglect of the idea is understandable, however, in light of its linkage to the job-shortage explanation of the problem of unemployment. Only during recessions is the existence of an aggregate job shortage taken for granted in the United States and, since the 1930s, Keynesian theory has tended to eclipse direct job creation as the preferred liberal strategy for closing the economy's job gap during such periods. The only time direct job creation commanded strong support in the post–World War II era was during the 1970s when unemployment rates rose sharply in an inflationary environment that seemed to checkmate Keynesian anti-cyclical measures.

This analysis suggests that support for direct job creation as a policy response to joblessness is likely to flourish only when two conditions are satisfied. First, the problem of joblessness must be perceived to flow from an aggregate shortage of jobs and not just from behavioralist or structuralist impediments to successful job-search activities. Second, the limitations of other policies designed to eliminate job shortages must be recognized.

The factual bases for both of these conditions appear to have been satisfied at virtually all times during the past four decades in the United States, but perceptions are another matter. The empirical evidence is compelling that job shortages are endemic in the United States economy, but liberals as well as conservatives tend to ignore the importance of aggregate job shortages as an explanation of joblessness except during recessions. In nonrecessionary periods, the problem is thought to have different roots— either structural barriers to equal employment opportunity (the liberal explanation) or behavioral problems on the part of the unemployed themselves (the conservative explanation). Like the social scientists in my parable of the dog-bone island, both liberals and conservatives have trouble seeing that the dimensions of the problem may have a different cause than the distribution of the problem among population groups.

Even if the importance of aggregate job shortages in causing the problem of joblessness were widely recognized, however, liberal support for direct job creation would remain weak as long as Keynesian measures were perceived to provide an alternative strategy for achieving that goal. This is a reasonable political stance. Macroeconomic measures tend to be less controversial than the creation of new government programs—especially government employment programs. To the extent that Keynesian macroeconomic manipulations can close the economy's job gap, such policies constitute a reasonable first choice for liberals seeking to combat joblessness.

You do not have to believe in a 6 percent "non-accelerating inflation rate of unemployment" (NAIRU), however, to acknowledge that driving unemployment down to the 2 percent level through macroeconomic stimulation alone is likely to cause serious inflationary problems. That is why some Keynesians now embrace direct job creation as a desirable, and possibly essential, component of an effective full-employment policy (see, for example, Mosler 1997–1998; Wray 1998). Direct job creation provides a useful complement to macroeconomic stimulation as a means of eliminating aggregate job shortages in the economy. Fiscal stimulation can be relied upon up to the point that inflation problems arise. From that point on, direct job creation is the logical choice to eliminate any remaining job gap.

Structuralist policies designed to achieve equal employment opportunity also would complement such a strategy, helping to ensure that the benefits of full employment are equally shared by all. In other words, support for direct job creation does not imply an abandonment of historical commitments either to Keynesianism or to structural labor market reforms. There is nothing inconsistent in pursuing those policies along with direct job creation. Indeed, a combined policy including Keynesian, structuralist, and direct job creation elements ought to be attractive to liberals once they recognize that the root cause of joblessness, in periods of prosperity as well as during recessions, is an endemic shortage of jobs relative to the number of persons seeking work in the economy.

References

Abraham, Katharine G. 1983. "Structural/Frictional vs. Deficient Demand Unemployment." *American Economic Review* 73 (September): 708–724.

Bailey, Stephen K. 1950. *Congress Makes a Law: The Story Behind the Employment Act of 1946*. New York: Columbia University Press.

Bureau of Labor Statistics. 1997. *Issues in Labor Statistics: Looking for a Job While Employed*. Washington, DC: Bureau of Labor Statistics, Summary: 97–114.

Burns, Arthur E., and Edward A. Williams. 1941. *Federal Work, Security, and Relief Programs*. Works Progress Administration Division of Social Research, Research Monograph 24.

Committee on Economic Security. 1985. *The Report of the Committee on Economic Security of 1935*, reprinted in *The Report of the Committee on Economic Security of 1935 and Other Basic Documents Relating to the Development of the Social Security Act*. Washington, DC: National Conference on Social Welfare.

Donohue, John J., and Peter Siegelman. 1991. "The Changing Nature of Employment Discrimination Litigation." *Stanford Law Review* 43 (May): 983–1033.

Employment and Training Institute, University of Wisconsin–Milwaukee. 1993. *Survey of Job Openings in the Milwaukee Metropolitan Area* (semiannual).

Hamilton, Dona Cooper, and Charles V. Hamilton. 1997. *The Dual Agenda: The African American Struggle for Civil and Economic Equality*. New York: Columbia University Press.

Harvey, Philip. 1989. *Securing the Right to Employment: Social Welfare Policy and the Unemployed in the United States*. Princeton: Princeton University Press.

———. 1993. "Employment as a Human Right." In *Sociology and the Public Agenda*, ed. William J. Wilson. Newbury Park, CA.: Sage.

———. 1995. "Paying for Full Employment: A Hard-Nosed Look at Finances." *Social Policy* 25, no. 3 (Spring): 21–30.

———. 1999a. "Joblessness and the Law Before the New Deal." *Georgetown Journal on Poverty Law and Policy* 6: 497–504.

———. 1999b. "Liberal Strategies for Combating Joblessness in the Twentieth Century." *Journal of Economic Issues* 33, no. 2: 1–41.

Holzer, Harry. 1989. *Unemployment, Vacancies and Local Labor Markets*. Kalamazoo, MI: W.E. Upjohn Institute for Employment Research.

———. 1996. *What Employers Want: Job Prospects for Less Educated Workers*. New York: Russell Sage Foundation.

Levitan, Sar A., and Gallo, Frank. 1991. "Spending to Save: Expanding Employment Opportunities." Occasional paper 2, Center for Social Policy Studies, George Washington University.

Mead, Lawrence. 1992. *The New Politics of Poverty*. New York: Basic Books.

Mosler, Warren. 1997–1998. "Full Employment and Price Stability." *Journal of Post Keynesian Economics* 20, no. 167 (winter).

Mucciaroni, Gary. 1990. *The Political Failure of Employment Policy 1945–1982*. Pittsburgh: University of Pittsburgh Press.

National Resources Planning Board. 1943. *Security, Work, and Relief Policies*. H.R. Doc. no. 128, Part 3, 78th Cong., 1st sess.

Rose, Nancy. 1994. *Put To Work: Relief Programs in the Great Depression*. New York: Monthly Review Press.

Sundquist, James L. 1968. *Politics and Policy: The Eisenhower, Kennedy, and Johnson Years*. Washington, DC: Brookings Institution.

United Nations. 1948. *Universal Declaration of Human Rights*. U.N. Doc. A/811.

Weir, Margaret. 1992. *Politics and Jobs: The Boundaries of Employment Policy in the United States*. Princeton: Princeton University Press.

Wray, Randall. 1998. *Money in the Modern Era*. Cheltenham, UK: Edward Elgar.

4

David Colander

Vickrey, Macro Policy, and Chock-Full Employment

There is work to do; there are men to do it. Why not bring them together? No, says Mr. Baldwin. There are mysterious, unintelligible reasons of high finance and economic theory why this is impossible. It would be most rash. It would probably ruin the country. Abra would rise, cadabra would fall. Your food would cost you more. If everyone were to be employed, it would be just like the war over again. And even if everyone was employed, how can you be perfectly sure that they would still be employed three years hence? If we build houses to cover our heads, construct transport systems to carry our goods, drain our lands, protect our coasts, what will there be left for our children to do? No, cries Mr. Baldwin, it would be most unjust. The more work we do now the less there will be left to do hereafter. Unemployment is the lot of man. This generation must take its fair share of it without grousing. For the more the fewer, and the higher the less. (Keynes 1931, 91)

Two aspects of Bill Vickrey's approach to economics are, for me, defining.* The first is that Vickrey was a deeply religious and moral individual. Because morality was fully integrated into his views of economics, understanding Vickrey's moral vision is important for an understanding of his support

---

*Bill Vickrey's twinkling eyes, spontaneous laugh, and warm smile made it clear to anyone who met him that he approached life in an open manner—no pretensions, no games—simply "here is the way I see it." I write this paper in that same spirit. Vickrey's passion was his hope that he could guide our society toward achieving "chock-full" employment. I supported and support him in that hope. This paper attempts to put his views on macro policy into perspective and to explain the reasoning that leads from economic theory to Vickrey's views.

for full employment policies and his approach to macroeconomic theory. The second is that Vickrey was an Old Keynesian, in the functional finance sense of the word. Like most true functional finance supporters, he had an almost visceral reaction to fear of deficits based upon some of the false arguments against deficits generally made. Those arguments do not logically hold water, and Vickrey wanted the world to know that.[1] In terms of policy, however, the deficit arguments of functional finance are only a sidelight. The central element of the functional finance approach is that one judges macro actions, such as running a deficit, in relation to "the results of these actions on the economy and not to any established traditional doctrine about what is sound and unsound" (Lerner 1943, 39).

Old Keynesians were somewhat of an anachronism in the 1990s, and in the last decade of his life, Vickrey was seen as the archetypal anachronism.[2] He was admired for his previous path-breaking work and tolerated for his current views. Vickrey did not care what the profession thought, and throughout the 1990s he went around to conferences urging a much more expansive monetary and fiscal policy than the then-current fashion allowed, and was seen as a bit of a crank for doing so.[3] I did not always agree with Vickrey's Old Keynesian views and, at times, I have to admit, I wished he would have been a bit less strident in his lectures. But he was always insightful, logical, and creative. Members of the profession knew that, and it scared them a bit that such a brilliant economist could differ significantly with conventional wisdom. It didn't scare them enough for them to reconsider their views, but it did scare them.

Even though I have not fully agreed with Old Keynesians, I have always found myself attracted to their approach to economics; there is a passion in their economics that is lost to today's techno-economists. That attraction led to my collaboration with Abba Lerner and with Vickrey. It also led me to do a set of interviews with Old Keynesians (Colander and Landreth 1996) on how Keynesian ideas came to America and spread throughout the profession. In those interviews, it is clear that Old Keynesians were passionately concerned with unemployment and saw the job of macroeconomics to be its elimination. It was also clear that their economic consciousness was shaped in the Great Depression. Their deep moral concern about unemployment was based on that experience and their gut feeling that unemployment must be eliminated.

I conducted that set of interviews to try to understand why Old Keynesianism fell out of favor and to gain a better understanding of how macroeconomic theory evolved the way it did. My conclusion was that Old Keynesians used and thought of macro theory in a different way than later macroeconomists did. Old Keynesians did not try to develop a full theory; they were interested in policy. They made whatever theoretical assumptions were necessary in their macro models to get them quickly to policy issues. In doing so, they developed what came to be known as neo-Keynesian theory, which was the macroeconomics taught to those of us educated in the 1960s and 1970s.

Unfortunately, while neo-Keynesians did not use it formally, they implied that Walrasian general equilibrium theory underlay their theory.[4] That made Keynesian theory dependent on fixed wages and prices. This connection, I believe, was the central cause of the downfall of Keynesian economics; it tied Keynesian economics to a theory that undermines its central insight.

Because of the way Old Keynesians used theory, they saw no problem with formally combining Walrasian general equilibrium theory with Keynesian economics, even though, in that theory, if there were perfect wage and price inflexibility, there would be no macro problem.[5] In the back of their minds they had a deeper, common-sense understanding that unemployment situations, such as those experienced in the Great Depression, were caused by something deeper than wage- and price-level flexibility. If it was necessary to assume wage and price inflexibility to fit Keynesian economics with general equilibrium theory, then do so and be done with it. The assumptions they made in their practical theories were acceptable because Old Keynesians knew there was a macro problem. They didn't need theory to tell them it existed; they needed theory to elucidate policies to solve the problem.

Old Keynesianism Falls Out of Favor

In mathematics, a proof is not a proof to everyone. Similarly with economics, an acceptable theory is not acceptable to everyone. What is acceptable depends on what one knows deep in one's gut. Whereas old Keynesian economists knew in their gut that there was a macro problem, later economists did not. Those of us born between 1940 and 1960 could accept it, even if we didn't feel it in our gut; we had heard the stories of the depression from our parents and grandparents. Those born after 1960, however, had a much harder time believing there was a macro problem. For them, if there were a macro problem, it would have to be pulled out of theory, and the theory that was passed down to them was Walrasian general equilibrium theory. It was here that the connection between Keynesian thinking and Walrasian general equilibrium theory undermined Old Keynesian ideas. One could not easily pull Keynesian ideas about significant unemployment from Walrasian general equilibrium theory without adding a whole number of assumptions that were hard to justify. By assuming sufficient wage- and price-level inflexibility, one could pull the ideas out, but the logical justifications of that wage and price inflexibility did not seem to fit the empirical reality.

The stagflation problem of the 1970s brought the differences between older Keynesians and younger macroeconomists home, as it required economists to adjust both the theory and the policy to accommodate simultaneous inflation and unemployment. Neo-Keynesian theory didn't really deal with such situations, and the rules of functional finance did not deal with it for policy. Old Keynesians went about developing policy and modifying their models to fit that stagflation by moving away from their Walrasian base. For them, inflation was caused by supply shocks and wage- and price-setting institutions. Unemployment was caused by nominal demand's failure to adjust to the higher nominal prices. Younger macroeconomists did not see it that way; they went about developing macro theory within a Walrasian general equilibrium system.

These younger economists would not believe that unemployment was a problem unless it could be shown formally that unemployment could exist in theory.[6] Most of these younger economists were taught in a Keynesian tradition and they tried to pull Keynesian insights—that involuntary unemployment can exist—from the Walrasian hat. The result was microfoundations, the New Classical revolution, the New Keynesian revolution, and the development of the natural rate and the non-accelerating inflation rate of unemployment (NAIRU) as the center of theoretical and policy discussions in macro. These theoretical developments arrived at the possibility of a temporary unemployment equilibrium, but it was a tortured path that was unsatisfying to many and since in the long-run theory said that the economy would return to its long-run growth path, these temporary problems seemed relatively unimportant. In short, when economists tried to pull a Keynesian rabbit out of a Walrasian hat, they got a classical rabbit with a few Keynesian stripes.

The Complexity Approach to Macro

My theoretical work in macro theory has been primarily designed around one simple assumption: There is no need to use a Walrasian hat, and it is much more intuitively satisfying to use an alternative foundation as the theoretical basis of macroeconomics. I have called that alternative foundation Post Walrasian, but the term has not caught on. I am currently working on the ideas within a complexity theory framework (such as that found in the work done at Santa Fe), so it might be called a "complexity foundation."[7] I do not care what it is called as long as it does not use the Walrasian general equilibrium assumptions of a unique aggregate equilibrium and global rationality; and as long as it does deal explicitly with the possibility of multiple equilibria, and incorporates into the framework an explanation of how and why markets develop, as opposed to simply assuming they exist.

These are grand requests for a theory of something so complex as macroeconomy, but I think they are reasonable ones. I fully recognize that they are requests that cannot be met with existing formal analytic theory. Standard theory—neo-Keynesian as well as classical—assumes the intractabilities away and develops a tractable formal theory. Joseph Schumpeter expressed the current economic approach when he wrote[8]:

> Multiple equilibria are not necessarily useless, but from the standpoint of any exact science the existence of a uniquely determined equilibrium is, of course, of the utmost importance, even if proof has to be purchased at the price of very restrictive assumptions; without any possibility of proving the existence of (a) uniquely determined equilibrium—or at all events, of a small number of possible equilibria—at however high a level of abstraction, a field of phenomena is really a chaos that is not under analytical control. (Schumpeter 1954)

Modern "macro theorists" have followed Schumpeter's lead in making macroeconomic theory an exact science, and, in doing so, have made it into a logical game with little direct application to the macro problems we face. The complexity approach is different. Since multiple equilibria are likely within such a complex system as the macroeconomy, the complexity approach concludes that economics cannot be an exact science.

The complexity approach requires that one not shy away from issues that make formal theory intractable. Thus, it does shy away from deductive theory for complex systems such as the macroeconomy. In its place, it offers an inductive approach, and a search for patterns that develop in nonlinear complex systems that might give us some insights into the problems we face. Had Keynesian economics been presented not as a grand theory but as a pattern that could sometimes develop based on existing institutions, there would have been no need to tie it in with Walrasian theory, and it would have been on much stronger footing.

One way to see the differences between the complexity approach to macro and other approaches is with the automobile metaphor used by Lerner to convey the idea of functional finance. Lerner portrayed classical economics as equivalent to driving the economy without a steering wheel. In Lerner's mechanistic specification of macro theory, Keynesian economics added a steering wheel to the economy; his functional finance put economists behind the steering wheel. That mechanical metaphor became the foundation for the building of neo-Keynesian models. They were models designed so that we could better understand the steering linkage between the steering wheel and the wheels. Through the 1960s, most macroeconomists accepted the need for a driver.

Conventional macroeconomics of the 1970s and 1980s incorporated that same metaphor, but questioned the old Keynesian picture. In its place was offered an image of a car with an exceedingly small steering wheel, sloppy linkages between the steering wheel and the wheels, and six people (none of them economists) fighting over who will steer, with economists advising them from the back seat. Luckily, by assumption, the car is going down a long-run road that it follows "naturally." Presented with this image, most modern economists returned to the classical "let the car drive itself" position.[9]

The complexity approach to macro suggests a different metaphor. The automobile we are in has an opaque windshield, so we have no idea what the road looks like. In fact, the only way we can induce that we are on, as opposed to off, a road, is by the vibrations we feel while in the car. And we can only see where we have been. Based on that history, some general principles that follow from the accounting relationships in the macroeconomy, and our current "feel" of the car, we must decide how, and whether, to steer the economy so that it tends to go in "desirable" directions.

How does one theorize about such a complex system? The best answer I can give is, "Very humbly and carefully." I suppose my biggest complaint about current macroeconomics has been that researchers of various persuasions have not been very humble. That said, within a complexity approach to macro, one goes on doing macro policy work much the same way most policymakers, as opposed to most macroeconomic theorists, currently do. The difference lies in which assumptions one considers ad hoc. From a neo-Walrasian perspective, assumptions considered ad hoc are inconsistent with instantaneously flexible wages and prices. Such characterization is a standard put-down of Old Keynesians by new classical macroeconomists. From a complexity perspective, such put-downs are meaningless. Observations about existing institutions must form the basis of one's assumptions, and guide the structure of the models.[10] The rationality of actors in the model is not assumed; it is inductively determined. This opens up the possibility of activist policy in those instances where collective rationality (collective results of individual decisions) differs from individual rationality.

In a complex world, there is no purely deductive theory that is going to answer a policy question. All we can do is to interpret the past data as best we can, and try to understand the patterns that have developed. Policy, in such a complex world, is an art characterized by rules of thumb, not by theoretically derived policies. The key to successful policy is finding previous patterns that match the current situation. There is no one model of the aggregate economy that will ever be "the right model." Instead, there will be a variety of models, and the art of macro policy involves choosing the relevant model as much as it does getting the policy right within the model.

I discuss the complexity approach because it provides for younger macro theorists, who use theory in a different way than did Old Keynesians, a theoretical foundation for understanding and appreciating Vickrey's, and other Old Keynesians', work in macroeconomics. Implicitly, Vickrey fully accepted the complexity approach to macro, and had little time for theorizing that did not. So too did most Old Keynesians. That is why little in what I specified as the complexity approach to macro would be problematic to most Old Keynesians. They simply ask: "Why spend the time belaboring the obvious?" I believe it is necessary to do so because, in their formal work, Old Keynesians always kept the Walrasian general equilibrium model as their vision of where the economy was going in the long run.

Differing Normative Assumptions

I am attracted to the complexity approach because it initially requires one to give up the notion of formal theory leading us to correct insights from first principles, and directs us toward building real-world institutions into our working models. Thus, it provides a theoretical foundation in which Vickrey's views on macroeconomics are defensible; they are as consistent, if not more consistent, with empirical evidence as are the conventional views. That said, it must also be said that the complexity approach to macro does not justify the old Keynesian approach. It simply provides a theoretical framework within which the old Keynesian approach has as much theoretical foundation as any other theory. The point is that abstract theory does not tell us whether Keynesian or classical economics is better; it simply provides a framework for thinking about problems.

Having explained the complexity approach, let me now return to Vickrey's theory of the macroeconomy and where it differs from conventional macro theory. Vickrey's theory starts with a normative sense that unemployment is bad and it directs the analysis toward finding ways to eliminate unemployment. The structure Vickrey and other older Keynesians place on their patterns reflects that normative sense; it leads them to create a model in which undesirable levels of unemployment are possible. Most modern theorists do not share the normative sense that unemployment is bad, and the structure they place on data interprets "unemployment" as natural and, in many ways, desirable—necessary for a dynamic, functioning economy. Complexity theory sees both patterns as possible. Given the empirical evidence and the logical structure of the arguments, one cannot formally reject either theory. Empirical evidence is simply too limited to reject a variety of patterns.

The above statement will, I suspect, be objected to by both modern theorists and Old Keynesians. But for me, this ambiguity of the evidence, and hence the need for one's policy agenda to guide the pattern one sees in the data, explains how brilliant economists on both sides can come to quite different conclusions.

As I have justified, at least to my mind, the need to consider Vickrey's views carefully, let me now turn directly to those views. Specifically, let me consider three aspects of his macro views as they relate to full employment. The first is the meaning of chock-full employment; the second is the relationship between inflation and unemployment; and the third is how he expected to achieve chock-full employment.

The Meaning of Chock-Full Employment

The key to understanding Vickrey's analysis of the macroeconomy is to recognize that in a complex system, the relationship between individual actions and aggregate results is too tenuous for any specific individual to take them into account. Thus, there is no presumption that individual decisions result in desirable aggregate results. Over time, institutions develop to improve the relationship between individuals' decisions and desirable aggregate results, but those institutions are endogenous to the system and can create problems of their own. Since these institutions are serving useful purposes, they cannot be assumed away in one's model; they are a necessary part of the system. Policy analysis is then directed at specifying alternative institutions that lead to preferable results. Therefore, before policy analysis can be undertaken, one must be clear about one's goals. There is no purely positive policy analysis.

For Vickrey, the desired policy outcome was an economy in which the labor market is a seller's market. That is what he meant by chock-full employment. Chock-full employment is not defined by a number, but instead by the choice set facing individuals. Chock-full employment means that there are many more employee seekers than job seekers—unfilled high-quality jobs exceed the number of unemployed.[11] The question is: How does one achieve such a state in the present institutional environment? Even now, at 4.2 percent unemployment, in many markets, job seekers exceed employee seekers, and Vickrey's definition of chock-full employment is not met.

Notice that the definition of chock-full employment has nothing to do with whether the unemployment is voluntary or involuntary. In complex system analysis, the two are indistinguishable, and any unemployment will have aspects of both. People, given institutions, make choices; those choices can result in unemployment. Had people made different choices, a different level of unemployment would have resulted, and, when there are multiple equilibria, those different levels of unemployment may be preferable to the one following from choice. Given the institutional structure, I am quite willing to say that all unemployment is in some sense voluntary. But so what?

The touchstone of what is right is not whether a situation is voluntary or involuntary. The real policy question is: Are the choices individuals are given appropriate? *The policy issue is not the choices individuals make; the issue is the choices they face.* It is an institutional structure issue. If an alternative institutional structure will achieve a preferred set of choices, then the result will be preferable, and whether unemployment is voluntary or involuntary is irrelevant. In Vickrey's view, we had tools to reduce unemployment significantly—expansionary monetary and fiscal policy—and unless we pushed those to the limit, we were not doing everything we could to reduce unemployment.

The Relationship Between Inflation and Unemployment

The thought that monetary and fiscal policy can expand the economy and reduce unemployment other than temporarily does not fit conventional theory, which sees a natural rate of unemployment determined independently of both monetary and fiscal policy. Conventional theory evolved to that view after trying initially to integrate simultaneous inflation and unemployment into its theory with a Phillips curve. In doing so, it found that, theoretically and empirically, the connection between inflation and unemployment is dubious. Vickrey fully agreed that the connection was dubious, but he had a quite different interpretation of that lack of connection.

Whereas standard theory built its view of a natural rate around a monetary theory of inflation, Vickrey built his around a *real theory* of inflation.[12] That real theory of inflation sees the price-setting process, and hence inflation, not as a monetary process, but as an institutional process: Individuals set their nominal prices according to institutional incentives. These institutional incentives are so removed from the aggregate employment-generating process that the two, within a wide range of unemployment rates—between approximately 3 percent and 9 percent—are so indirectly related as to be separable. Vickrey accepted this, as did Lerner and many other Old Keynesians.

The real theory of inflation is not an administered price theory, nor is it a cost-push theory. It is an institutional process theory of inflation. Institutional process can present problems for our real economy because it lacks a coordination mechanism to see that individual nominal wage and price decisions lead to a desirable collective decision. Our real economy lacks a direct price-level anchor and therefore must rely on the indirect anchor working through aggregate nominal demand. In this theory, inflation becomes a systemic problem because there is no direct institutional connection between an individual's decision on pricing and the price level; no individual takes into account the effect of his or her price-setting decision on the price level.

The real theory of inflation emphasizes the potential instability of the price level since expectations of others' nominal prices and wages play a central role in setting the price. This means that a small change in desired relative price changes can lead to much larger swings in the price level. Institutions smooth out the process, but leave the real economy subject to swings because of nominal price shocks.

The real theory of inflation does not hold that there is no relationship between inflation and unemployment, only that within the economy's normal range the connection is weak. Thus, in terms of unemployment, it might be called a *natural range of unemployment theory*, a theory that sees a range of accelerating inflation rates of unemployment equilibria as possible.

The level of unemployment the economy can achieve within this range depends on the result of the inflation-generating process. If little inflation is generated, the low end of the range of unemployment is possible; if significant inflation is generated, the high end is possible. Alternatively expressed, this theory holds that, within the natural range, the Phillips curve is flat, and aggregate demand has little effect on inflation.[13] If this theory is true, it suggests that the relationship between deviations of unemployment and inflation are nonlinear, and the statistical fit we get between increases in inflation and unemployment comes primarily from the extremes, not from small deviations.

Unlike the standard Phillips curve, or the natural rate theory, a natural range theory is consistent with the experiences of the economy in both the 1970s and the 1990s. The 1970s rise in the achievable rate of unemployment was caused by major nominal upward price shocks, combined with wage- and price-setting institutions conducive to inflation, both of which became built into expectations of inflation. The 1990s fall in the achievable rate of unemployment, in spite of expanding aggregate demand, is due to (1) nominal downward price shocks; (2) wage- and price-setting institutions experiencing significant international competition; and (3) the building of the above structural characteristics into expectations of declining inflation.

How Chock-Full Employment Can Be Achieved

Seeing inflation and unemployment as the results of separable real processes leads one to think of macro policy in a quite different way. One needs two separate tools to deal with two separate problems: inflation and unemployment. It is where my free-market solution to inflation, which Lerner and I later renamed the Market Anti-inflation Plan (MAP), came in (Lerner and Colander 1980).

The idea behind MAP is simple and closely tied to Vickrey's separation of the inflation and unemployment problems. If inflation is a problem of coordinating nominal price changes, then its solution is to devise a coordinating mechanism compatible with a market economy. MAP does that. It is a market-based incomes policy. It creates property rights in value-added input prices and thereby controls the aggregate price level while leaving individual prices free to fluctuate.

MAP establishes, by law, rights in value-added input prices, and allows firms to raise or lower the value-added input prices they pay only if they buy the right to do so.[14] Thus, it is a direct control over the price level, while leaving each individual firm free to set whatever price it wants. MAP simply makes sure that that decision does not contribute to inflation. Vickrey saw MAP as the institutional change needed to guarantee chock-full employment.

To understand the idea behind MAP, consider the following questions: Assuming there were property rights on value-added prices, what would the price of raising price be? And: What implication for the economy's natural rate would a positive price of raising price have? The answers are simple. By definition, assuming there were no inflationary pressures, the price of raising price would be zero. If there were a positive price of raising price, then MAP would be eliminating inflation pressure. The higher the price of raising price, the more inflationary pressure it would be eliminating, and the lower the unemployment rate achievable via expansionary monetary and fiscal policy.

To emphasize that the purpose of this program was to allow real growth, in his recent work, Vickrey had started to call the rights to change prices "growth warrants." Here is how the growth warrants were allocated: All firms in the program are allowed warrants equal to their level of value-added at the initial starting period. Each year firms receive additional warrants equal to the average increase in productivity in the economy. Thus, all firms are allowed nominal raises in input prices consistent with a noninflationary economy—that is, increases in growth warrants equal to the average total factor input productivity.

When firms hire additional workers, or invest more, they receive additional growth warrants equal to the value of those inputs in their previous use. This means that firms increasing their inputs would receive additional growth warrants, and firms decreasing their inputs without lowering their value-added price would be forced to buy additional warrants. This would create inflows of capital to growing firms from firms that were monopolizing, increasing their value-added per input. That is why the plan can also be seen as a tax on monopolization.

There are many technical and practical issues that need to be answered before these plans can become reality. Concern about these issues kept many economists who supported the plan in principle from supporting it in practice. However, no serious attempt has been made to deal with these issues. Vickrey felt that all of these practical and technical issues had solutions—not perfect solutions, but solutions—and that a major effort should be undertaken to resolve them. It never was undertaken because, politically, such a major institutional change was not in the cards. But if one is serious about achieving chock-full employment, significant effort is needed to solve these technical and practical problems.

The higher the price of these growth warrants, the higher the cost in administrative expenses and misallocated resources. But the higher the price of these growth warrants, the lower the achievable unemployment rate. Thus, the imposition of this plan would present government with a new trade-off—the systemic gain in aggregate efficiency of achieving chock-full employment against the administrative costs of the plan.

The plan has one other major advantage: It will allow a much more reasonable use of monetary policy. This follows since the price of growth warrants would give us a direct measure of the inflationary pressures in the economy. We would no longer need to operate monetary policy blind; instead we could set a monetary rule based on the price of these growth warrants because that price tells us the level of inflationary pressure in the economy.

Vickrey was much more of a visionary than I, and much more willing to argue that MAP was ready for prime time. I do not know whether MAP actually is workable in practice, or whether the politics of inflation control could ever change sufficiently so that it could be tried. However, I will argue that it should be explored in much greater detail than it has been. I will also say that it offers large potential gains, and that it was precisely the type of policy that Vickrey could see working in actual practice that other economists could not.

Conclusion

This paper has covered a lot of territory. Were Vickrey here, I'm sure that he would have corrected a number of points and would have offered different interpretations of others. But he would agree with its central claim: Macro policy should be directed toward making the labor market a seller's market, and economists should work on solving the practical and administrative problems of market-based incomes policies.

In explaining his approach to dealing with unemployment, and contrasting it with the microfoundations approach, Vickrey liked to use the analogy of a sinking ship. The important policy issue is not the allocation of seats in existing lifeboats; it is seeing that there are more lifeboats than there are people. That requires pushing existing monetary and fiscal policies as far as we can, and developing new institutions to directly stop inflation if those policies lead to inflation. Unemployment is not the natural lot of humans. There is no abra, no cadabra about unemployment. Unemployment is the result of institutions, and it is the economists' job to change institutions so that unemployment, as we know it, disappears.

Notes

1. The Old Keynesian functional finance view was first stated by Abba Lerner (1941). See Colander (1979) for a discussion of how functional finance might be adjusted to include inflation.

2. In the late nineties, as threats of global depression spread, Vickrey's views are becoming less and less anachronistic.

3. Robert Eisner, a strong advocate of many of the same ideas held by Vickrey, told me that he always appreciated speaking at a conference with Vickrey because it made Eisner seem like a moderate.

4. What is Walrasian is subject to some ambiguity. Robert Clower argues that what we call Walrasian is really neo-Walrasian.

5. When I asked James Tobin about a possible incompatibility of Keynesian economics with the Walrasian model, he responded, "[I]t just recognizes that (Walrasian general equilibrium theory) might be a good start for a model of a full employment economy over a long period of time. In that sense, neo-Keynesian economics regards the business cycle as a departure from a Walrasian market economy, and explicitly says that that's what it is—situations of excess supply and excess demand existing at existing prices and wages."

6. This tendency of economists toward abstract theorizing has led to the joke that economics is the only profession in which economists spend all their time trying to show what is obvious in reality is possible in theory.

7. For a discussion of the Santa Fe complexity approach, see Arthur et al. 1997, and Waldrop 1992.

8. This approach is still followed by most neo-Walrasian models. In his 1994 book, *Structural Slumps*, Edmund Phelps assumes away multiple equilibria by asserting "a divine hand guiding the economy to that solution exhibiting the largest output level" (198).

9. The nature of that road is somewhat in debate. The conventional view is that it is straight: Potential income is exogenously growing at 2.5 percent per year in the long run, regardless of the policies followed. That provided a basis for policy when income deviated from its potential. Recently, real business cycle theorists have suggested that the road is actually curved, and that even when there are cycles, the aggregate economy is still best left to drive itself.

10. Blinder's (1998) recent study of prices suggests that the institutional structure is one in which firms set prices and wages. It is the type of work that complexity theorists would find interesting, and which standard macroeconomists would downplay.

11. It should be noted that this goal was stated early on by Lord Beveridge when he argued that "Full employment is sometimes defined as a state of affairs in which the number of unfilled vacancies is not appreciably below the number of unemployed persons, so that unemployment at any time is due to the normal lag between a person losing one job and finding another. Full employment in this *Report* means more than

that in two ways. *It means having always more vacant jobs than unemployed men, not slightly fewer jobs. It means that the jobs are at fair wages, of such a kind, and so located that the unemployed men can reasonably be expected to take them.* It means, by consequence, that the normal lag between losing one job and finding another will be very short" (Beveridge 1945, 18 italics mine).

12. See Colander (1992) for a further discussion of a real theory of inflation. The complexity view is important to macro policy because it is consistent with an alternative interpretation of the inflation/unemployment problem—one that the Walrasian-based general equilibrium theory rules out.

13. See Lerner (1972) for a discussion of this view of the Phillips curve and of high-level and low-level unemployment.

14. Input prices are used so that general advances in productivity that are not the result of investment are instituted as rights of society and not as rights of sellers. Firms receive additional property rights when they invest in new technology. For a further discussion of the technical aspects of MAP, see Colander (1986).

References

Arthur, W., S. Durluaf, D. Lane, eds. 1997. *The Economy as an Evolving Complex System.* Redwood City, CA: Addison-Wesley.

Beveridge, William. 1945. *Full Employment in a Free Society.* New York: W.W. Norton.

Blinder, Alan, et al. 1998. *Asking About Prices.* New York: Russell Sage Foundation.

Colander, David. 1979. "Rationality, Expectations and Functional Finance." In *Essays in Post Keynesian Inflation,* ed. James Gapinski. Cambridge, MA: Ballinger.

———. 1992. "A Real Theory of Inflation." *American Economic Review* 82, no. 2 (May).

———. ed. 1986. *Incentive Based Incomes Policies.* Cambridge, MA: Ballinger.

Colander, David, and Harry Landreth. 1996. *The Coming of Keynesianism to America.* Brookfield, VT: Edward Elgar.

Keynes, J. M. 1931. *Essays in Persuasion.* New York: W.W. Norton.

Lerner, Abba. 1941. "The Economic Steering Wheel." *University Review* (June).

———. 1943. "Functional Finance and the Federal Debt." *Social Research* (February): 38–51.

———. 1944. *The Economics of Control.* New York: Macmillan.

———. 1972. *Flation.* New York: Penguin.

Lerner, Abba, and David Colander. 1980. *MAP: A Market Anti-Inflation Plan.* New York: Harcourt Brace Jovanovich.

Phelps, Edmund. 1994. *Structural Slumps: The Modern Equilibrium Theory of Unemployment, Interest, and Assets.* Cambridge: Harvard University Press.

Schumpeter, Joseph. 1954. *History of Economic Analysis.* New York: Oxford University Press.

Vickrey, William. 1963. *Metastatics and Macroeconomics.* New York: Harcourt Brace.

———. 1992. "Chock-full Employment Without Increased Inflation: A Proposal for Marketable Markup Warrants." *American Economic Review* 82, no. 2 (May).

Waldrop, M. Mitchell. 1992. *Complexity: The Emerging Science at the Edge of Order and Chaos.* New York: Simon and Schuster.

5

Edward J. Nell

The Simple Theory of Unemployment

Introduction

Defenders of macroeconomics today have a tendency to make it all very complex. New Keynesians, for example, set out to show that unemployment can exist and government fiscal policy can be effective when agents are rational and markets competitive, provided that agents are not too rational, nor markets too competitive. Realistic "imperfections" make it possible for unemployment to exist and for governments to have an impact on markets (Mankiw and Romer 1993). David Colander goes even further; he wants to base macroeconomics on literal complexity (Colander 1996), proposing to treat markets as complex processes in the technical sense, which means that market systems are allowed to have multiple equilibria, some or all of which are likely to be unstable.

Yet, in practice, unemployment does not seem to be at all complex. Lots of people, adequately skilled, often with relevant experience, would like a job, but cannot find one. There are not enough jobs; in the aggregate, businesses do not need any more workers. It is really quite simple. Businesses do not need any more workers because they do not need to produce any more goods and services than they are currently turning out. What they are presently turning out is what the public, in the aggregate, including business itself and the government, wants to buy. If the public wanted to buy more, business would produce more, offering more jobs and hiring more workers. But the public doesn't, so business won't. This is perfectly simple; only after long years of graduate study does it become difficult.

This is easily reflected by a simple and instructive model that makes use of the following ideas:

- Aggregate output is a simple linear function of the level of aggregate employment, given the presently existing productive facilities that operate at constant marginal productivity as their degree of utilization varies. The implication—supported by many empirical studies—is that marginal and average variable cost curves have long flat sections.

- Household consumer spending depends on household wage income; all household income is spent.
- Investment spending depends largely on long-run factors and, as a first approximation, can be taken as autonomous.
- Income consists of wages and profits; expenditure consists of spending on consumption and investment.

These propositions are based on a significant level of abstraction from reality. They leave out or smooth over important features of the economy. Even so, it is easy to see how to relax these abstractions. Output could be disaggregated, for example, into investment and consumption goods; increasing or diminishing returns could be explored; workers could be assumed to save; other categories of income can be added; besides workers and firms, we may wish to add other categories of agents, and so on.

In addition, however, in contrast to much economic theorizing, nothing has been *idealized*. No agents are assumed to have superhuman powers or supernatural foresight; no processes are assumed to work in unimaginably perfect ways; no adjustments are instantaneous. Figure 5.1 shows how this looks when diagrammed.

Simple as this is, it provides us with a number of powerful insights. Admittedly, as they derive from very great abstractions, they cannot be expected to prove literally true. But they may nevertheless give us genuine guidance in investigating the way the world works. For example:

- Investment and profits are equal here; this suggests that we should expect to find them closely correlated in practice, which we in fact do. (Nell 1998a, ch. 7)
- Investment determines profits here; investment being the driving force. We should expect to find something like this in reality, which many studies suggest that we do.
- The multiplier here will equal $1/(1 - w/a)$, where w is the real wage. That is, the multiplier will reflect the distribution of income, and will not be very large. Again, this seems plausible.
- Real wages and the level of employment and output are *positively* related. This can be seen by drawing in a steeper wage line, with the same level of investment. The C+I line will then also be steeper, intersecting the output line at a higher level of output and employment. In fact, most empirical studies of the postwar era do find real wages and employment to be positively related (Figure 5.2). (Nell, ed. 1998)

Figure 5.1

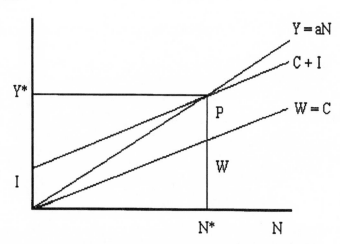

Figure 5.2

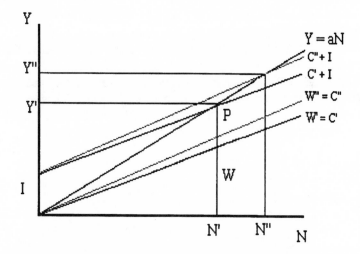

- Household savings *reduce* output, employment, and realized profits.
  (Obviously, qualifications are needed, such as that this is a short-run
  analysis, but the long-run may never come. If this proposition seems
  hard to accept, think about what has been happening in Japan recently.)
  (Figure 5.3)
- Unemployment is indicated by marking off the level of full employment on the horizontal axis. It clearly results from deficiency in demand. That is, either investment is too low or wages are too low, which
  implies that unemployment can be reduced by increasing either.

Figure 5.3

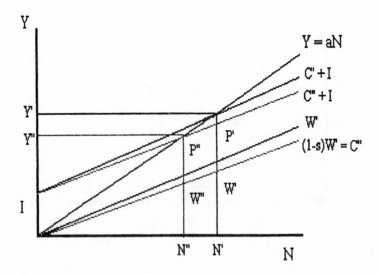

- The model must be expanded to include government spending and taxation. Taxes may be levied at a fixed rate on wages, t, and government spending, G, added on to investment. For given t and G and a given output function, whether the government is in deficit or surplus will depend on investment and the real wage. Unemployment can be reduced or eliminated by increasing G or lowering t (Figure 5.4).

From:

$$Y = W + P$$
$$E = C + I + G$$
$$Y = E$$
$$C = (1-t)W.$$

We then have:

$$W + P = C + I + G$$
$$= (W - tW) + I + G,$$

so,

$$P = I + (G - tW), \text{ so that } dP/dI = 1 - tdW/dI, \text{ normally} > 0.$$

Figure 5.4

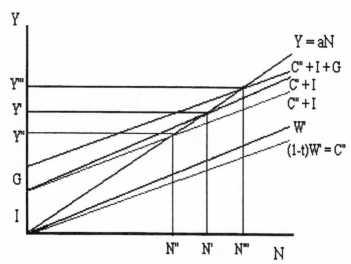

A government deficit therefore increases business profits; a government surplus reduces them. Rearrange the equation:

$$I - P = tW - G$$

A public-sector surplus implies an equal and opposite private-sector deficit.[1] This can be shown on a simple diagram. I is plotted on the vertical axis, the others on the horizontal, and a 45–degree line is drawn in. G is marked off as a vertical (alternatively, it could fall slightly as I increased, since a higher I will reduce the need for unemployment compensation). When $I = 0$, $P = G - tW$, so mark off P_0; then indicate tW_0. The line is drawn representing the increase in profits as I increases. It will intersect the 45-degree line at a certain level of I. At that level, G and tW must be equal. That is, at low levels of I there will be a public-sector deficit and a corresponding private-sector surplus. Then, at a certain level of I, both will be in balance, but at higher levels there will be a public-sector surplus and a private-sector deficit (Figure 5.5).

The preceding list covers major topics of policy concern—growth, profits and wages, unemployment, and the government budget. The propositions advanced are both important and empirically interesting. They cannot be claimed to be "true," for they are based on an analysis that is too simple and too abstract. But they point in the direction of empirically true hypotheses. Perhaps even more importantly, they suggest plausible market mechanisms that might underlie such hypotheses. The very simplicity of the abstraction

Figure 5.5

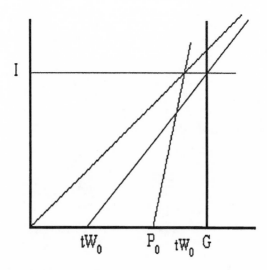

helps to suggest how the model might be made more complex and more realistic.

Adding a Monetary Sector

This simple model is easily extended to include money and interest. The rate of interest may be assumed to have some influence on both business and household spending. When interest is relatively high, businesses are likely to curtail or postpone investment projects, and households may cut back on consumer durables. Thus, when interest rises, the investment line will shift down to a lower intercept, while the households' consumption line will swing down, reducing its angle. Similarly, of course, when interest rates are relatively low, investment and household spending will be correspondingly higher (Figure 5.6).

So a downward sloping demand relationship can be drawn relating I and N (Figure 5.7).[2] To this we add a flat line, indicating the interest rate chosen by the Federal Reserve Board.

Scarcity, Value, and Factor Prices

But among many economists in leading circles today, this approach is not possible and such simplicity is nowhere to be found. To the contrary, explaining unemployment is for them a complex problem, requiring an under-

Figure 5.6

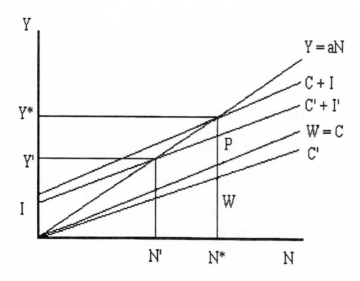

Figure 5.7

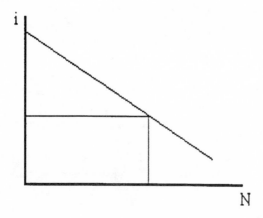

standing of the many ways in which markets may fail to reach the right kinds of equilibria.

In fact, the reason for the problem is easy to find: It lies right at the heart of mainstream economics. But to solve it will require radical surgery. Value reflects scarcity, according to the dominant tradition. That is, prices rest on preferences, technology, and endowments; prices will measure relative scarcities. Factor prices, in particular, will reflect the extent to which the limited endowment of the factor permits the realization of agents' preferences. The number of agents in the system is taken as given—indeed, the matter is considered so obvious that the point is hardly even mentioned—it comes up when the subscripts are defined, for example, n for the number of individual agents.

First, this all leads to a fundamental theorem that states that if a factor is not binding, it will not have a positive price. It will be priced at zero. By the same token, if it has a positive price, the amount of that factor is a binding constraint on economic activity. It is scarce relative to demand. That is, the amount that is available in the endowment is fully employed.

The problem this poses for the theory of unemployment should be evident. Society has an "endowment" of labor—the labor force that is able and willing to work. Wages are positive. But for some part of the labor force, there are no jobs available, so the labor constraint is not binding. But then wages should be driven down to zero, or at the very least, we should see them falling. In fact, however, wages are positive and often quite steady in periods of even high unemployment. Indeed, in many periods we have seen unemployment together with rising wages.

In short, if wages are positive, the labor constraint must be binding so that what appears to be unemployment really must be something else, for example, some kind of voluntary unwillingness to work. Thus, workers who appear to be unemployed may "really" be searching for acceptable jobs, or may be actually unwilling to work at the prevailing wage, even if they claim otherwise.[3]

Moreover, a second point follows from the fact that the number of agents is given. The traditional approach tells us that the demand for labor will depend on preferences and technology. The number of agents and their preferences are given. The technology is given, which tells us how productive agents will be. *So the scale of the system is given.* That is, the position of the demand curve for labor is fixed, so that the actual level of the demand for labor depends only on the real wage. Keynes defined his problem as "a study of the forces which determine changes in the scale of output and employment as a whole" (Keynes 1936, vii).

Determining scale means determining who takes part in the activities of the economy. People are not part of the political system just because they exist; they have to obtain citizenship, or alien residency. Likewise, to become part of the economic system, to take part in the circular flow of money, a person must own property or have some other set of rights, in particular, a job. But the set of agents who are part of the system is not *given*; it varies with economic conditions and must be determined. The traditional approach fixes the scale by assumption, leaving no room for Keynes's problem.

Chart 5.1

	Tools	Food		
Tools	3/8 T	1/2 F	$\rightarrow$	1 T
Food	5/8 T	1/2 F	$\rightarrow$	1 F
	1 T	1 F		

Value Based on Reproduction

An alternative is to reject the scarcity theory of value.[4] If value is not based on scarcity, then the implication that positive wages must imply full employment disappears. But it will not do just to *reject* the traditional approach. Macroeconomics needs a theory of what determines the stable, normal, or long-term levels of prices. These need to be known in order to aggregate the various goods and services into the usual macroeconomic categories. Moreover, we typically assume that the agents in our macroeconomic models know and make use of such prices, for example, in calculating the "marginal efficiency of capital" in various industries, or in drawing up household plans for consumption.

Instead of relying on the theory of scarcity, long-term prices can be derived following the classical approach. This implies that value (price determination) reflects the interdependence of production. Different industries, each producing its distinctive product, use each other's products and labor in their production processes. Labor is supported by consumer goods, which are produced using capital goods and labor. This permits us to base value, that is, the determination of benchmark or long-term prices, on the technical conditions of production, together with the normal pattern of distributing the net output generated where net is over and above what is needed to replace what is used up and consumed during the process.

Using a simple numerical example, we can see how this works out (Chart 5.1). Suppose initially that we have two mutually dependent industries:

Each industry *produces* one unit each period of production, and the economy as a whole *consumes* one unit of each during that period. At the end of the period, tool producers will keep 3/8 of their output and be ready to exchange 5/8 for the ½ F that they need. Food producers will keep ½ their output, and be ready to exchange the other for the 5/8 T they need. Hence 5T exchange for 4F; the price of tools in food is 4/5.

Now suppose that, through cajoling or coercing, the workers in each industry are persuaded to move faster. The labor input will therefore be only half as much (Chart 5.2).

Chart 5.2				
	Tools	Food		
Tools	3/8 T	1/4 F	→	1 T
Food	5/8 T	1/4 F	→	1 F
	1 T	1/2 F		

A *surplus* has emerged consisting of 1/2 F. If the workers were paid in proportion to their increased productivity, the wage would be doubled and would absorb the whole surplus. The price would then be unchanged.

But suppose that the surplus were appropriated by the *owners* of the industries to be invested in expansion. Each industry will have to "plow back" a combination of the two goods in the proportion in which it uses them. So the surplus will have to consist of *both* goods, in the proportions in which they are used overall. So the relative sizes of the two industries must change; we will assume *constant returns to scale* here. That means that changing the relative sizes of the industries will not change the coefficients. (This is an extreme assumption, but it simplifies the story a lot, and, anyway, is not so wrong for mass production.) Given the coefficients, we have to determine at what rate the system can grow. Let the growth rate be G, and the relative size be q (Chart 5.3).

The best way to understand this is to imagine that all of the profit will be *invested* back into each sector. But if there is no technical change, each sector will need for its investment a bundle of the same goods it already uses as means of production. So, in the aggregate, the surplus has to consist of the *same goods* in the same proportions as the aggregate means of production. That way each sector can have the goods it needs for investment. Hence, the ratio of the surplus to means of production is a *pure quantity ratio*; since the bundles making up numerator and denominator consist of the *same* goods in the *same* proportions, they can be compared without recourse to prices. So this ratio—the surplus being invested to the present bundle of means of production—will be the rate of growth, that is, the ratio of net investment to physical capital.

Solve each equation for q and set them equal. Then, rearranging, we will get

$$2/32 \ G^2 + 5/8 \ G - 1 = 0,$$

which is quadratic. Applying the formula, we find that the positive root is

$G = 1.403$, and solving for q, $q = 13/7$.

Chart 5.3

	Tools		Food		
Tools	G[3/8 T]q	+	G[5/9 T]	→	q
Food	G[1/4 F]q	+	G[1/4 F]	→	1

Chart 5.4

	Tools	Food		
Tools	39/56 T	26/56 F	→	104/56 T
Food	36/56 T	14/56 F	→	56/56 F
	74/67 T	40/56 F		

That is, the net rate of growth is 2/5, and the tool industry should be 13/7 the size of the food industry. To see how this works out, the tool industry is multiplied by 13/7 (Chart 5.4). This will change the relative sizes. (In this comparison of systems, we are *not* asking how this comes about or how goods and labor, transferred from one sector to the other, shift the economy from a stationary to a growing system. That is a separate and important line of inquiry; instead we are comparing the systems.)

The ratio of the output of tools to the total used up is 104/74, and the ratio of food produced to food consumed is 56/40. Allowing for rounding, both are equal to 1.4. So in the aggregate, the output is now in the right proportions to be invested!

What about exchange? Profits must be considered in *value* terms. In each sector, the output—food and tools, respectively—multiplied by price is the revenue. Revenue minus replacement costs—the food and tools to replace what was used up in production—equals profits. The rate of profits is the ratio of profits to replacement costs. So *prices* have to be such that the ratio of the net output of each sector to its means of production is the rate of profit. But if all profits are invested, then the rate of profit *has* to equal the pure quantity ratio defined above. It is easily seen that if this is true, then the net output of each sector will exactly exchange at these prices for the bundle of means of production each sector needs for investment.[5]

Taking the equations above, with both sides multiplied by 56 to clear the fractions, and R written for the rate of profit, and p for the price of tools in terms of food, then,

$$R[39p + 26] = 104p$$
$$R[35p + 14] = 56.$$

We know that $R = 1.4$. Substituting and doing the arithmetic, $p = .74$. In intuitive terms, this means that tool producers hold back $1.4 \times 39 = 54.6$ units, and exchange 49.4 units for $1.4 \times 26 = 36.4$ units of food. Food producers hold back 19.6 units and exchange 36.4 units for 49 tools. Allowing for rounding off, this gives us the price ratio, determined by investment and the requirements of production.

In the long run, these prices will be fixed so long as the economy has a given real wage. Neither preferences nor endowments figure in the story. Scarcity plays no role. By implication, labor is paid what is necessary to enable it to work and to be productive. Nothing is implied about full employment, one way or the other. Fluctuations in investment will lead to changes in output and employment rather than in prices.[6]

Advantages of the Reproduction Theory of Value-Evolution and the Market as Selector

One significant advantage of the reproduction theory of value is that it enables us to see the economy as an evolving system. In each period it reproduces itself. Of course, such reproduction will never be exact but will demonstrate random differences. More importantly, there will be deliberate attempts to improve both products and processes. Innovation will itself be directed by market forces. The market will act as a selector; it will support the good changes and reject the bad. As a result, there will be a constant drift, persistent small changes reflecting the pressures of competition.

This is important when we come to consider the implications of the distinction between "long run" and "short run." Mainstream economics, at least among its "New Keynesian" practitioners, acknowledges that aggregate demand influences the level of employment and output and, perhaps, even productivity. Thus, an increase in the propensity to save could be expected to lower output and employment. But in the long run, it is argued, an increase in savings will raise the growth rate; or, if not, it will raise capital-intensity.[7] In the short run, it is admitted that Keynesian relationships hold, but in the long run the propositions of the traditional theory—that is, scarcity theory—must predominate.

Figure 5.8

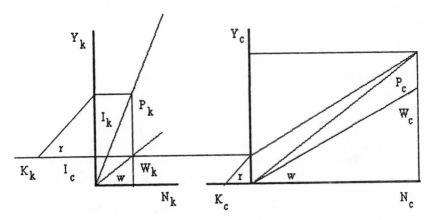

It has always been difficult to make sense of this. Why should the economy work one way (that is, be demand-determined) in the short run, and another (be resource-determined) in the long run? How exactly do these two ways of working fit together? The mystery disappears when we replace the traditional scarcity theory of value with the reproductive approach. The economy does not work differently in the long run. On the contrary, over the long run we can see the patterns of growth and change: the decline of agriculture's share in output; the rise of government's; the increase in capital goods in manufacturing; the decline of household services; the rise of business services; and so on. The economy transforms itself as it grows; the process is one of *transformational growth*, and it is market-driven.

The Theory of Effective Demand Based on Reproduction

Now let us see how it all works out when we base the theory of effective demand on the classical theory of reproduction. We have two sectors: they earn the same rate of profit; they pay the same wage rate. It is reasonable to assume that the capital-goods sector is relatively capital-intensive. Then we can draw the diagram in Figure 5.8:

All aggregates are expressed in monetary values. The rate of profit is the same in both sectors, as is the wage rate: $P_k/K_k = P_c/K_c$, and $W_k/N_k = W_c/N_c$. The diagram on the left shows output of capital goods on the vertical axis and, measuring to the right, capital goods employment, N_k on the horizontal. The steeper line is the output function, the shallower the wage bill, assumed equal to consumption by capital goods workers, C_k. Investment demand $I = I_k + I_c$ is marked off on the vertical axis; this determines output and employment in the sector, and so its wage bill. This wage bill represents demand for consumer goods, and so is mapped onto the diagram on the right, showing output of consumer goods as a function of employment in the consumer goods sector. It is clear that the wage bill of the capital goods sector equals the gross profit of the consumer goods sector, $W_k = P_c$. Total output is $Y = Y_k + Y_c = W_k + W_c + P_c + P_k$, and total expenditure $E = C_k + C_c + I_c + I_k$, where all profits are saved and all wages consumed, so that $P = I$.

Inventories of consumer goods are assumed to be on hand, the result of production in the previous period. New capital goods and replacements have been sold and are in place. This is the starting point, and also must be the end point. Production times in the two sectors are coordinated, and all firms act in concert. If production times were not coordinated, some firms would have a competitive advantage. Profits are retained and used to finance investment purchases.

The crucial relationship here is between the wage bill of the capital goods sector and the capital requirements of the consumer goods sector. This becomes the basis for the multiplier.

Implications: the Proposal for an "Employer of Last Resort"

As an example of the usefulness of this simple way of thinking about unemployment, let us consider a proposal to eliminate unemployment. The suggestion has been made that the government might act as an "employer of last resort (ELR)," offering a job at a living wage to anyone who wishes to work.

Stabilizing the Money Wage Rate

By adopting this approach, the lower end of the wage spectrum can be stabilized as the state-established program providing "employment of last resort" will also help to stabilize money wages. Workers who have lost their jobs or are otherwise unemployed can sign up to receive a basic wage in return for various kinds of work, including training in basic and advanced skills, and socially useful environmental or other public work.

The actions of the state as employer of last resort would be similar in formal respects to those of the managers of a commodity reserve. When market employment falls, the state hires labor at a fixed wage; when employment rises, the state allows workers to be bid away. The ELR would constitute a labor reserve, for which the state would provide training in jobs of various kinds in order to maintain and upgrade the skills of the labor force. (The aim would be to offer useful work while upgrading skills. Both the successes and failures of President Jimmy Carter's Comprehensive Employment and Training Act [CETA] program might provide an instructive example.) This would tend to fix and stabilize a low-end money wage. Importantly, it would also add to overall purchasing power.

In addition, the movement of labor in and out of the ELR can be used to trigger other policies. When the ELR pool is being emptied, indicating high private-sector demand, the discretionary aspects of fiscal and monetary policies can be gradually adjusted to cool things down. When the ELR pool is filling up, fiscal and monetary policies can be set to generate a higher stimulus. Likewise, incomes policies can be used to offset inflationary pressures, and they can be adjusted to the level of the ELR pool. For example, when the ELR pool has been run down to a certain level, mandatory across-the-board wage-bargaining might be required, with tax penalties for nominal wage or price increases beyond certain limits.

Macroeconomic Aspects of the ELR

The principal focus of an ELR program would be on employment—it would in effect provide jobs as an entitlement. Figure 5.9 helps to show how the scheme would work. Measure output on the vertical axis and employment on the horizontal. The "constant returns" utilization function shows the relationship between them. Private employment is measured from left to right; ELR employment from right to left. Private employment generates output, as shown by the heavy black line rising from left to right. ELR employment will be assumed to consist largely in training and environmental maintenance. There will be some output, but productivity will be much lower than that of the private sector. When ELR employment is zero, private output will be at a maximum; when private employment is zero, ELR output will reach its maximum. Actual output at any other level will be the sum of the outputs of the ELR and the private sector, and will be shown by the heavy black line running from max ELR output to max private sector output. The slope of this line measures the difference in productivity between the private sector and the ELR.

The introduction of an ELR program may well increase productivity (that is, raise the angle of the private-sector output-employment line), but once it is established, shifts of labor from the private sector to ELR activity and back will raise or lower output as indicated by the heavy black line.

The private wage line rises from left to right; the ELR wage line rises from right to left. When full employment is reached, ELR employment will be zero. At zero private employment, the ELR wage bill will be at a maximum; at full employment, the ELR wage bill will be zero. The wage-consumption line therefore runs from the ELR maximum point on the vertical axis to the point representing the maximum private wage bill. Notice that the higher the level of the ELR wage relative to the private sector wage, the

Figure 5.9

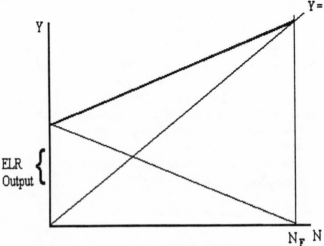

Figure 5.10

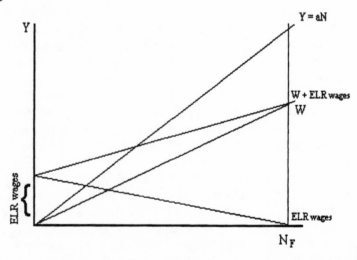

lower will be the multiplier effect of shifting labor to the private sector (Figure 5.10).

When investment is added to the private wage-consumption bill, effective demand is determined at N', with output Y', where N_F is full employment (Figure 5.11). With an ELR system operating, the same private wage rate and level of investment will generate overall employment of N'', with output Y''. Employment in the ELR program will be $N_F - N''$.

Obviously, the ELR improves the lot of the working population. If workers

Figure 5.11

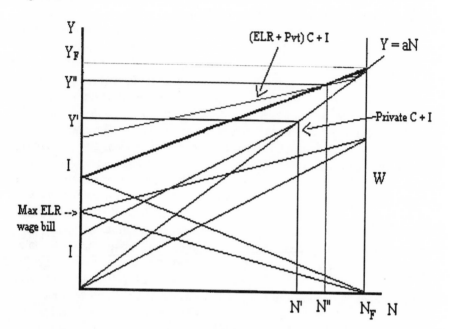

lose their private sector jobs, they can immediately enroll for ELR jobs. Such jobs will provide them with training or socially useful activity, for example, running day care centers, acting as nurses' and teachers' aides, helping care for the aged and infirm, and performing various jobs involved with cleaning up and maintaining the environment. Care must be taken to ensure that these jobs do not displace private employment. In addition, an important aspect of ELR employment—perhaps the most important—will be to ensure that workers' skills are maintained and upgraded.

Equally, or perhaps even more important, are the macroeconomic consequences of ELR employment. The program will tend to raise the level of employment and output for a given private wage and level of investment; it will also stabilize private employment. The fact that it raises private sector employment and output is evident from comparing N' and N''. Of course, an equal amount of any kind of government spending would add to the same degree to effective demand. The advantages of an ELR program lie in the fact that the addition to effective demand is both *automatic* and *stabilizing*, automatic because workers laid off from their private-sector jobs will be driven by self-interest to apply for ELR jobs. Because ELR employment will rise automatically as private-sector employment falls, responding to a rise in unemployment does not require pushing a bill through Congress or a new spending program in the executive branch.

The stabilizing effects on employment and output can be seen by comparing the slopes of the solid $C + I$ line, which intersects the private-sector output-employment function at N', with the dotted $C + I + ELR$ line, which intersects the combined output line at N''. In the first instance, a given fluctuation in investment will have a comparatively large effect on income and output, reflecting the initial value of the multiplier. But it will have a much smaller effect in the second case where the more shallow aggregate demand line reflects the effect of ELR wages on household consumption spending, which lowers the multiplier. (The multiplier will be large when workers go from being employed to being unemployed and earning no wages, resulting in drastic cuts in household spending. But when workers go from being employed in the private sector to ELR employment, their income (and household spending) changes by the amount of the difference between private sector and ELR wages. So, other things being equal, the multiplier will be smaller.) Note, however, that the reduction of the multiplier may be offset in part, or even wholly, by the effect of ELR output on total output. The ELR flattens the aggregate demand line, thereby lowering the multiplier, but it also tends to flatten the output line, which *raises* the multiplier, making the system more volatile.

Secondly, comparing the slopes of the aggregate demand lines in the two cases, the latter, being more shallow, implies that a given fluctuation in productivity will have a smaller impact on employment than in the case of the steeper line. *Without* ELR, the macroeconomic consequences of a rise in productivity could be a large rise in private sector unemployment. *With* ELR, the increase in unemployment will be smaller, and laid-off workers will be provided something useful to do as well.

With primary prices and the lower end of the wage scale stabilized, the chief causes of variation in manufacturing prices will be eliminated by, in effect, a closed economy, or one with exchange rates that are flexible within limits, supplemented by capital controls and modest trade barriers. Wage differentials could change, and so could the markup. But such changes would most likely be once-and-for-all adjustments leading to adaptations, and not necessarily to setting off a wage-price spiral. Even if such a policy did not work perfectly (no policies ever do), it would improve upon the present tendency to rely on austerity and unemployment to support the value of money.

Conclusions

Unemployment can be explained quite simply: The level of employment directly reflects the level of aggregate demand. When the latter falls short, unemployment emerges. The economy is "demand driven," that is, the scale on which it operates and the rate at which it grows depend respectively on the level and growth of demand. But conventional theory tries to explain prices and values in terms of resource constraints, implying that the economy always operates at a level that pushes up against factor endowments, in particular, that of labor. In fact, this rarely happens. Modern economies always operate with a margin of excess capacity and a reserve of unemployed or underemployed labor.

Long-run prices and capital values have to be grounded in the structure of production. Exchange values reflect the division of labor; exchanges are made in order to permit production processes to be repeated while the proceeds are distributed in proportion to claims of various kinds. This approach both provides a basis for macroeconomics and encourages an evolutionary view of growth and technological development. It allows us to understand why prices are not very responsive to cyclical fluctuations. The result is a simple but highly suggestive analytical framework that can easily be made as detailed as is necessary for empirical work. There is no need to appeal to complexity.

Notes

1. Notice that the public sector's surplus must be made available to the private sector in order for the latter to carry out its planned investment spending. This will happen automatically as the tax receipts in excess of government spending drain reserves from the banking system, requiring either for the Treasury to retire bonds, or for the Fed to purchase them on the open market. Either way, the private sector will acquire the funds to make up the difference between its planned investment and its net earnings by running down its holdings of government bonds. It makes no sense to talk of "investing the surplus," as so many politicians do.

2. It is important to note that this relationship is not very reliable. Businesses need not increase their spending when interest rates fall. For example, if future sales prospects do not look good, low rates will not lead businesses to spend on new capacity. What use is capacity, however cheap, if it is not going to be used? Similarly households will not buy a new car, even if the payments are low, if they fear unemployment or hard times.

3. Lucas's (in)famous comment stems from this same presumption: "Involuntary unemployment is not a fact or phenomenon which it is the task of theorists to explain. It is . . . a theoretical construct which Keynes introduced in the hope that it would be helpful in discovering a correct explanation of a genuine phenomenon: large-scale fluctuations in measured, total employment" (Lucas 1977, 354) Here again an utterly unnecessary difficulty is introduced. In the ordinary sense of the term, "involuntary unemployment" obviously is a fact that needs to be explained. But since it is impossible in Lucas's framework, it must be a theoretical idea that Keynes and Keynesians have foisted on the world.

4. And cast away a century of theoretical work? Not at all. Neoclassical theory has developed models that can be used effectively in prescriptive analysis. Shadow prices

have an important role to play, but they are not descriptive and they are not what markets aim at (Hollis and Nell 1975; Nell 1998).

5. The ratio of aggregate net output to the aggregate means of production is known as the Standard Ratio, or sometimes as the Von Neumann Ray (Sraffa 1960; Pasinetti 1977; Bharadwaj and Schefold 1992).

6. For a fuller discussion, see Nell 1998, chaps. 9 and 10. Studies of prices using input-output tables show that real prices are stable and that changes in prices are almost wholly explained by changes in labor productivity (Ochoa 1984).

7. According to this perspective, Japan, with its very high saving rate, should be growing much faster these days than the United States, where the household saving rate has fallen to zero, or even become negative.

References

Bharadwaj, K., and B. Schefold. 1992. *Essays on Piero Sraffa*. New York: Routledge.

Colander, David, ed. 1996. *Beyond Microfoundations: Post Walrasian Macroeconomics*. Cambridge, UK: Cambridge University Press.

Hollis, Martin, and Edward J. Nell. 1975. *Rational Economic Man*. Cambridge, UK: Cambridge University Press.

Keynes, J. M. 1936. *The General Theory of Employment, Interest and Money*. London: Macmillan.

Lucas, Robert. 1997. "Understanding Business Cycles." In *Stabilization of the Domestic and International Economy*, ed. K. Brenner and A. Meltzer. Carnegie Conference on Public Policy.

Mankiw, N. Gregory, and David Romer, eds. 1993. *New Keynesian Economics, Imperfect Competition and Sticky Prices*. Vol. 1. Cambridge: MIT Press.

———. 1993. *New Keynesian Economics, Coordination Failure and Real Rigidities*. Vol. 2. Cambridge: MIT Press.

Nell, Edward J. 1998. *The General Theory of Transformational Growth: Keynes After Sraffa*. Cambridge, UK: Cambridge University Press.

Nell, Edward J., ed. 1998b. *Transformational Growth and the Business Cycle*. New York: Routledge.

Ochoa, E. 1984. "Labor Values and Prices of Production: An Interindustry Study of the U.S. Economy, 1947–72." Ph.D. diss. New York: New School for Social Research.

Pasinetti, Luigi. 1977. *Lectures on the Theory of Production*. New York: Columbia University Press.

Sraffa, Piero. 1960. *The Production of Commodities by Means of Commodities*. Cambridge, UK: Cambridge University Press.

6

C. LOWELL HARRISS

Fuller Employment

William Vickrey's Challenge to Economists

Every hour of undesired idleness is a waste. There are many such hours. Who suffers? (1) The persons who do not get compensation. (2) The persons who do not get what might be produced. Thus, there are two kinds of losers—a sort of opposite of the mutual beneficiaries of voluntary exchange. The losses are real, but they are inadequately recognized—especially when 95 percent or so of the labor force has employment.

The Challenge

William Vickrey, before, during, and after his 1993 presidential address to the American Economic Association, challenged the economics profession to do more to help reduce the losses from unemployment. The challenge deserves more attention than I see it receiving—for two kinds of reasons.

Obvious must be any person's desire to help reduce human distress. This audience needs no demonstration of the existence of poverty and deprivation in our own country—to say nothing about other parts of the world. The extent, the nature, the causes, the hopes for alleviation, these and other aspects, do call for discussion. One looks for potentials for improving the human condition by replacing undesired idleness with purposeful employment (helping the other fellow, someone who needs help!).

A second reason for professional concern stems from the reality that as members of groups—from families, to nations, to the world—we will benefit from more as against less total income. ("No man is an island," and so on!) The concern here, let me emphasize, is not a redistribution but an enlargement of *real* income by the fuller use of resources. And the calculation of "real" should be truly inclusive. Effects on freedom belong in that calculation—elusive, perhaps intangible, but an element of the good life.

Government Action and Personal Freedom

Some, most, proposals for "doing something" about (un)employment imply, or require, action by an authority that has and will use broad powers: the government. Government can, and often does, coerce. Human beings are compelled, or at least induced, to act differently from what they would otherwise do.

Politics and bureaucracy have many characteristics. Enough experience has been accumulated in this country and elsewhere to make clear that results are not always beneficial, that realities can differ from dreams. The admonition "Do no harm" should be respected.

The individuals and groups compelled by a governmental (political) requirement vary enormously in uncountable characteristics. What may serve well in moving toward some estimable objectives can work hardship in other respects. Use of the term "bureaucratic" will remind one that adaptation to differences in circumstances and conditions, today and as conditions change, can (will) leave much to be desired. Correction by voluntary adjustments as conditions differ and change cannot overcome the rigidities of governmental determination.

Personal freedom, not always clearly definable, is both an end and a means. Limits on the coercion of politics (government)—liberalism in the nineteenth-century sense—will be identified with freedom. Sweeping generalizations run the risk of irresponsibility. Yet I venture to assert that proposals for new employment practices almost inevitably embody restrictions on freedoms— of the "other fellow," for some "greater good." Explicit attention to personal freedom considerations will raise complex concerns, but they are important.

Macroeconomics

Professor Colander's essay in this volume deals at greater length, and very well indeed, with macroeconomic elements of William Vickrey's work. When Vickrey and I began graduate study of economics at Columbia more than six decades ago, macroeconomics as we now know it did not exist. But mass employment plagued the world. Monetary economics seemed inadequate. Keynes's *General Theory* stimulated new thinking. And sixty years later, discussion, inquiry, and research continue. Without presuming to present a systematic discussion of Professor Vickrey's challenge to us economists, I venture a few points.

First, as just noted, the acting agent usually assumed is some central authority, that is, human beings with broad power. A major element of that power seems to me to be the ability to create or destroy money. Today, attention focuses on interest rates. So be it. But is not the instrument to be used (to change or stabilize an interest rate) the money-creating power? One lesson from history—and perhaps even more from knowledge of human beings—is that the ability to change the quantity of money can be used with both good and bad effects, in amounts large and small. (Are there any exceptions to the conclusion that over time the sovereign has always debased the currency?)

If a society (not a term of precise meaning!) decides to increase employment, pumping more money into the system (trying to reduce those interest rates that are influenced by the central bank) can bring some change in the real economy, probably in the desired direction. We can stipulate this conclusion. But that is not enough. How much? Over the longer run the results may—or may not—be undesirable. There are major problems about amounts, to say nothing of specifics.

There will be doubts about what serves the functions of money. The use of funds (velocity) may present surprises. Government (monetary) officials having authority must operate in a world of uncertainty. America is anything but a closed economy.

A second point is a concern that runs through the whole range of employment issues, but it is one that seems to me to get less attention, less explicit attention, than its importance deserves. What is the relation between (1) the quantity of labor demanded (employment) and (2) wage (plus fringe) costs? Understandably, attention goes to the relation of wage rates to the price level (inflation)—Phillips curve, and others. But the total consists of specific parts—this person in his or her location at a time.

Vickrey outlined a grand (but, I believe, impossible) program for preventing inflation; his exposition indicates some of the economic, albeit not all of the political, problems. Continuing study warrants serious effort. I ask, "Would explicit attention to relative wage rates (not aggregates) help to sharpen discussions of employment policy?" Yes.

The point just made leads on. The quality of public consideration of macroeconomic actions leaves much to be desired. Vickrey tried to get better understanding of budget realities. One could sense his frustration over the inadequacies of discussion of federal budget issues and choices even at the highest levels. When the statements of leaders fall short of reasonably professional competence in public "discussions" about "the" budget, can we expect the best of attainable results? The public deserves more rationally discriminating guidance. But who will listen?

Discussions of budget balancing, surplus, and deficit could benefit from more explicit consideration of the relation to money creation. Virtually all popular treatments with which I am familiar fail in making clear if, when, and how budget changes will influence the monetary system—and the significance. Some complication arises from the separation of power between the political branches and the Federal Reserve. And other realities, near- and longer-term, include some near certainties and many reasons for doubt, sometimes in direction and frequently in amount.

We live in a world in which the creation of money is not tied to something hard to get, for example, gold. One result is freedom to expand the money supply—for good or ill. For years now, our leaders have avoided the temptation to spur employment by irresponsible monetary actions. But what is "responsible"?

The term means as least taking all the evidence into account, considering all aspects and weighting each as appropriately as possible, looking to the long run as well as the short, considering the entire public, and doubtless other elements. Authorities, for example, can determine such things as a fixed rate of change in some key monetary variable or make adjustments as the economy moves along, but inevitably economic life has uncertainties. There will be surprises. If monetary action is subject to discretion, this fact in itself constitutes an element of uncertainty, one that is man-made; its existence brings costs.

One can always dream of the wisdom of those with power combined with a rational desire to improve upon what would exist under a fixed rule. Persons holding authority can be expected to prefer to retain power as against living by a rule. Moreover, changes in conditions may make even a good rule obsolete. In any case, discretionary power will continue indefinitely.

Federal Budget Deficits to Offset Otherwise Unused Funds (Savings)

Vickrey's last work was a bit of "This is where we came in." In the 1930s, the prospect of oversaving was a prevailing concern. Funds withdrawn from the flow of income savings—instead of being spent for consumption—acted as a drag on the economy unless spent on capital investment goods. Velocity (in equation of exchange terms) declines, thus reducing the flow of income. Employment then suffers. The economy stagnates. When wage rates are inflexible downward, the processes of market adjustment will involve more, relatively, of falling employment and output than of falling prices.

In the mid-1990s, looking ahead not so many years, Vickrey calculated that there would be more saving than would be used for any investment at any (very low) level of interest rates. He did not, as I recall, explicitly consider profit levels as an inducement and reward for nondebt investment. Stagnation threatens but can be prevented by federal action.

I have seen no professional analyses of Vickrey's forecasts. Of course, forecasting has its pitfalls. Persons with only short memories will recall that not long ago we were told to expect federal budget deficits indefinitely; at present, we witness a surplus (using federal accounting) and hear of much more in the years ahead. But surprises are inevitable. "Be prepared" is a guide to be respected. Such preparation requires understanding of conditions as they develop over time.

If oversaving does appear, economists can do their part to suggest remedies. No agreement can be expected. There will always be ample scope for tax reduction. Persuasive support will exist for many ways of increasing federal spending. President Nixon advocated revenue sharing with state and local governments to use federal receipts.

One point does seem deserving of attention: Somehow there should be thought about preparing public understanding. One cannot know how influential popular opinion will be in future macroeconomic policy. But to serve best, professional knowledge must move beyond the ivory tower. New realities may call for policies whose justification rests on unfamiliar economic analysis.

Nonmacroeconomic Approaches

Employment actions involve specific persons and situations. "Macro" forces work themselves in "micro" realities—"nuts and bolts," as it were. Policies affecting the conditions of living and work can be modified for the better.

Job discrimination (for example, gender, age, ethnic background) receives continuing attention. Information needs are enormous. Mere mention of training and education can remind one of a wide range of past and present policies with results that suggest the need for continuing research. Statutory minimum wages (at some level) can hamper employment. Labor union agreements influence employment totals, perhaps excluding persons who would work for lower pay. Many factors influence mobility, for example, housing, family attachments, and seniority. The best of macroeconomic policies cannot "deal" with the myriad of details that can impede the achievement of truly "full" employment.

Jobs programs of a micro nature can have tempting appeal. Uncountable numbers exist—uncountable because some are elements of dual- or multipurpose programs. Job encouragement is one reason given in support of programs when they are not necessarily the most important aspect—highways, time-and-a-half for overtime, child care, local subsidies to attract or hold employers, aid to exports. The list could go on and on. Much experience has been accumulated. Analyses of the job aspects of past, existing, and proposed programs should be studied before new projects are adopted or existing ones modified for their possible employment results. "Have we been there before?" Cost-benefit results may be calculable, at least approximately.

An economist can see merit in proposals that would use the coercive power of government to take money from someone ("the other fellow") to subsidize the employment of some persons under some conditions. Modest changes might have significant and welcome results at the margin—no appreciable harm to large numbers of taxpayers, each paying only a tiny amount to get otherwise idle persons productively occupied. (That is, total net output effects could be positive; the use of otherwise idle labor and capital could bring benefits that exceed any decline in desired output due to the extraction of funds to finance subsidy.)

Measurement

What is the size of "the" problem when it is being examined and as time passes? Measures of employment may be reasonably satisfactory—with guesses as to the amount of "off the books," hidden, and black-market activity. But measures of unemployment (undesired idleness) leave much to be desired. Critics of present figures are correct, I believe, in asserting (1) that quite large numbers of part-time workers would prefer to work more, and (2) that many persons who have withdrawn from the labor market would welcome employment of some kind. What would really be the magnitude?

The potentials for benefit seem substantial—net, that is, above money and employment costs. But, one must ask, what are the near certainties and the complicating uncertainties of estimates? How would the quantity offered (supply) be affected by the price (wage) offered?

How many employers? Around 7 million "establishments," mostly small, now operate. Federal, state, and local governments do "deal" with them. How well? The IRS has some experience. Implementing a subsidy to employers would depend, of course, upon the specific features. Obviously, costs (burdens) of administration would be added. To do the job well, I believe, would require more funds than Congress would appropriate. Is there not a history of providing less than needed for high-quality administration? Some of the added work would certainly be done by the shift of resources from other IRS responsibilities or those of whatever agencies are involved. Some of the real cost would be largely unidentifiable deterioration in the administration of taxes or other responsibilities and, for the Treasury, revenue loss. Employers, of course, would have added work. Compliance problems call for study to help in formulating the structure of any program. Such would not necessarily be a formidable undertaking, but it would be more than merely incidental.

The tax system already brings justified complaints about its complexity.

The experience with the Earned Income Tax Credit can illuminate problems and suggest precautions to be taken. The early years witnessed much evasion, abuse, and strains on the IRS in its efforts to administer a tax provision that invited deception. A gap, large indeed, existed between the dreams of advocates and the realities of life. Problems of a subsidy would also include inducement to mislead and lie.

The persons involved—employers and workers—would be distributed over the whole country. Programs well suited to rural Alabama would not always be appropriate for older urban cities.

The geographical dispersion would complicate somewhat efforts for systematic scrutiny of reports, depending, of course, upon the details of any plan. Normal, expected pressures to elaborate, refine, and adapt to a myriad of real-life circumstances would invite complicating provisions. The population involved would include poorly educated, poorly trained, poorly motivated persons. Rather more than for the Social Security payroll tax, the subsidy would encounter such problems as language and mobility. In a world that is inevitably imperfect, the defects to be added might seem small—even at the margin. I would not predict an administrative-compliance nightmare. But per hour of net added employment, the full costs could be worse than merely troublesome.

Current Changes in Public Assistance (Welfare)

Major changes are now (1999) being made in public assistance (welfare) programs, state by state. Many of the new efforts do directly affect persons needing more work—much of the "target group" of employment proposals. The processes of the work aspects differ fundamentally from those that are the substance of macroeconomics. Fortunately, general economic prosperity provides conditions for adjustment that are about as generally favorable as possible. Undoubtedly, many lessons are being learned. It is trite, of course, to observe that any new program should take advantage of experience and coordinate rather than conflict with positive elements.

As employment programs get closer to the personal, as distinguished from the macro, level, more and more caution is required for any generalizing that hopes to be responsible. In principle, one would hope, flexibility would permit adaptation to changing circumstances. But inertia will inevitably delay governmental adjustments—the approach of the social service case worker with two or three dozen "clients" as contrasted with the academician with the best of equations! The case worker at the individual level and the makers of law (statute and regulation) can exert compelling pressure on human beings—to enable, to prod, to compel, to prohibit, to frustrate. Advocates will picture benign results. If there are burdens (taxes or other costs), they will not always be forecast with accuracy nor measured fully. (I understate.)

More Intrusion of Government

The term "intrusion" may seem colored (conforming to my earlier references to freedom). Be that as it may, an increase in government direction would result from an employer subsidy (or somewhat comparable programs). Government is not some single entity with a mind and a heart. It is human beings, like all of us, except that the actions of government employees can utilize the coercive power of government. A new program would tell elected officials, the civil service, the judiciary, and perhaps the military to do things they are not now doing, with effects on other persons, effects that are not necessarily reflective of voluntary decision!

It would be wrong of me to appear to demonize added government just as it is erroneous to idealize voluntary aspects of market choices. But there *are* significant differences. The mutuality of expected benefit from voluntary choices will not necessarily be realized as superior in actual results to what will be accomplished through the compulsion of politics. At many margins, the quality of results will call for scrutinizing and often for modification of practices. Enough experience has now been accumulated to provide guidance and to call for discriminating caution if there is new action.

Encroachments on freedom are numerous and extensive. Proposals for new programs, for example, the president's 1999 State of the Union address, are meant to be tempting without examining the real-life aspects of implementation. There may not be even a pretense of *general* public benefit as distinguished from group favoritism. Nor do advocates feel compelled to demonstrate any reasonable assurance that benefits will exceed costs. Much is hidden—in today's terminology, lacking "transparency." Inflexibility hampers (often prevents) efficient adaptation to changes in conditions. Inflexibility reduces the ability of governmental agencies to profit from a "learning curve" of experience.

Any missionary can be expected to make a persuasive case for his or her brand of salvation. Identifying a laudable objective can elicit support. But achievement calls for more, including respect for other worthy goals. Projections of favorable job results may tip a balance for adoption of a program without adequate weighting of, or even knowledge of, the total results.

An audience like the one for this symposium, myself included, embodies praiseworthy desires to "do good." For a century or more, proposals for "doing good" have quite generally involved government. (Productive businesses account for much of the "good" done in raising levels of living, but this reality tends to get less explicit recognition than is probably justified.) Generations of experience can teach us more about the use, and the misuse, of government.

International Trade and Immigration

Two topics with employment aspects deserve mention. Each invites oversimplification.

Recent decades have seen much reduction of governmentally imposed barriers to international trade. Yet there are unending pressures to use the power of government to obstruct this or that import. A prominent reason given is that domestic jobs would be protected or saved. In specific cases in the short run, employment here and there can be helped, but over the whole population, the net results in the longer run can (will) be very different. For present purposes I merely note the point and assert one conclusion: The *net* employment effects call for more sophisticated analysis than usually accorded. Trade barriers are at best a costly way to improve net employment. (Almost certainly any net increases will be at the expense of human beings as consumers.)

Immigration policy has its own complexities. Employers—perhaps in high-tech industries or for back-breaking agriculture—may press for immigrants to meet a demand for labor. And human beings from many parts of the world seek to come to the United States. Objections may be raised by unions or others who would face the competition of immigrants. The considerations that need to be taken into account in immigration policy include, but are by no means limited to, the direct effects on jobs.

Entrepreneurship and Property Tax Change

Two topics are too important to escape explicit mention, but they are rather beyond the realistic boundaries of this paper.

(1) The sources of successful entrepreneurship deserve attention. Most employment will be in business firms. Governments impose obstacles. One is the taxation of corporate earnings. Vickrey wrote about the desirability of shifting the financing of government to other revenue sources. Governments impose regulations, some of which hamper employment. Their existence creates the need for unending effort to make regulation as rational as possible.

(2) All employers operate in one or more localities and each local govern-

ment uses property taxation. Economically, this revenue source consists of two significantly different elements. One is the space on the earth (land) whose quantity (with minor exceptions) has been fixed by nature. The other consists of structures, machinery, and other man-made capital. Taxes on man-made capital must impede investment. Vickrey joined with other economists, past and current, who recognized that lowering tax rates on buildings and getting more revenue from land would encourage capital formation without reducing the quantity of land. Doable. And doable in a system far more extensive and rational than the "special deals" of some cities and states to encourage industry and housing.

Employment as an objective of public policy deserves continuing support as appropriate to conditions. With employment as high as the levels of early 1999—in the United States—a challenge of fuller employment does not seem pressing. But things could be better now. What means would bring net benefits? A professor can be expected to reply, "We need more study." We do.

7

GERTRUDE SCHAFFNER GOLDBERG

Full Employment and the Future of the Welfare State

William Vickrey gave little thought to the subject of this article—the welfare state and its relationship to full employment.[1] In Vickrey's view, full employment would obviate some of the mess that the welfare state would otherwise have to mop up, that is, the direct and indirect consequences of unemployment—crime, poverty, homelessness, and sickness. His position on the budget deficit—that balancing the budget would not only retard economic growth but hurt the people who need social services—implies support for the welfare state. On the other hand, though he preferred borrowing for health care to investing in space stations, he said in "Today's Task for Economists" (1993) that either would serve the primary goal of "income recycling," a statement that suggests he thought of the welfare state primarily as a fiscal stimulus. Nonetheless, in supporting and working closely with the National Jobs for All Coalition, Vickrey accepted its position that a welfare state, albeit one different from one that is burdened by unemployment and its attendant ills, is an integral part of a strategy for economic justice. There is no doubt, however, that Vickrey's principal, overriding interest was full employment, or what he liked to call "chock-full employment."

Full Employment and the Welfare State

Full employment and the welfare state were twin peaks of domestic policies in Western Europe from the mid-1940s until at least the mid-1970s. In Sweden, the commitment to full employment ended later. These economic and social policies were integrally related and mutually reinforcing in the conceptions of Sir William Beveridge in his plan for the British welfare and full-employment state. The same is true of the postwar program of the Swedish government.

Because he wrote so eloquently about both full employment and social welfare and influenced countries throughout the world—perhaps some of these more than his own—I call this period in the development of the welfare state the Beveridge Full Employment Phase. However, it might just as well be called the Swedish Model. Writing in the early 1980s, Helen Ginsburg (1983, 122) pointed out, "Full employment is the linchpin of Sweden's comprehensive social-welfare policy."

During this middle phase of welfare-state development, the United States did not adopt a full-employment policy. Despite the intentions of the New Dealers who planned the Social Security Act, the U.S. welfare state, itself chronically underdeveloped, had to limp along without full employment (Skocpol 1990; Goldberg and Collins, forthcoming). The architects of the American welfare state thought that mass unemployment would continue to be a serious problem and wrote that "public employment projects should be recognized as a permanent policy of the government and not merely as an emergency measure" (Committee on Economic Security 1935, 89). Only a few months before the passage of the Social Security Act, New Dealers succeeded in enacting the Works Progress Administration (later Work Projects Administration), the largest job creation program in history. The WPA, however, was terminated when war began to employ the labor force more fully, and twice—in 1946 and 1978—Congress rejected the concept of a genuine entitlement to employment (Bailey 1950; Ginsburg 1983). Although price stability won out in the competition for top priority, maximum employment continued to be an aspiration of U.S. policy until the 1980s. While the United States had an entitlement to welfare for certain population groups, it never had an entitlement to work or to an opportunity for everyone who wanted a job to practice its much-touted work ethic. Employment and social-welfare policy were not well integrated in the United States during the years when they were two sides of the same coin in Europe. By contrast, in countries with relatively egalitarian social policies, or in advanced welfare states, "social policy is in some measure absorbed into general economic policy" (Wilensky 1983, 53). Of course, relief and labor market policies were hardly separate in the minds of Americans who sought to maintain a low economic and social wage.[2]

Throughout the postwar period, Japan took an approach different from either Europe or the United States. If Europe was committed to both a strong welfare state and full employment and the United States pursued weak versions of each, Japan favored full employment and a minimal public welfare apparatus. Though by no means without social provision and considerably ahead of the United States in health insurance, Japan placed much more emphasis on achieving low levels of unemployment for male breadwinners than on building a welfare state, particularly one that would permit women to be economically independent. Indeed, labor force participation and both the economic and social wage of Japanese women remain quite low (Axinn

1990). Depending on how one draws the boundaries of the welfare state, however, Japan might be said to have undertaken policies—and not only its particular brand of male-breadwinner full employment—that serve a function similar to social welfare (Gould 1993; Nomura and Kimoto, forthcoming).[3]

The Introductory or Proto-Welfare-State Phase

The Beveridge, or Full Employment Welfare State in Europe, was preceded by a period of experimentation with social insurance, but not full-employment policies, dating roughly from the last third of the nineteenth century through the 1930s. In neither the experimental phase nor the present post-Beveridge stage, has full employment been an integral component or equal partner of the welfare state. During the experimental phase, various forms of social insurance—protection against industrial accidents, sickness, unemployment, and old age—were invented and implemented in the countries of Western Europe.[4] As Heclo (1981, 389) points out, these social insurance programs were seen as deviations from established economic doctrines, and few saw them as good economics. The political motivations are clear in the case of German Chancellor Otto von Bismarck, who regarded the social insurance programs that he introduced in late nineteenth-century Germany as insurance against socialism (Pflanze 1990, 145–184). The demise of state socialism in the third phase of the welfare state may make it easier to resist "welfare statism" now that capitalism is unchallenged. One hopes reform will not have to wait for deregulated capitalism to sink itself again.

In this era too, the United States exhibited its usual exceptionalism. Prior to the 1930s, it initiated only a workers' compensation program; first, for federal employees in 1908, followed by the adoption of insurance programs against industrial injury in forty-three states between 1909 and 1920 (Lubove 1968). Theda Skocpol (1992) has made the case that pensions for Civil War veterans of the Union army can be compared to social insurance programs adopted by the European nations in this period, but these were not social insurance and lasted only as long as the veterans did.

The experimental era ended with mass unemployment in most of these countries. Sweden began to recover earlier because the ruling Social Democrats employed public policies that would later be associated with Keynsianism, whereas Germany, Britain, and the United States required the preparation for war or war economies to cure depression.

How serious a problem was unemployment during the first phase of the welfare state? Beveridge had this to say about it: "Unemployment before the first World War appeared as an evil calling for remedy, but not as the most serious economic problem of its time. That it was this between two wars will be denied by few" (1945, 105–106). Nonetheless, Beveridge observed that in Britain, which was among the nations that had inaugurated social insurance policies in this early phase, it was arguable that for only a little more than three years, between 1883 and 1914, was there adequate demand for the products of industry and hence the conditions for full employment (ibid., 108). Study of the development of unemployment insurance in Western Europe reveals that "extensive unemployment . . . wracked Europe in the mid-1880s and early 1890s" (Alber 1981, 152). Whether one considers the period before 1914 or the period between the two wars, this early, experimental phase of what would later be called the welfare state was not a full-employment state.

Economic and Social Benefits of Full Employment

Beveridge wrote *Full Employment in a Free Society* when "unemployment . . . [was] being melted away in the heat and fury of war." For Beveridge, it was the "spectacular achievement" of the "planned war economy" that demonstrated the possibility of full employment (Beveridge 1945, 117–118, 120). Beveridge believed it would not be necessary or desirable to attempt in peacetime to drive the economy at the pace of war. However, if peace should bring back education, leisure, and other desirable amenities that are thrust aside in order to stave off defeat, it should not "bring back the misery and waste of mass unemployment":

> But if full employment is to be attained, the target for peace must be such as to set up effective demand for the products of labour constantly exceeding the supply. In war, men and women become an asset, not a liability, because the urgency of the needs of war is effectively recognized by the people and by the Government. The bringing about of the same condition in peace depends upon a recognition of the needs of peace, which is equally effective in guiding the policy of government. Thus and thus alone will it be possible *to ensure to the people the first condition of happiness—the opportunity of useful service.* (Beveridge 1945, 122, emphasis added)

It is this emphasis on the "opportunity of useful service" that is one of the central components of the Beveridge approach to both the welfare state and full employment. "Idleness," wrote Beveridge, "is not the same as Want, but a separate evil, which men [and it was largely men and male breadwinners on his mind] do not escape by having an income. They must also have the chance of rendering useful service and of feeling that they are doing so" (ibid., 20). That meant useful and productive work. Probably in response to Keynes, he wrote that "Employment which is merely time-wasting, equivalent to digging holes and filling them again, or merely destructive, like war and preparing for war, will not serve that purpose" (ibid., 90). Similarly, income transfers were not considered a solution for persons who wanted to work. For the Swedes, full employment was also much more than economic security. The concept of *normalization* was fundamental to the Swedish social welfare system, and work was the key to a normal life, a means of reducing isolation, loneliness, and alienation (Ginsburg 1983, 123).

Beveridge, who proposed his comprehensive plan for Social Security two years before publishing his full-employment manifesto, considered the two policies mutually supportive. One of the assumptions of Social Security was that employment would be maintained and mass unemployment prevented (Beveridge 1945, 17). "The actual financing of Social Security," Beveridge wrote, "will be affected materially by the successful adoption of a policy of full employment" (ibid., 160). Full employment meant that "larger benefits in terms of money can be provided for materially lower contributions by all parties concerned" (ibid.). Whereas the social interventions of the experimental phase of the welfare state were seen as deviating from sound laws of political economy, the Beveridge phase held that social policy was not only good economics, but that the economic and social spheres of public policy were integrally related with each other" (Heclo 1981, 389). Even though Beveridge thought that full employment made it easier to finance the welfare state, he nevertheless held that "maintenance of employment is wanted for its own sake and not simply to make a Plan for Social Security work more easily" (Beveridge 1945, 17).

Socially useful jobs were preferable to income maintenance for persons of working age who were not caring for the young and the frail in their families, but full employment did not obviate their need for social welfare, even in economies with adequate wages. It required a different kind of welfare state, particularly as both parents became employed and many women became single parents. Study of the feminization of poverty in seven industrial nations leads to the conclusion that single mothers in all of these countries need the welfare state to escape poverty (Goldberg and Kremen 1990). In Sweden, which had an unemployment rate of 2.5 percent in 1981 and 2.1 percent in 1987 (U.S. Department of Labor 1997), the pre-transfer poverty rates for single-mother families were nonetheless 23.5 percent and 29.1 percent (Smeeding and Rainwater 1991, Table 7). In Germany, the single-parent poverty rate was 26.1 percent in 1981 when its unemployment rate was 5.5 percent. These were high rates of pre-transfer poverty, albeit considerably lower than in the United States, Canada, Britain, and the Netherlands, where the rates were 50 percent or more. In the early 1980s, the welfare state or income transfers reduced the poverty rates of single-parent families by 75 percent in Sweden and 93 percent in the Netherlands. By sad contrast, the reductions of single-parent poverty in Canada and the United States were so low that poverty rates for these families were 50.6 percent in the United States (1979) and 45 percent in Canada (1981) (ibid.).

In addition to alleviating the poverty of vulnerable populations, a full-employment welfare state can—and did—offer benefits different from those of nations that do not pursue full-employment policies. The full-employment state can pursue welfare in the broadest sense of the term rather than primarily prevent destitution and poverty. The Nordic countries that hewed to the full-employment goal differed from the more residual approach of the United States. The social wage and the market wage were adequate in the Nordic countries, and interestingly, it was this welfare-state model, with its commitment to full employment, that was most "decommodifying," that is, most likely to guarantee economic security irrespective of market status (Esping-Andersen 1990).[5]

The welfare state in which full employment is a full or senior partner is one with less public assistance, less need to supplement wages of the working poor in the way that we do increasingly in the United States, less unemployment insurance, and less money spent for the indirect costs of unemployment or the pernicious social ills that Vickrey sought to curtail.[6] In the United States, such a welfare state would introduce universal health insurance, family allowances, quality, subsidized child care, paid parental leave, and guaranteed child support for single-parent families.

The Post-Beveridge Welfare State

We are now in a third stage, one of both retreat from full-employment policies or aspirations, and declining confidence in either the affordability or effectiveness of the welfare state. This third phase of the welfare state—the post-Beveridge phase—has been variously labeled as one of welfare-state crisis, retrenchment, or dismantling, but is *none* of these, at least not yet (Pierson 1994; Pfaller, Gough, and Therborn 1991). Dismantling does not even describe the current status of the U.S. welfare state, which was one of the last to rise and, expectedly, the first to fall. I say this in full recognition of how dispiriting and ominous were the losses of the federal entitlement to welfare for poor, single-mother families in 1996, and the effort to create a phony Social Security "crisis" in order to privatize the huge bundle of money annually contributed to the Social Insurance Trust Funds.

The Budgetary Burdens of Unemployment

Throughout the postwar period, the combination of full employment and expansive social policies that has been called "welfare statism" fulfilled im-

portant functions for the system of capital production—"the efficient reproduction of manpower and the formation of human capital or stablization of
demand" (ibid., 2). The welfare state was recognized as an economic stabilizer, keeping up consumption when unemployment increased, helping to
prevent the kind of mushrooming depression experienced in the United States
before the New Deal. Particularly in the Nordic or social-democratic model,
the welfare state also employed large numbers of people, especially women
(Esping-Andersen 1990; Alestalo, Bislev, and Furåker 1991). In the current
era, however, "welfare statism" is said to have lost its "functionality" and to
have become a "costly luxury that nations could afford as long as they were
immune from competition from countries who do not have this luxury"
(Pfaller, Gough, and Therborn 1991, 2). This is not the case, however, if full
employment is maintained. For example, Ginsburg (1996) found that shortly
before cuts were made, Sweden had a strong welfare state and a hefty budget
surplus. "To understand why Sweden began to hack away at its social safety
net," Ginsburg holds, "one needs to examine the power of business interests,
the pressures of globalization, the implementation of neo-liberal policies and
the abandonment of the historic commitment to full employment" (ibid., 22).
These factors were the principal contributors to the demise of social safe-
guards, not the allegedly unsupportable weight of the welfare state.

With the abandonment of full-employment policies, the welfare state, as
Beveridge would have predicted, has become harder to finance. Even a small
amount of unemployment is costly for public treasuries. The Congressional
Budget Office estimated that a sustained rise of only one percentage point in
unemployment from 1995 through 2000 would cost the United States treasury a cumulative loss—in revenues and benefits—of more than $400 bil-
lion (Ginsburg 1995). The major loss would be in the revenues of the
unemployed, many of whom would otherwise be contributing to general
revenues and, in all cases, to the Social Insurance Trust Funds. Compensation in direct benefits to the unemployed costs the Treasury less than these
revenue losses but is nonetheless a drain.

Fuller employment and faster economic growth would also put an end to
the phony Social Security crisis or force the proponents of privatization to
come up with another problem. Lower unemployment means that fewer
people are forced to retire early and more workers pay into the Social Insurance Trust Funds; so do more employers. Just one year of lower unemployment has increased the Social Insurance Trust Funds so much that its projected
insolvency has been delayed by three years. The best insurance for Social
Security is full employment at decent wages. In predicting the Social Security "crisis," the Funds' trustees used three levels of unemployment, the lowest being a long-term rate of 5 percent (still above current levels) and what

Robert Eisner called "somber intermediate projections based on a six percent unemployment rate" and "gloom-and-doom" high-cost projections of around 7 percent (Eisner 1997, 46; Ginsburg 1998; Board of Trustees OASDI 1996). Whereas these latter "gloom-and-doom" rates predict bankruptcy in 2020, the intermediate rates anticipate a bare cupboard in 2030, and our offspring are safe beyond 2070 with the seldom-cited projections based on low (but not as low as current) unemployment rates. With any of these projected unemployment rates, we would have more to worry about than the solvency of the Social Insurance Trust Funds.

More evidence of the effect of unemployment on the welfare state comes from abroad. Two German analysts recently observed that "high unemployment almost inevitably pushes the welfare state into a financial crisis" (Bäcker and Klammer, forthcoming). (Germany's unemployment rate, which was under 0.7 percent in 1965, was 9.0 in 1986, considerably before unification, and was 11.4 percent in mid-1997 [U.S. Department of Labor 1997]). In the years when joblessness returned to a country whose previous mass unemployment was cured by Hitler's preparation for World War II, the government's response was to tighten the terms of entitlement to income support by increasing the periods of employment required prior to becoming eligible for benefits; lower payment levels for both unemployment insurance and the public assistance program available for the long-term unemployed after their insurance entitlement expired; abolish the bad-weather allowance for outdoor workers; and, most recently, lower unemployment assistance benefits by 3 percent (Bäcker and Klammer, forthcoming). Despite these cutbacks, unemployment expenditures, as measured by the proportion of gross domestic product (GDP), rose 39 percent between 1980 and 1990 and, with the added problem of unification, more than doubled in the next five years (OECD 1998b). As Jörg Huffschmid writes, "The loss in tax income and social insurance premiums diminishes the revenue side of the budget, whereas unemployment and welfare benefits burden the expenditure side, the cuts in benefit levels notwithstanding." The German Labor Agency estimates that the costs of unemployment amount to nearly 30 percent of total federal expenditures (Huffschmid 1997, 70–71). In Canada, too, unemployment has soared, coverage of the jobless has declined precipitously—from 88 percent of the unemployed in 1980 to 43 percent in mid-1997—and the cost of financing unemployment benefits has nonetheless risen somewhat over these years (Evans, forthcoming; OECD 1998b).

Diminishing Real Welfare

Welfare in the general sense of economic and social well-being is declining, but less from a reduction in the welfare state than from the effects of unemployment and low wages. The economic wage has deteriorated more than the social wage. My colleagues and I are completing a study of what we began by calling *Diminishing Welfare* (Goldberg and Rosenthal, forthcoming). This is an appropriate title if we consider welfare in the broader sense of the term, but not if the reference is to a substantial decline in overall social expenditures. The nine countries in the study, which are on three continents and include the largest economies in the world, are Canada, France, Germany, Hungary, Italy, Japan, Sweden, Britain, and the United States. On average, the proportion of GDP spent on social welfare increased by just over one-fourth (26 percent) between 1980 and 1995 in eight of these nine countries (OECD 1998b). (Data for Hungary were not available in this series.) The lowest increase in the proportion of GDP going to social welfare was 11 percent in Sweden, which still has the highest expenditures of the group; the largest increase, 40 percent, was in Japan, still the lowest spender.

Total social expenditures are questionable indicators of welfare effort or welfare outcomes. For example, public expenditures for health costs in the United States consume a much larger proportion of GDP than they did in 1980, but more people are without any health insurance coverage at all—43 million people or 16 percent of the population in 1997—and the rise is largely a function of escalating health costs and demographic changes (Bennefield 1998; Weiss and Lonnquist 1994, 295–301). Cash benefits to families have dropped 28 percent, causing great hardship among a hard-pressed population, but these expenditures amounted to less than 0.5 percent of GDP to begin with. Japan is using 57 percent more of its wealth for old-age cash benefits, whereas its total expenditures in 1995 consumed 40 percent more of the GDP than they did fifteen years ago. Aggregate spending can be misleading, but, on the other hand, these data from the OECD social expenditure database do not lead one to compose a requiem for the welfare state—at least not yet.

Paul Pierson (1994) examined trends in a number of countries and concluded that the welfare state remains intact, even in Britain where the ideology and power of the Thatcher regime would have made dismantling or substantial reduction a likely outcome. Pierson reasons that welfare states develop strong constituencies of beneficiaries that resist cutbacks. Even if the constituencies originally responsible for the rise of the welfare state, such as left political parties and labor movements, have declined in strength, beneficiaries are able to protect their interests.

National Wealth or National Will

Although it is easier to finance Social Security with less unemployment, the nations that carp about welfare burdens and plead poverty are richer than they were in the Beveridge phase when social welfare was both expansive and less burdened by market failures. The pace of growth has slowed, but the problem is not national wealth or capacity to finance social welfare. According to the Bureau of Labor Statistics (U.S. Department of Labor 1998, Table 1), the U.S. real GDP per capita more than doubled between 1960 and 1996 and increased by 29 percent between 1980 and 1996. The percentage increases for the last sixteen years ranged from a high of 53 percent in Japan to a low of 17 percent in Sweden.[7] The increase in social expenditures was lower than the increase in GDP per capita in Japan, Britain, Germany, Sweden, and the United States, and higher in Canada, France, and Italy. In the United States, the very elites who devoured the lion's share of gains in recent years are those who have successfully lobbied their governments for lower income taxes. And European elites, overlooking the price that the United States pays for its great economic inequality, talk of emulating the "American model."

Despite the growth in national resources and increased welfare spending, there is a concomitant upswing in inequality and poverty. In the United States, which has much higher rates of family and childhood poverty than most Western European nations, an already high poverty rate for families with children is 38 percent higher than it was thirty years ago, even after economic recovery and a year or two of the lowest rates of unemployment in a quarter century (Dalaker and Naifeh 1998, Table C3). The U.S. rise in inequality is appalling; the Gini ratio has increased 14 percent since 1980 and, in 1997, the last year for which data are available, was at its highest since 1947. The share of income of the top one-fifth of households is nearly fourteen times that of the lowest fifth, compared to about ten-to-one in 1980 (U.S. Bureau of the Census 1998, Table B3). In Britain, the number of people living in poor households more than doubled between 1979 and 1993/1994 (Millar, forthcoming). Between 1980 and 1990, Germany was an economic success, its share of world exports rising almost 14 percent, and the profit rate of German corporations up more than one-third. But in the same decade, the number of unemployed and poor people more than doubled (Huffschmid 1997, 74). Regardless of the level of social-welfare spending, economic welfare for lower-income groups was declining.

The welfare state did not eliminate poverty or inequality, but it came close with respect to poverty and, where it was most advanced and included full employment, did more to reduce inequality than elsewhere. In the mid-1980s, those regimes that were most encompassing or social-democratic (Finland, Norway, Sweden) had mean rates of poverty of 4.2 percent for the total population and 2.6 for the elderly, compared to 14.0 percent and 10.5 percent in the liberal regimes of Canada, the U.K., and the United States. The Gini coeffficients of the three Nordic countries averaged 0.226, compared to 0.302

in the liberal regimes. France and Germany, classified by Esping-Andersen as conservative-corporatist, were in the middle on both counts (overall poverty rate of 7.2 percent and 3.6 percent for the elderly); mean Gini coefficient of 0.268 (Korpi and Palme 1998, using data from the Luxembourg Income Study).[8]

Ethan Kapstein of the Council on Foreign Relations has observed that "Just when working people are most in need of the nation state as a buffer from the world economy, it is abandoning them" (1996, 16). As a matter of fact, the welfare state is not being dismantled, but it appears that it would have to grow very substantially to provide such a buffer. Cross-national study suggests that the welfare state is not rising to the occasion even though, as already indicated, social expenditures have increased. As Ian Gough concluded, in referring particularly to Britain, "The social welfare system must run hard simply to stand still. In the event it hasn't run hard enough" (1991, 146). However, the consensus seems to be that the prime culprit is unemployment and, in the United States, low wages. As Jane Millar (forthcoming) writes of Britain, "It is changes in the labor market that have been the underlying cause of rising poverty rates. Put simply, there has been a significant increase in the number of people who are unable to achieve an adequate and secure income from employment."

Consequences of the Welfare State Minus Full Employment

It is economically possible for rich nation-states to buffer high rates of unemployment and low wages, but is it politically feasible or socially desirable? France, Sweden, Germany, and Italy had unemployment rates ranging from 6.5 percent to 12 percent in 1995 (and continued to experience high unemployment in 1998) (OECD 1998a; U. S. Department of Labor November 1998). At the same time, they were spending from about one-fourth to one-third of GDP on social welfare. France, which is not the wealthiest of the rich countries nor the one with the greatest growth in national wealth, spends 30 percent of its GDP on social welfare and has increased that proportion 28 percent since 1980. Sweden, though its growth rate has slowed since 1980, still spends almost one-third of its GDP on social welfare.

"Political mobilization pays," concludes political scientist Mark Kesselman in an assessment of welfare in France. "The French tradition of broad social provision primarily distributed on a universalist basis has survived intact in the 1990s, thanks to the intense mobilization protesting possibilities of retrenchment, including, of course, the immense strikes of late 1995 that toppled the government of Alain Juppé" (personal communication, September 18, 1998). In Germany, cutbacks have also been resisted but not as successfully as in France. A protest in Bonn, almost equal in size to the population of the city itself (Cowell 1996), was the response to Chancellor Helmut Kohl's proposal to cut $5 billion from the welfare state—including reductions in sick pay and unemployment benefits and a postponement of scheduled increases in children's allowances. Protesting cuts of $1 billion in Ontario's budget that would drop 180,000 persons from the welfare rolls, Canadians staged a two-day protest in Toronto, the fifth and largest in a series of "Days of Action." The protest "tangled highway traffic and shut down mass transit"; a third of the city's public school teachers did not show up for work; and police were needed to keep hundreds of protesters from disrupting the Toronto Stock Exchange (DePalma 1996).

This political support for the welfare state is a far cry from the scant protest over the loss of the entitlement to welfare for poor women and their children in the United States. However, welfare mothers are the weakest, most stigmatized, and least well organized of welfare state beneficiaries and are perceived to be overwhelmingly women of color. Their loss of benefits does not challenge Pierson's theory. A better test lies ahead with the response to the proposed privatization and cutbacks in the large, universal Social Security system that does have an organized constituency. The volatility on Wall Street, which at first seemed to have saved us the trouble of taking to the streets, has not led either the administration or many members of Congress to abandon their advocacy of partial privatization of the Social Security system.

One important question is whether there are economic penalties for a country like France that responds to political pressures and maintains the welfare state pretty much intact. Is maintaining an extensive welfare state with such high unemployment an economic burden? When asked this question, Kesselman responded that this policy seems to be working pretty well, with inflation low, the budget generally balanced, and the franc stable. The welfare state is, of course, a fiscal stimulus that can help to keep up consumption and to throttle unemployment. However, even though the welfare state was thriving, unemployment in France was still nearly 12 percent as recently as the summer of 1998 (U.S. Department of Labor November 1998).

One problem with financing the welfare state in nations with growing inequality is that the burden of paying for it falls on the working classes. They, in turn, may be getting fewer benefits because, in order to save money, programs may become more residual. It is these groups that are burdened by what James Galbraith (1998) calls the "transfer state." They pay heavily to finance the big-ticket insurance programs with regressive payroll taxes and also to borrow to pay the debts that pile up as their incomes fall short. With the former, they subsidize the elderly, and with the latter, the lenders or the well-to-do. The culprit, the underlying cause of low wages, concludes Galbraith after careful analysis of income data from several sources, is the declining commitment to full employment since the 1970s.[9]

An alternative to the present system of paying for the welfare state would be to depend more on taxing those who have grown wealthier in recent years— like the richest 1 percent of U.S. families who got 60 percent of the nation's substantial after-tax income gains in the years between 1977 and 1989, and the top one-fifth as a whole who grabbed 94 percent of those gains (Nasar 1992, A1). However, their resistance to progressive taxation has risen in proportion to the increases in their incomes, and so has the political clout to get away with it. Another difficult alternative politically, though not economically, is to collect the long overdue "peace dividend" and to convert that government spending to domestic investment and employment, expenditures that would lead to more growth and more jobs (Aschauer 1990; Melman 1974, 1989).

Maintaining the welfare state in the absence of full employment or with high rates of unemployment appears incompatible with maintaining economic well-being. The welfare state continues but poverty, inequality, and their attendant ills and risks increase. That, in turn, leads to dissatisfaction with the welfare state. "We are spending billions and poverty is still rising" is a likely complaint. On the other hand, substantial cuts in welfare could threaten political legitimacy.

In the United States, the failure to pursue genuine, full employment and to attack the labor-market deficiencies that exist in economically disadvantaged areas in good times and bad (U.S. Department of Labor 1967; U.S. Senate 1972) has consigned millions of people, particularly young men and women of color, to economic and social marginality.[10] The results have been crime, family breakdown, and the various forms of self-destruction that those who are denied socially useful roles inflict on themselves and others. Individual deviance and crime have been the expressions of this economic deprivation in recent years, but, particularly if the welfare state declines further, it may once again take the more political routes of riot and rebellion.

Jobs for all at decent wages are, as Robert Heilbroner and Lester Thurow put it, the best "benefit" an economy can provide (Heilbroner and Thurow 1981, 50–51). The National Jobs for All Coalition has formulated and promulgated a plan for an updated, full-employment welfare state, or "welfare statism" that is suited to a globalized economy (Collins, Ginsburg, and Goldberg 1994). The Coalition's program has also been updated from the earlier focus of Beveridge, though not of Sweden, on a male breadwinner model. No longer a gendered concept, "jobs for all" means fully employed men and women of working age. Full employment means jobs at a living or family-supporting wage. A policy of jobs for all is also the best way to maintain a welfare state that can provide for women who support their families, the young, the elderly, the frail, and those who perform vital work by caring for them in the home. An updated full-employment program would also reverse the regrettable trend toward longer hours for women and dual-earner families by reducing the work week and allowing more time for community, family, and fun.[11]

Full employment was the senior partner of a progressive welfare state in parts of Europe during the postwar decades. For a time, these economic and social policies were integrated with felicitous consequences for the reduction of poverty and inequality, and, if resumed and modified to meet new economic and social conditions, they would once again be conducive to social welfare or well-being. The same would be true of a similar partnership in the United States, which has been a "reluctant" or "semi-welfare" state and has only experienced full employment in times of war.[12] We would not only enjoy significantly less poverty, homelessness, sickness and crime, but reduction of our egregious inequality.

Notes

1. I base this on my reading of some of his writings and my firsthand experience with him in the National Jobs for All Coalition, several articles reviewing his career (Canova 1997; Colander 1998; Holt, Colander, et al. 1998), and an e-mail exchange with David Colander.

2. For example, during the debate on the Family Assistance Plan proposed by President Richard Nixon, Representative Phil Landrum revealingly objected that "there's not going to be anybody left to roll those wheelbarrows and press those shirts" (Burke and Burke 1974, 147). Daniel P. Moynihan (1973, 378) reported Governor Lester G. Maddox as saying, "You're not going to be able to find anyone willing to work as maids or janitors or housekeepers if this bill goes through."

3. These might broadly be termed occupational welfare and include not only substantial private provision for more privileged groups of employees, but also such government interventions as protecting family businesses and the self-employed against competition from large-scale businesses, import restrictions and subsidies for agricultural products, and large government investments in public works that aid the construction industry. "Not by Social Security, then, but by investment and protection has the government successfully maintained an adequate standard of living for the self-employed and employees in family businesses" (Nomura and Kimoto, forthcoming).

4. By the outbreak of World War I, twelve countries had some kind of workers' compensation schemes, ten had introduced either compulsory or subsidized voluntary sickness insurance programs, eight provided for old age, and five had some kind of unemployment insurance. At the start of World War II, most had compulsory accident and sickness insurance, all had some kind of unemployment insurance, and all but one provided for old age (Alber 1981).

5. Esping-Andersen classifies welfare states according to the extent to which they accomplish the goal of decommodification. The least decommodifying are the liberal welfare-state regimes, the United States, Canada, and Britain. Midway between liberal and social-democratic models are the "corporatist/conservative" welfare-state regimes of France, Germany, and Austria, which, though providing substantial protection, tend to maintain status distinctions established by the market and other social institutions.

6. In his presidential address to the American Economic Association in 1993, Vickrey wrote that full employment would mean "a major reduction in the ills of poverty, homelessness, sickness and crime" (1993, 10).

7. The increases were: Japan, 53 percent; the United States, 29 percent; Germany, 28 percent; Italy, 23 percent; the United Kingdom, 22 percent; France, 19 percent; Canada, 18 percent; Sweden, 17 percent.

8. Korpi and Palme were specifically interested in the extent to which social insurance institutions in these countries were targeted, or universalism. Their findings were roughly categorized according to the regime types identified by Esping-Andersen. Poverty was itself conceptualized in relative terms, that is, as below 50 percent of the median income, adjusted for family size. Esping-Andersen (1990, 27) describes the corporatist regimes as preserving differences of class and status. Ramesh Mishra (1996, 323) describes Germany as committed to social welfare "but more from the viewpoint of security and stability than equality."

9. Galbraith tends to overstate U.S. commitment to full employment, but certainly the attainment of maximum employment as a policy goal has declined since the 1960s. For a discussion of trends in U. S. unemployment, see Ginsburg 1983, 34–54; Collins, Ginsburg, and Goldberg 1994, 44–47.

10. In November 1966, when national unemployment was 3.4 percent, the lowest for that month in thirteen years, the Department of Labor intensively surveyed ten urban slum areas to determine their rates of subemployment (includes the number who are officially unemployed or involuntarily employed part-time; the estimated number of discouraged adult male workers, that is, who want a job but have stopped looking for one; an estimate of the male "undercount," assuming half the missing males to be subemployed; and full-time workers with annual incomes under the government's poverty threshold). Whereas official unemployment in these areas averaged nearly 10 percent, subemployment was, on average, more than three times as prevalent, reaching a high of 47 percent in slum areas of San Antonio (U. S. Department of Labor 1967). A Census Employment Survey (CES) using a similar subemployment index was administered in fifty-one urban areas as part of the 1970 Census. Analyzing the voluminous data from the CES, the Senate Subcommittee on Employment, Manpower, and Poverty found an average subemployment rate of 30.5 percent for the fifty-one areas (U.S. Senate 1972). This was very close to the 1966 results of the smaller survey by the Department of Labor.

11. Barry Bluestone and Stephen Rose (1997) examined several sets of data, both cross-sectional and longitudinal, and found a modest increase in work time for the labor force as a whole over a recent twenty-year period, a figure that includes a slight reduction in men's hours, but a large addition to women's. During the 1980s, a substantial minority of prime-age workers were what these researchers termed "overworked and underemployed," experiencing at least one year of substantial overtime (average work week of forty-six hours or more) and one year of significant underemployment (average of less than thirty-five hours—which they interpret as feasting

before anticipated famine). Dual-worker families have substantially increased their combined hours of work.

12. Harold L. Wilensky used the term "reluctant welfare state" in an introductory essay, "The Problem and Prospects of the Welfare State," to a paperback edition of the influential book that he co-authored with Charles N. Lebeaux, *Industrial Society and Social Welfare* (1958/1965). Michael B. Katz wrote that "By the 1940s, America had acquired a unique, unsatisfactory, semi-welfare state" that compromised rather than superseded the local basis of relief, did not erase distinctions between the worthy and unworthy, preserved class distinctions in creating walls between social insurance and public assistance, and failed to redistribute income (1986, 247 and passim).

References

Alber, J. 1981. "Government Responses to the Challenge of Unemployment: The Development of Unemployment Insurance in Western Europe." In *The Development of Welfare States in Europe and America*, ed. P. Flora and A.H. Heidenheimer. New Brunswick, NJ: Transaction Books.

Alestalo, M., S. Bislev, and B. Furåker. 1991. "Welfare State Employment in Scandinavia." In *The Welfare State as Employer*, ed. J.E. Kolberg and G. Esping-Andersen. Armonk, NY: M.E. Sharpe.

Aschauer, D.A. 1990. *Public Investment and Private Sector Growth*. Washington, DC: Public Policy Institute.

Axinn, June. 1990. "Japan: A Special Case." In *The Feminization of Poverty: Only in America?* ed. G.S. Goldberg and E. Kremen. New York: Praeger.

Bäcker, G., and U. Klammer. Forthcoming. "The Dismantling of Welfare in Germany." In *Diminishing Welfare: A Cross-National Study of Social Provision*, ed. G.S. Goldberg and M.G. Rosenthal. New York: Praeger.

Bailey, S.K. 1950. *Congress Makes a Law: The Story Behind the Employment Act of 1945*. New York: Columbia University Press.

Bennefield, R.L. 1998. "Health Insurance Coverage: 1997." *Current Population Reports*. P602002, September. Washington, DC: U.S. Bureau of the Census.

Beveridge, W.H. 1945. *Full Employment in a Free Society*. New York: W.W. Norton.

Bluestone, B., and S. Rose. 1997. "Overworked and Under-Employed." *American Prospect*, March–April: 58–69.

Board of Trustees, OASDI. 1996. *1996 Annual Report of the Federal Old-Age Survivors Insurance and Disability Insurance Trust Funds*. Washington, DC: U.S. Government Printing Office.

Burke, V.J., and V. Burke. 1974. *Nixon's Good Deed: Welfare Reform*. New York: Columbia University Press.

Canova, T. 1997. "The Macroeconomics of William Vickrey." *Challenge* 40 (March/April): 95–109.

Colander, D.C. 1998. "Macroeconomics: Was Vickrey Ten Years Ahead?" *Challenge* 41: 72–76.

Collins, S.D., H.L. Ginsburg, and G.S. Goldberg. 1994. *Jobs for All: A Plan for the Revitalization of America*. New York: Apex Press.

Committee on Economic Security. 1935, 1985. *The Report of the Committee on Economic Security of 1935, 50th Anniversary Edition*. Washington, DC: National Conference on Social Welfare.

Cowell, A. 1996. "Germans Stage Huge Protest on Budget Plan." *New York Times*, June 16, A8.

Dalaker, J., and M. Naifeh. 1998. *Poverty in the United States: 1997*. U. S. Bureau of the Census, *Current Population Reports*, P60201. Washington, DC: U.S. Government Printing Office.

DePalma, A. 1996. "Protesters Take to Streets to Defend Canada's Safety Net." *New York Times*, October 10, 3.

Eisner, R. 1997. *The Great Deficit Scares: The Federal Budget, Trade, and Social Security*. New York: Century Foundation Press.

Esping-Andersen, G. 1990. *Three Worlds of Welfare Capitalism*. Princeton: Princeton University Press.

Evans, P.M. Forthcoming. "Downloading the Welfare State: The Canadian Case." In *Diminishing Welfare: A Cross-National Study of Social Provision*, ed. G.S. Goldberg and M.G. Rosenthal. New York: Praeger.

Galbraith, J.K. 1998. *Created Unequal: The Crisis in American Pay*. New York: Free Press.

Ginsburg, H. 1983. *Full Employment Policy: The United States and Sweden*. Lexington, MA: Lexington Books.

―――. 1995. "Increasing Unemployment Increases the Deficit; Reducing Unemployment Reduces the Deficit." *Uncommon Sense*, Part 1. New York: National Jobs for All Coalition.

―――. 1996. "Sweden: Fall from Grace." *In These Times*, December 23.

―――. 1998. "Social Security: The Phony Crisis." Testimony before the New York City Council. New York: National Jobs for All Coalition.

Goldberg, G.S., and S.D. Collins. Forthcoming. *Washington's New Poor Law: Welfare Reform and the Roads Not Taken, 1935–1996*. New York: Apex Books.

Goldberg, G.S., and E. Kremen. 1990. *The Feminization of Poverty: Only in America?* New York: Praeger.

Goldberg, G.S., and M.G. Rosenthal. Forthcoming. *Diminishing Welfare: A Cross-National Study of Social Provision*. New York: Praeger.

Gough, I. 1991. "The United Kingdom." In *Can the Welfare State Compete? A Comparative Study of Five Advanced Capitalist Countries*, ed. A. Pfaller, I. Gough, and G. Therborn. London: Macmillan.

Gould, A. 1993. *Capitalist Welfare Systems: A Comparison of Japan, Britain and Sweden*. London: Longman.

Heclo, H. 1981. "Toward a New Welfare State." In *The Development of Welfare States in Europe and America*, ed. P. Flora and A.J. Heidenheimer. New Brunswick, NJ: Transaction Books.

Heilbroner, R., and L. Thurow. 1981. *Five Economic Challenges*. Englewood Cliffs, NJ: Prentice-Hall.

Holt, R.P.F., D. Colander, et al. 1998. "William Vickrey's Legacy: Innovative Policies for Social Concerns." *Eastern Economic Journal*, 16.

Huffschmid, J. 1997. "Economic Policy for Full Employment: Proposals for Germany." *Economic and Industrial Democracy* 18: 67–86.

Kapstein, E.B. 1996. "Workers and the World Economy." *Foreign Affairs* 75 (May/June): 16–37.

Katz, Michael. 1986. *In the Shadow of the Poorhouse: A Social History of Welfare in America*. New York: Basic Books.

Korpi, W., and J. Palme. 1998. "The Paradox of Redistribution and Strategies of

Equality: Welfare State Institutions, Inequality, and Poverty in the Western Countries." *American Sociological Review* 63: 661–687.

Lubove, Roy. 1968. *The Struggle for Social Security, 1900–1935.* Cambridge: Harvard University Press.

Melman, S. 1974. *The Permanent War Economy.* New York: Simon and Schuster.

———. 1989. "The Peace Dividend: What to Do with the Cold War Money." *New York Times*, December 17.

Millar, J. Forthcoming. "Diminishing Welfare: The Case of Britain." In *Diminishing Welfare: A Cross-National Study of Social Provision*, ed. G.S. Goldberg and M.G. Rosenthal. New York: Praeger.

Mishra, R. 1996. "The Welfare of Nations." In *States Against Markets*, ed. R. Boyer and D. Drache. London: Routledge.

Moynihan, D. P. 1973. *The Politics of a Guaranteed Income.* New York: Random House.

Nasar, S. 1992. "The 1980s: A Very Good Time for the Very Rich." *New York Times*, March 5, A1, D24.

Nomura, M., and K. Kimoto. Forthcoming. "Is the Japanese Style Welfare Society Sustainable?" In *Diminishing Welfare: A Cross-National Study of Social Provision*, ed. G.S. Goldberg and M.G. Rosenthal. New York: Praeger.

OECD. 1998a. "OECD in Figures." Supplement to the *OECD Observer* 212 (June/July).

OECD. 1998b. *OECD Social Expenditure Database.* Paris: OECD.

Pfaller, A., I. Gough, and G. Therborn, eds. 1991. *Can the Welfare State Compete? A Comparative Study of Five Advanced Capitalist Countries.* London: Macmillan.

Pfaller, A., with I. Gough and G. Therborn. 1991. "The Issue." In *Can the Welfare State Compete? A Comparative Study of Five Advanced Capitalist Countries*, ed. A. Pfaller, I. Gough, and G. Therborn. London: Macmillan.

Pflanze, O. 1990. *Bismarck and the Development of Germany.* Vol. 3. Princeton: Princeton University Press.

Pierson, P. 1994. *Dismantling the Welfare State: Reagan, Thatcher and the Politics of Retrenchment.* Cambridge: Cambridge University Press.

Skocpol, T. 1990. " 'Brother, Can You Spare a Job?' Work and Welfare in the United States." In *The Nature of Work: Sociological Perspectives*, ed. K. Erikson and S. Vallas. New Haven: Yale University Press.

———. 1992. *Protecting Soldiers and Mothers: The Political Origins of Social Policy in the United States.* Cambridge: Belknap Press of Harvard University Press.

Smeeding, T.M., and L. Rainwater. 1991. "Cross-National Trends in Income Poverty and Dependency: The Evidence for Young Adults in the Eighties." Working paper no. 67, *Luxembourg Income Study.* Syracuse, NY: Maxwell School of Citizenship and Public Affairs, Syracuse University.

U.S. Bureau of the Census. 1998. *Money Income in the United States: 1997.* Current Population Reports, P60200. Washington, DC: U.S. Government Printing Office.

U.S. Department of Labor, Bureau of Labor Statistics. February 1998. "Comparative Real Gross Domestic Product per Capita and per Employed Person, Fourteen Countries, 1960–1996." Washington, DC: U.S. Department of Labor.

———. November, 1998. "Unemployment Rates in Nine Countries: Civilian Labor Force Basis Approximating U. S. Concepts." Washington, DC: U.S. Department of Labor.

U.S. Department of Labor, Bureau of Labor Statistics, Office of Productivity and

Technology. September 1997. "Comparative Civilian Labor Force Statistics: Ten Countries, 1959–1996." Washington, DC: U.S. Department of Labor.

U.S. Department of Labor. 1967. *A Sharper Look at Unemployment in U. S. Cities and Slums*. Washington, DC: U.S. Government Printing Office.

U.S. Senate, Committee on Labor and Public Welfare, Subcommittee on Employment, Manpower and Poverty. 1972. *Comprehensive Manpower Reform Hearings*, Pt. 5, 92d Cong., 2d sess. Washington, DC: United States Government Printing Office, 2276, 2280.

Vickrey, W. 1993. "Today's Task for Economists." *American Economic Review* 83:110.

Weiss, G.L., and L.E. Lonnquist. 1994. *The Sociology of Health, Healing, and Illness*. Englewood Cliffs, NJ: Prentice-Hall.

Wilensky, H.L. 1983. "Political Legitimacy and Consensus: Missing Variables in the Assessment of Social Policy." In *Evaluating the Welfare State: Social and Political Perspectives*, ed. S.E. Spiro and E. Yuchtman-Yaar. New York: Academic Press.

8

HELEN LACHS GINSBURG

A Humanistic Concept of
Full Employment Transcends
the Welfare State

Gertrude Goldberg, in her paper "Full Employment and the Future of the Welfare State," provides a unique, comprehensive analysis of the interplay between full employment and the welfare state over time and in different places. She shows that William Vickrey's vision of full employment is one that enriches nations and hence *enables* them to provide generous benefits. But Goldberg also points out that, in many advanced industrial nations, the lack of capacity to finance social welfare is not the real problem.

My remarks in the following four areas expand on topics that Goldberg covered in her paper only briefly or not at all: (1) how a humanistic concept of full employment transcends the welfare state; (2) why real full employment means decent wages; (3) how full employment enhances human welfare by making it easier to transform workplaces; and (4) how unemployment can lead to negative ideological shifts, while full employment makes it easier to maintain social and intergenerational solidarity.

How a Humanistic Concept of Full Employment Transcends
the Welfare State

It has often been said that the United States has attained full employment. But though unemployment is lower than in decades, numbers can deceive (Collins, Ginsburg, and Goldberg 1994, 42–48).

The narrow concept of full employment presently embraced by many economists and others focuses exclusively on an unemployment rate and thus obscures a broader, humanistic tradition. The latter is expressed, for instance, in documents such as Franklin Delano Roosevelt's Economic Bill of Rights, the United Nations Charter, and Article 23 of the Universal Declaration of Human Rights, and by economists such as William Beveridge in his seminal work *Full Employment in a Free Society* (1945) and Vickrey in "Today's Task for Economists" (1993). In this tradition, full employment is explicitly or implicitly considered an aspect of human welfare that includes but goes beyond the welfare state's cash transfers and provision of services. It stresses that greater utilization of human and other resources means rising living standards; and, with some exceptions—for example, women in earlier conceptions—this approach leaves out no individual or group (Ginsburg 1991; Ginsburg, Zaccone, et al. 1997). Vickrey, for one, was disturbed not only by unemployment, but also by its unfair, unequal distribution that strikes hard at some groups while leaving others relatively unscathed. This humanistic concept of full employment recognizes the social as well as the economic role of work and the havoc that ensues when unemployment runs rampant. It is no accident that efforts to promulgate full employment as an overriding goal flourished while embers of World War II still burned, and in that war's aftermath. Full employment was considered a necessary ingredient in the recipe for a just and peaceful world.

In the early 1990s, when U.S. unemployment seemed stuck in the 7 percent range, Bill Vickrey (1993) was a voice in the wilderness of the economics profession. Probably based on his World War II experience, Vickrey set the figure for full employment at 1.5 percent unemployment, and actively advocated attainment of that goal. For Bill, who was driven by moral concerns and his Quaker beliefs, there was simply no alternative, since, above all, he recognized the social and human destruction caused by unemployment. In his 1993 presidential address to the American Economic Association, he told his fellow economists, "We simply cannot carry on as we have been doing without falling apart as a community" (Vickrey 1993, 100).

Today, with unemployment hovering around 4.5 percent, we are far from real full employment. To those who say the United States now has full employment, we can ask, full employment for whom? Despite the welcome reduction in unemployment, about 15 million people remain officially or unofficially unemployed; that is, they want jobs and do not have them, or are working part-time involuntarily. Another 1.7 million people are in jail, a figure that has doubled in a decade. A disproportionate number of these inmates are minority men, and many of them would be jobless if they were not incarcerated. Robert Cherry (1998) has estimated that if a portion of these men were out of prison and counted as unemployed, the 1997 unemployment rate for twenty-to-sixty-four-year-old black men would triple—from 8.5 to 25 percent. Not just in the United States, but also in Germany, France, Sweden, and elsewhere, there is a differential impact on minorities or immigrants. And in many countries, women are harder hit than men. As for the disabled, their massive hidden unemployment, along with their human right to a job, is largely ignored.

Why Real Full Employment Means Decent Wages

Slavery is not full employment; neither are jobs at poverty wages. Both Vickrey and Beveridge, as well as Roosevelt's Economic Bill of Rights and the Universal Declaration of Human Rights, recognized that full employment means jobs at living wages. Yet in 1997, about 16.8 million full-time workers earned less than the meager poverty level for a four-person family (Ginsburg and Ayres 1998). As James Galbraith (1998) has shown, much wage erosion and widening inequality in recent decades is attributable to high unemployment.

In the 1960s, with unemployment in the 3 percent range, many thought that full employment had arrived, only to have urban riots shatter that myth. The Kerner Commission, appointed by President Lyndon Johnson to investigate the cause of the riots, concluded that depression levels of subemployment—that is, unemployment, underemployment, and work at poverty wages—in the nation's ghettos were major causes of the riots (National Advisory Commission on Civil Disorders 1968).

How Full Employment Enhances Human Welfare by Making It Easier to Transform Workplaces

A whole strand of thought argues against work and the vision of full employment because work is said to be degrading. But full employment makes it easier to unionize, makes workers more likely to demand workplace democracy, and forces employers to provide better working conditions. Full employment in Sweden was accompanied by high worker turnover in the automobile industry, and that induced Volvo to eliminate the assembly line in one of its plants (now closed). Unemployment creates on-the-job stress and deteriorating working conditions for the *employed* as well as increased overall mortality (Brenner 1995). Employers welcome unemployment not only for its ability to restrain wages, but also because it disciplines workers, while full employment tilts power from capital to labor.

How Unemployment Can Lead to Negative Ideological Shifts, While Full Employment Makes It Easier to Maintain Social and Intergenerational Solidarity

Goldberg demonstrates how Germany restricted eligibility to unemployment benefits and cut their level when it became an unemployment rather than a full-employment state. I would add that rising unemployment weakens welfare states because it increases the need to maintain working-age people while simultaneously reducing the revenue to do so. It can also lead to erosion of political and social solidarity and spawn racism, as fewer workers must support more of the jobless. Under such conditions, ideological myths are easier to introduce or to perpetuate: "They" are taking away our jobs, or "they" are lazy. When there are not enough jobs, the need to preserve work incentives is used to justify benefit cuts and implicitly shift blame for unemployment onto its victims, especially when they are disproportionately minorities and immigrants.

Contrary to assumptions of the neoclassical model, in Sweden when the wage replacement for jobless benefits was 90 percent, it was not a disincentive to work (Ginsburg 1983; 1996). But when mass unemployment came to Sweden, benefits were cut and official documents now talk of restructuring benefits—that is, cutting or restricting them—in order to maintain the incentive to work (Sweden, Ministry of Finance 1995, 65). Never mind that there are simply not enough jobs for all!

Similarly, nations with aging populations project deficits in pension funds, then justify reductions in pensions because of a projected decrease in the ratio of workers to retirees. But demography is not necessarily destiny. Full employment means higher output and less need to support people of working age.

When Sweden had full employment, it was generously supporting a large elderly population—about 18 percent of Swedes were 65 years of age or older. (That proportion—about 40 percent more than the 12.8 percent of the United States population currently 65 years and over—is one that the United States is not projected to attain for decades.) Yet their support did not push Sweden into an economic crisis. What did do that were factors like deregulation of financial markets, currency decontrol, and the shift in the government's main priority from full employment to price stability (Canova 1994; Edin and Andersson 1995; Ginsburg 1996; Hermele 1993; Meidner 1993, 1997, 1998; Olson 1991; Pontusson 1992).

In the United States, there is much hype about a pending Social Security "crisis," with deficits looming down the road. But this gloomy scenario is based on Social Security trustees' wildly pessimistic mid-range assumptions (DuBoff 1999; Ginsburg 1998; Board of Trustees 1998). Annual gross domestic product (GDP) growth is projected to average only 1.4 percent for the next seventy-five years—less than half of the 3.5 percent average for 1920 to 1995, years that include the Great Depression. Even in the sluggish 1973–1995 era, growth averaged 2.5 percent. The trustees also assume 6 percent unemployment for most of the next seventy-five years. Using these projections, in 2032, when it is presumed the Trust Fund will be emptied and benefits dependent on insufficient payroll taxes paid at that time, the number of jobless—around 6 million at the end of 1998—would surge to 9.5 million (Spitz 1998).

But what happens when the trustees use more realistic but only slightly less dismal assumptions? In their "low cost" estimate, annual GDP growth is assumed to average 2.5 percent for a decade, but thereafter, through 2075, only around 2.1 percent. These rates are still far lower than for most of this century. Unemployment, it is assumed, will rise to 5 percent within a few years and remain there until 2075. Using these assumptions, which are not part of the public debate, there are no deficits at all during the entire seventy-five-year period. Why? Because more jobs (and higher wages) substantially increase revenues flowing into the Social Security Trust Fund. Just one year of faster growth and lower employment (in 1997) increased revenues enough to delay the insolvency the trustees originally projected for 2029 by three years to 2032.

To put this in perspective, we should recall that in 1978, Congress passed the Humphrey-Hawkins Full Employment and Balanced-Growth Act making a 4 percent *interim* unemployment rate, to be attained in five years, national policy. The act, which is still the law of the land, clearly states that 4 percent unemployment is not the final goal. But it has taken two decades just to come close to the interim goal. That law has been ignored, if not violated. If it were adhered to, Social Security would be even more flush with funds than it is now and there would be discussions of how to raise the incomes of those who receive benefits that are too low. Thus, the fight for jobs for all at decent wages is an integral part of the fight for a secure Social Security system.

With full employment, it would be far easier to provide for the elderly, some of whom might even prefer to work. Jobs for all at decent wages would prevent the decay of intergenerational bonds, which are so politically essential for maintaining a system of decent old-age benefits. This is especially necessary because so many youth are jobless in European countries, or, as in the United States, earn considerably less than their parents did when young. As they may say, "Why tax my low wages to maintain those geezers?"

Toward a Commitment to Full Employment and the Welfare State

Neither Professor Goldberg nor I have dealt in these papers with the specific pressures in the global economy working against both full employment at decent wages and the welfare state. It is not because we think these are unimportant. On the contrary, we, with others from the National Jobs for All Coalition and the Columbia University Seminar on Full Employment, have written about them in *The Challenge of Full Employment in the Global Economy* (Ginsburg, Zaccone, et al. 1997). Our analysis counters prevailing defeatist attitudes that hold that full employment is no longer a realistic goal for governments of industrial economies and that welfare states must be trimmed back. We present a program of concrete solutions and call for an international meeting led by concerned academics and other allies to dramatize the employment crisis and secure the welfare state. Our volume is dedicated to William Vickrey. A broad movement and political commitment to full employment are needed, and we are proud that Bill Vickrey was an active member of the Advisory Board of the National Jobs for All Coalition and co-chair of the Columbia Seminar on Full Employment. We are especially grateful to Dean Aaron Warner for his Herculean efforts to stimulate the necessary intellectual foundation for reviving interest in full employment.

References

Beveridge, William. 1945. *Full Employment in a Free Society*. New York: W.W. Norton.
Board of Trustees, Federal Old-Age and Survivors Insurance and Disability Trust Funds. 1998. *The 1998 Annual Report*. (Transmitted to the 104th Cong., 2nd sess., H.R. Doc. 104–228). Washington, DC: Government Printing Office.
Brenner, M. Harvey. 1995. "Political Economy and Health." In *Society and Health*, ed. Benjamin C. Amick III, Sol Levine, Alvin R. Tarlov, and Diana Chapman Walsh. New York: Oxford University Press, 211–246.
Canova, Timothy A. 1994. "The Swedish Model Betrayed." *Challenge* 37, no. 3 (May/ June): 36–40.
Cherry, Robert. 1998. "Black Men Still Jobless." *Dollars and Sense*, no. 220 (November/December): 43.
Collins, Sheila D., Helen Lachs Ginsburg, and Gertrude Schaffner Goldberg. 1994. *Jobs for All: A Plan for the Revitalization of America*. New York: Apex Press.
DuBoff, Richard B. 1999. "Social Security Is Not in 'Crisis.'" *Uncommon Sense* 21 (February). New York: National Jobs for All Coalition.
Edin, Per Olaf, and Dan Andersson. 1995. *7 Myths About Sweden's Economic Crisis*. Stockholm: Swedish Trade Union Confederation.
Galbraith, James K. 1998. *Created Unequal: The Crisis in American Pay*. New York: Free Press.
Ginsburg, Helen Lachs. 1983. *Full Employment and Public Policy: The United States and Sweden*. Lexington, MA: Lexington Books.
———. 1991. "Changing Concepts of Full Employment: Divergent Concepts, Divergent Goals." *International Journal of Social Policy* 11 (1/2/3): 18–28.
———. 1993. "Jobs for All: Values, Concepts and Policies in the United States, Germany and Sweden." Paper presented at the Columbia University Seminar on Full Employment, (October).
———. 1996. "Sweden: Fall from Grace." *In These Times*, December 23, 21–23; 34.
———. 1998. "Social Security: The Phony Crisis." Testimony to the New York City Council, 29 April. New York: National Jobs for All Coalition.
Ginsburg, Helen Lachs, and Bill Ayers. 1998. "Employment Statistics: Let's Tell the

Whole Story." *Uncommon Sense* 4 (November). New York: National Jobs for All Coalition.

Ginsburg, Helen Lachs, June Zaccone, Gertrude Schaffner Goldberg, Sheila D. Collins, and Sumner M. Rosen. 1997. "The Challenge of Full Employment in the Global Economy." In *The Challenge of Full Employment in the Global Economy*, ed. Helen Lachs Ginsburg, June Zaccone, Gertrude Schaffner Goldberg, Sheila D. Collins, and Sumner M. Rosen. Special issue, *Economic and Industrial Democracy* 18, no. 1: 5–34.

Hermele, Kenneth. 1993. "The End of the Middle Road: What Happened to the Swedish Model?" *Monthly Review* (March): 14–24.

Meidner, Rudolph. 1993. "Why Did the Swedish Model Fail?" In *Real Problems, False Solutions, Social Register, 1993*, ed. Ralph Milliband and Leo Panitch. London: Marlin Press, 211–227.

———. 1997. "The Swedish Model in an Era of Mass Unemployment." In *The Challenge of Full Employment in the Global Economy*, ed. Helen Lachs Ginsburg et al. Special issue, *Industrial and Economic Democracy* 18, no. 1: 87–97.

———. 1998. "An Alternative Design of Macroeconomic Policies Aiming at Restoring Full Employment." Working paper 11/9. Thematic Network: Full Employment in Europe. http://www.barkhof.uni-bremen.de/kua/memo/europe/tser/.

National Advisory Commission on Civil Disorders. 1968. *Report of the National Advisory Commission on Civil Disorders.* New York: Bantam Books.

Olson, Greg. 1991. "Labour Mobilization and the Strength of Capital: The Rise and Fall of Economic Democracy in Sweden." *Studies in Political Economy* (spring): 109–145.

Pontusson, Jonas. 1992. "At the End of the Third Road: Swedish Social Democracy in Crisis." *Politics and Society* 20, no. 3 (September): 305–322.

Spitz, George N. 1998. "Social Security Doesn't Need Saving." *Social Policy* (fall): 19–28.

Sweden, Ministry of Finance. 1995. *The Swedish Budget 1995/96. Budget Statement and Summary. July 1995–December 1996.* Stockholm: Ministry of Finance.

Vickrey, William. 1993. "Today's Task for Economists." *American Economic Review* 83 (March): 1–10.

9

Sumner M. Rosen

Economics and the Welfare State

Many economists are uncomfortable when asked to address serious welfare-state issues. While they recognize that income support serves as a countercyclical buffer and helps to reduce inequalities in the distribution of income, their focus seldom goes deeper. This in turn is reflected in the media and in popular understanding. When I studied social welfare programs in Scandinavia in the 1980s, an informant concluded her explanation of the expansive scope and generous level of social welfare provision with a caveat: "Remember that these are the fruits of economic growth." Her implication was clear: When growth slows, the welfare state must curtail its generosity. Many economists would find it difficult to integrate in their analysis Justice Holmes's response to a clerk who wondered if he objected to paying high taxes: "On the contrary; with my taxes I buy civilization." Holmes would have appreciated the achievements of modern social democratic societies.

Other chapters in this volume, notably Gertrude Goldberg's comparative historical study, "Full Employment and the Future of the Welfare State," and Helen Ginsburg's, "A Humanistic Concept of Full Employment Transcends the Welfare State," an analysis of the retreat from full employment in the 1990s, demonstrate the vulnerability of even the most fully developed social welfare programs to the political effects of economic decline. But in Sweden's economy during the twenty-year period (1962–1981) when it led the capitalist world in successfully keeping unemployment below 3 percent, extensive social supports were required to prevent substantial poverty among the working population. Universally provided, they made an important difference in the economic well-being of women employed part-time because of the need to take care of families, young people, immigrant workers, people with handicaps, and workers in labor-intensive low-productivity sectors. Much of this work was in the provision of state-supported benefits to the elderly, the mentally ill, the homebound, mothers and their young children, and others—that is, work in the social welfare sector essential to the functioning of modern economies and societies.

In social democratic regimes that held power in most of the postwar period, at their interface, economic policy and social welfare provision were mutually interactive and interdependent in theory and practice. In the future, as populations age and vulnerabilities to chronic illness, occupationally based limits of activity, and other hazards increase, social welfare provision that ensures basic functioning of individuals, families, and communities cannot be held hostage to economic policy makers and large, private economic entities that exert disproportionate influence on labor market dynamics and national political deliberations. Full-employment economies cannot flourish without major and continuing investments in education and training, preventive and public health, affordable housing, and a range of social services that meet the needs of not only the young, the old, and the poor, but the working-age population as well.

Social democracy, widely admired in earlier decades, has lost much of its effectiveness in the recent past. Some point to this record as evidence that social democracy is an inherently flawed model for social control of modern capitalism. But Sweden, competing globally with Germany, the United States, Britain, Italy, Japan, and other modern capitalist economies, was able for many years to combine full employment and comprehensive social welfare provision with impressive records of economic performance. A nation of only eight million could boast of two world-class automobile manufacturers and equally proficient—and profitable—firms across a wide spectrum of industries. Swedish unions negotiated wages that matched or exceeded those anywhere. The system worked.

The tools that were developed in the 1940s and 1950s by the Social Democratic economists—notably Rudolf Meidner and Gösta Rein—modified and extended Keynesian concepts to reduce reliance on fiscal and monetary policy by deploying extensive and comprehensive labor market policies. Principal among them were:

- Tax incentives to induce firms to integrate their capital investment planning and seasonal variations in production with the need to regulate business cycle fluctuations;
- Extensive and continuing adaptation of the labor force, mature and young, to the requirements of changing technology and product design;
- Incentives to limit overconcentration of economic activity around Stockholm and other large cities in the south of the country;
- Extensive support for access to information about jobs, mobility assistance, accurate matching of job openings and job seekers, and other methods to ensure maximum flexibility in adaptation of the labor market to changing patterns of economic activity.

Sweden's expenditures on these labor-market measures, as a share of gross domestic product, far exceeded those of comparable economies. They were managed by the National Labor Market Board, a government agency with a tripartite board led and staffed at high levels of competence. They played a central role in the record briefly summarized here.

The political and institutional foundations for these policies grew out of heated class struggles early in the twentieth century that ultimately persuaded both labor and capital that an alternative system was needed. Tripartite economic and social policy making achieved national consensus in the 1930s. Social democracy came to power in the postwar years and, with some exceptions, remained in power until the late 1980s. Its base of power was a trade union movement representing more than 90 percent of the industrial and 80 percent of the white-collar and clerical labor force. Social democratic governments convened and chaired a national tripartite consultative process with labor and employers, the "social partners" that in essence negotiated the terms under which labor–management relations and social welfare policies would be implemented. Social democracy's long tenure made it possible to develop, test, modify, and, only then, extend the policies cited here, negotiating with the centers of employer power that, though having international dimensions, were rooted in and committed to national welfare. Labor and capital negotiated national agreements that linked wage increases to overall increases in productivity and, through a "solidaristic" wage structure, distributed the national wage increment relatively equally, so that wages in labor-intensive, low-productivity sectors—for example, social services—kept pace with those in the leading, high-productivity sectors to ensure improved living standards for the working class as a whole.

Counterarguments to social democracy's steady enlargement began among Sweden's intellectual circles in the late 1960s, stimulated in part by similar developments in the United States, the United Kingdom, and other countries. The Social Democrats' control was interrupted in the 1970s; conservative ideas and resistance to further increases in taxes and limits on capital's freedom of investment decisions won a foothold in Sweden's political arena. The long process of steady enlargement of social control of capital came to an end. Key elements in the conservative program included freedom from foreign exchange controls and autonomy for the central Riksbank to set interest rates and monetary policy without the constraints that social democracy had required.

The trigger that began the process of dissolution of the Swedish social contract was the adoption by the Social Democrats of Meidner's "wage earner fund" proposals in 1981, in essence a scheme that would transfer corporate profits to the funds providing pensions and other benefits to workers. Swedish capital saw this as a thinly disguised effort to socialize ownership, and mobilized in opposition with unprecedented strength and solidarity. The steady unraveling of the tripartite social contract proceeded; employers withdrew from the centralized negotiating structure and labor–management negotiations were shifted to the company level. Tripartism ended and, with its end, the national consensus in support of Sweden's full employment and social welfare state ended as well. Swedish labor split; Sweden's wealthy and highly capable capitalists turned their focus to the emerging opportunities for profitable investment in the new global economy assisted by the relaxation of exchange controls and a more restrictive monetary-policy regime.

Social democracy achieved much, as long as capital retained its identification with and commitment to a peaceful and mutually rewarding relationship with national labor, reinforced by constraints on international capital mobility, and labor could sustain both solidarity and political hegemony. When both these preconditions erode, as they have in many if not most of the advanced capitalistic economies, social democracy, in one small country, appears to be destined to lose its power to define and shape the basic contours of the economy and social order. Yet Sweden's record over decades tells us that full employment, comprehensive social welfare protection, national prosperity, and steadily rising living standards could be achieved and sustained for a long time. What is needed now is an understanding of how to adapt to these principles in the era of globalization. Global challenges will require global remedies as well as institutions capable of exerting influence to ensure that the combination of prosperity and equity becomes the criterion for the management of the new global economy. Sweden's social democratic era may still have much to teach us.

10

HEATHER BOUSHEY

Rethinking Full Employment

Unemployment, Wages, and Race

Introduction

Is discrimination an issue appropriate for discussions of full employment? Discrimination is a microeconomic issue, one might answer, an issue addressed by evaluating differences in human capital, differences in "soft skills," or in the hiring and promoting practices of employers. These are not macroeconomic issues, and gender and race differences in the labor market do not hinder us from thinking about a full-employment economy. I will argue here, however, that to ignore discrimination is to be blind to the true difficulties in reaching a full-employment economy. Discussions of full-employment policy often overlook the fact that discrimination, primarily racial discrimination, is a major impediment to full employment in the United States.

Discrimination is often excluded from discussions of full employment because we too frequently look only at aggregate data and ignore by what means government statistics claim to reflect true economic trends. Economists see a national unemployment rate of 4 percent as indicative of full employment. However, the aggregate unemployment rate does not tell the whole story. First, unemployment for African Americans has consistently been twice that of white Americans. Even in the current boom, as white unemployment averaged 3.9 percent over the first nine months of 1998 and reached a low of 3.6 percent in April of 1999, African American unemployment averaged 9.1 percent, and decreased to only 8.2 percent in June 1999. Second, over the past three decades, the official unemployment rate demonstrates an expanding undercounting of true joblessness (Murphy and Topel 1997). The nonparticipation that increased among prime age males in the 1990s was higher for African American than for white males (Juhn 1998) (see Figure 10.1). Third, those at the upper end of the income spectrum in

Figure 10.1 **Labor Force Participation, Males by Race**

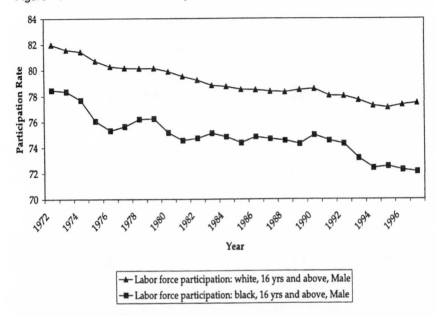

more profitable or stable industries, and those who are better educated, are less likely to experience unemployment (see Figure 10.2). Thus, the official unemployment rate does not reflect accurately the unemployment situation. The fact that we need to look to alternative, disaggregated numbers to get the full picture of who is "not working"[1] must be incorporated into our definition of full employment.

A further reason for discrimination's being overlooked as a barrier to full employment is that our models of discrimination, and income inequality in general, are usually based on microeconomic mechanisms. Our theoretical models prevent us from seeing how the dynamics of discrimination are macroeconomic in nature. Standard labor-market theory argues that workers will be paid their marginal product based on their endowments of human capital, including "unobserved productivity characteristics." In this view, discrimination is the "residual" once all productivity-related characteristics (both observed and unobserved) have been accounted for. This model leaves no room for macroeconomic fluctuations to affect labor market outcomes. Framed in this way, research on inequality and discrimination is perceived to be about the characteristics of individuals rather than about the process of the economic system that creates inequality. Discrimination is situated beyond the purview of macroeconomists who focus on movements in aggregate variables such as unemployment.

Figure 10.2 **Unemployment by Education and Race, September 1997 and 1998**

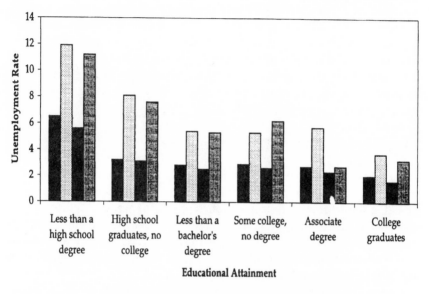

Neglecting discrimination in our empirical and theoretical analyses of full employment leads to second-best policy prescriptions. Policies aimed at discrimination tend to focus on human capital and other microeconomic issues, rather than seeing discrimination as related to full employment and macroeconomic policy. Seen as microeconomic issues, labor market discrimination and its resulting income inequality are dealt with through judicious social policies aimed at individuals, such as education, training, or affirmative action. Discrimination is not seen as something to be alleviated through interest-rate or full-employment policies. However, once understood from an alternative perspective, it becomes clear that the problem of ending discrimination is actually tied up in the problem of moving to a full-employment economy, and the implications for policy become very different. Full employment has been elusive for African American workers even in a boom. Full employment has also been elusive for many workers near the bottom end of the income spectrum, those with little education. The facts indicate that the microdynamics of labor markets are affected by macroeconomic trends. Theory and policy should reflect this.

This chapter begins with the question of whether we can commit to full employment without simultaneously committing to ending systemic discrimination in the labor market, and then argues that the answer to this question must be "no." Seeing discrimination and full employment as linked requires a rethinking of our models of the labor market. This essay offers a model, based on an understanding of the dynamic between unemployment and wages, in which "the social structures of insulation" shape labor market outcomes. The model is followed by empirical tests. The theory and empirics presented here promote an analysis that links the macroeconomy and microeconomic outcomes. In so doing, we see how macroeconomic processes drive discrimination, a microeconomic outcome.

Discrimination and the Macroeconomy

Discrimination serves as a conduit for keeping wages down. It is a concrete, allocative mechanism for the unemployment–wage trade-off. A theory accounting for the role of discrimination in regulating wages is a theory better equipped to address the attainment of a full-employment economy. The very nature of the capitalist process of growth engenders inequality, with the result that discrimination rears its ugly head as a way to allocate workers along the income spectrum. The macroeconomy and discrimination are intimately related.

The method for understanding the relationship between unemployment, discrimination, and wages begins with the premise that unemployment regulates wages. Concretely, unemployment keeps wages in check through downward pressure at the bottom end of the income spectrum. Workers have different degrees of "insulation" from the market and from unemployment or underemployment and are therefore not equally threatened by rising unemployment rates. The placement of workers within the wage structure, and thus the degree of insulation a worker has from unemployment and its deleterious effects on wages, is determined by multiple factors, including, in the United States, gender and race. Taken together, these factors form the social structures of insulation.

The social structures of insulation against unemployment and low wages exhibit three characteristics. These are (1) unemployment's regulation of pay—that is, the relationship between unemployment and the wage level; (2) differing processes of regulation for different worker groups—that is, the relationship between unemployment and wage differentials. The process of regulation will differ among workers depending on the extent of labor market discrimination and the ways that social policy does or does not insulate workers from unemployment. And (3) the degree of insulation determined by family structure. The structure of the family, the number of family members working in the paid labor market, and the interaction between social policy and family structure all affect a worker's degree of dependence on the market. The social-structures-of-insulation theory is based on an understanding of the labor market and its relationship to the macroeconomy and takes the Marxian economic model as its starting point. This model sees unemployment as the regulator of wages, a starting point based on the observation that unemployment is a permanent feature of the capitalist economy. Individuals, due to their race ethnicity, gender, marital status, age, disability, education, or other characteristics, do not all have the same relationship to unemployment and paid labor. The theory of the social structures of insulation seeks to explain how social structures and safety nets insulate workers to varying degrees from unemployment and its effects on wages.

Two points of departure from mainstream economic theory are necessary to an understanding of how the social structures of insulation affect the relationship between unemployment and pay.[2] First, the standard neoclassical model of the labor market is rejected in favor of an approach that situates the labor process historically and institutionally. In Marx's economic analysis—and in the analyses of many modern economists[3]—the normal functioning of the capitalist economy leads to a continual regeneration of unemployment. Unemployment is not an "imperfection" but is endemic to the capitalist system; its role is to regulate wages. Because some workers are more likely to experience unemployment, unemployment regulates wages through creating income inequality. Second, once we understand that labor markets are institutionally and historically situated, the next step is to place gender and race at the center of the analysis. The systems of gender and race oppression are a fundamental part of what is "institutionally and historically situational." Gender and race serve as allocative mechanisms for determining the degree of insulation one has from unemployment and underemployment. This is evidenced by the fact that unemployment does not appear uniformly across gender and race groups in the American economy. Thus, we see discrimination as the result of not simply a microeconomic process whereby individual characteristics matter, but as the result of a macroeconomic process that systemically creates inequality and assigns workers, based on their ascriptive characteristics, to different places in the employment/unemployment hierarchy.

Unemployment and Wages

The tradition of negatively linking unemployment and pay goes back to the classical economists and includes Keynes and Kalecki, both of whom began with the premise that unemployment may not be transitory and may exist in equilibrium. Keynes (1937) objected to the ideas that real wages depend on the money-wage bargain and that labor can reduce its real wage and increase the volume of employment by accepting a lower money wage. Kalecki saw unemployment as a general feature of capitalist economies. Unemployment serves to discipline workers, thereby restraining wages and maintaining work intensity on the shop floor. Kalecki (1971 [1943]) concludes that demand-management policies are not used by governments to achieve permanent full employment because they would hamper the disciplinary function of unemployment. These heterodox models share the view that unemployment may be a permanent feature of the labor market. In such a model, wages may or may not fall in response to a shift in the labor-supply function.

Marxian Economics: The Nature of the Relationship Between Unemployment and Pay

The notion that unemployment disciplines wages has an early and clear formulation in Marx's theory of the reserve army of labor. Marx argued that unemployment and pay are inversely related. The dynamics of capitalist accumulation regulate both the supply of and demand for labor to continually reproduce an excess labor supply.[4] As accumulation proceeds, capitalists will purchase additional labor power, lowering the rate of unemployment to increase output. As the pool of available workers shrinks during a healthy phase of accumulation (as the economy nears "full employment"), workers may be able to effectively organize to increase wages. Increases in wages may occur, but if the rate of accumulation is beyond the point of profitability, accumulation will slow. In neo-Keynesian terms, Marx argues that labor-saving, or non-Harrod neutral technical change, is the dominant form of technical change under capitalism. The dominance of this form of technical change is supported empirically (Foley and Marquetti 1997).

The process of accumulation not only puts pressure on capitalists to cheapen labor to maintain profitability, but also puts pressure on labor to work and organize to sustain living wages and employment. As the unemployment rate rises in a local labor market, employed workers feel increased downward wage pressure from employers and pools of unemployed workers. In a region of high unemployment, the probability that an employed worker will find a new job—if she is fired, laid off, or quits—decreases. Therefore, employed workers may be less likely to demand higher wages and less likely to quit if working conditions are unsatisfactory in a high-unemployment region. Concurrently, in a high-unemployment region, employers may find many suitable applicants for each job opening. The task of replacing workers becomes easier and employers have less of an incentive to pay a "wage premium" or to acquiesce to worker demands for higher wages or better working conditions.

Modern economists have done extensive work on the way that unemployment serves as a labor discipline device, relying on, but not explicitly arguing, Marx's general notion of the reserve army of labor. Blanchflower and Oswald's (1994) research on the wage curve is a good example of this type of analysis. Blanchflower and Oswald document the existence of a stable, negative relationship between unemployment and the level of pay, which they term the "wage curve." Through random samples of nearly 4 million people from sixteen countries, they find that the local unemployment rate affects pay level such that "A worker who is employed in an area of high unemployment earns less than an identical individual who works in a region with low joblessness" (5).[5] The formula for the wage curve is:

$$\ln w = -0.10 \ln U + \textit{other terms} \tag{1}$$

where $\ln w$ is the natural log of the wage, $\ln U$ is the natural log of unemployment in the worker's local region, and other terms are control variables for worker and sectoral characteristics. Their major finding is that the log of wages is a monotonically decreasing and convex function of local unemployment rates. The unemployment elasticity of pay is -0.10 so that, hypothetically, a region with an unemployment rate one percentage point higher than another region will have wages that are 10 percent lower.

The Macro Origins of Income Inequality

Marx's theory of the reserve army of labor contains within it a second dynamic between unemployment and pay that explores the mechanism by which inequality is continually recreated in the labor market. The analysis of aggregate labor markets suggests that movements in the wage level tend to be limited by both movements in the productivity of labor and by movements in the reserve army of labor. Differential costs of production will essentially form "centers of gravity" around which actual wage rates will fluctuate. Labor organization is a crucial component of this process because it is only through struggle with capital that labor may be able to garner wage gains from increased productivity or limit the impact of the reserve army of labor on wages.[6] Wage differentials are, then, the result of three dynamics: (1) the accumulation process, which continually regenerates the reserve army of labor of the unemployed; (2) capitalist competition and technical change, which create differentials in the conditions of production, productivity, and profitability; and (3) the uneven effects of organized labor, which affect worksite conditions and bargaining power among groups of workers. Thus, the Marxian model finds inequality, in terms of both wages and employment, to be endemic to the general process of accumulation. The continual regeneration of a reserve army is a part of the process of maintaining a steady labor supply.

Under capitalism, wage differentials are realized through the process of competition. Competition, among labor, among capital, and between labor and capital, mitigates against the equalization of wage rates (Botwinick 1993). This notion of competition is antithetical to the notion of competition in neoclassical models (Shaikh 1980). First, under capitalism, firms compete against one another for market shares and profits (Marx 1986). Marx's distinctive analysis of capitalist competition allows us to see how persistent and substantial differentials in profit rates can be explained. This extends to an analysis of wage differentials in that a particular firm's or industry's conditions of access to potential labor reserves conditions the overall range of wage differentiation in any particular labor market. Second, workers and capitalists compete against each other over the extraction of surplus value. In the initial stages of capitalist development, capitalists increased the rate of profit through increasing absolute surplus value—increasing the length of the workday without equal increases in wages. In the modern era, surplus value, though increasing the productivity of labor,[7] is generally increased relatively. The struggle between labor and capital will determine what amount of surplus value capital is able to appropriate.

The relationship between unemployment and wage inequality has recently received a good bit of attention from the economics profession. In his recent book, *Created Unequal: The Crisis in American Pay*, James Galbraith (1998) argues that unemployment, among other macroeconomic variables, is an important driver of income inequality. He tests the hypothesis that, over time, macroeconomic events determine the movement of wage inequality. He finds, in a linear regression of macroeconomic variables on inequality from 1920 to 1992, that "unemployment turns out to be a key variable: it has a significant, positive effect on inequality in all three measures and is the variable with the largest effect on the measure of wage dispersion in the manufacturing wage structure" (141). He explains this by pointing to the concrete ways that unemployment regulates wages:

> A high rate of unemployment, we ought to expect, produces more pressure on wages in low-wage, weakly organized, and competitive industries than in high-wage, strongly organized, and cartelized or monopolistic sectors. Rising unemployment therefore undermines the position of low-wage workers, while leaving earnings structures in the higher strata alone (Galbraith 1998, 140).

Thus the reserve-army-of-labor model contains two interactive dynamics: (1) the regulation of the wage level, and (2) differentiation creating inequality among workers' pay. Through exploring the links between the wage level and wage differentials, this analysis sheds light on the interaction between the macroeconomy and microeconomic processes.

We began the analysis of the social structures of insulation with a general discussion of persistent wage inequality because to launch a complete theory of labor market discrimination, a lens must be devised through which we can see the simultaneous and interactive processes of oppression that occur within capitalism. Because of its high level of abstraction, this analysis thus far has ignored the concrete characteristics of social formations. Using this analysis of abstract, theoretical processes, the theory of the social structures of insulation can now elucidate how the labor market will look in any particular historical configuration. In our current era, the allocation of workers to unemployment and underemployment is determined, to some extent, by gender and race. Through showing how gender and race discrimination permeate the labor market, the theory will elucidate how social structures of insulation affect the macroeconomic relationship between unemployment and pay.[8]

Discrimination in the Labor Market

Unemployment does not occur randomly across the spectrum of occupations and industries. Workers in certain occupations and industries are more likely to experience unemployment than are other workers. Wage inequality, then, is not neutral with respect to gender and race. Social institutions and practices that discriminate against women and people of color shape the labor market.

Discrimination in the labor market means that, all else being equal, women and people of color do not have access to the same opportunities in employment as do men and whites. Labor market discrimination takes three forms: (1) wage inequality; (2) employment inequality; and (3) occupational segregation. Although women and minorities both experience discrimination in the labor market, the form it takes for each group is not identical; rather, it is historically contingent. Work on labor market discrimination has found that the ascriptive characteristics of gender and race are determining factors in wages and employment (Albelda 1985; Bergmann 1989; Boston 1988; Fuchs 1988; Howell and Gittleman 1994; Kirschenman and Neckerman 1991; Reich 1981; Reskin and Hartmann 1986). Labor market discrimination against women and minorities is sustained and recreated through the creation of wage differentials (Mason 1993; Williams 1991). Thus, to sustain a constant supply of low-wage labor, some workers are systematically excluded, based on their gender or race, from higher-paying segments of the labor market.

In the United States, labor markets have always been segregated by race, even after legal separation of the races was abolished. During the 1970s, there was a period of convergence of African American and white incomes. However, by the 1980s, this trend had reversed itself (Bound and Freeman 1992). Darity, Dietrich, and Guilkey (1997), in a longitudinal study of the dynamics of racial ethnic group differences in economic performance, conclude that "despite the collapse of Jim Crow and the apparent successes of the Civil Rights movement, by 1980 and 1990 black males continued to face the highest relative losses in socioeconomic status due to lower returns for given characteristics" (304).[9] Seitchik (1989) found that data from the Current Population Survey (CPS) Displaced Worker Survey shows that over the period 1981–1986, African Americans constituted a disproportionately high 11.2 percent of displaced workers, and 16.6 percent of those experiencing long-run postdisplacement unemployment.

In the United States, the labor market is also segregated along gender lines. The most important reason for wage inequality between men and women is that they hold different jobs. In 1994, close to one-half of all women worked in clerical and service sector jobs (Albelda and Tilly 1997). Sex segregation characterizes the majority of employment in the United States. Although women have moved into new jobs since the advent of affirmative action, they are still segregated into the lower-paying segments of these jobs.[10] Bielby and Baron (1984) found that out of 373 firms surveyed, 60 percent had perfect sex segregation by title. King (1992) finds that nearly two-thirds of men or women would have to change jobs to achieve gender integration, and 30 percent of white or African American women would have to change jobs to achieve within-gender racial integration. Sex segregation by occupation contributes to sex- and race-based earnings disparities (Boushey and Cherry 2000). Groshen (1991) finds that the largest source of the female/male wage gap is the association between wages and the proportion of women in the occupation, which accounts for one-half to two-thirds of the wage gap. Job cells are far more segregated than establishments or occupations, although wages of women and men in the same job cell were found to differ by only 1 percent. The association between wages and the proportion female is stronger for establishments than for occupations. Thus, segregation among establishments is more detrimental to wage equality than segregation by occupation.[11]

Women and African Americans experience different forms of discrimination in the labor market. Discrimination against African Americans tends to take the form of employment discrimination, whereas, for women, discrimination primarily takes its form in the distribution of jobs, although both groups experience both forms of discrimination. Both groups experience wage discrimination. It is this common component—wage discrimination—that interests capitalists. Gender and race are used systematically to pay some workers less for qualitatively identical labor. Ascriptive characteristics are used to allocate workers to locations in the hierarchy of unemployment and employment. Workers are thus insulated to varying degrees based on their ascriptive characteristics and on the extent to which racism and sexism permeate the labor market.

Policies of Exclusion: The Reserve Army of Labor in Its Concrete Form

Having established that capitalism in general recreates wage and employment inequality and that this process capitalizes on differences in gender and race, we can now explore the systematic ways that social structures insulate workers from unemployment and underemployment.[12] The generation of jobs with substandard working conditions and their assignment to women and minorities are both consistent with capitalist competition. The conditions for discrimination derive from capitalism in general. Negative labor market outcomes for women and people of color are the result of the inequality that capitalism engenders. The actual dynamics of discrimination are driven by the systems of gender and race oppression. Wage differentials result from the concrete mechanism of discrimination. As discrimination pulls down the wages of some workers, the entire spectrum of wages erodes, negatively affecting the wage level. Thus, discrimination against some workers is an effective tool to keep down the wages of all workers. It is important to note that, in this view, the genesis of the reserve army of labor is not simply reducible to actions of the capitalist class. Workers compete with each other for good jobs, and thus they too are implicated in the dynamics of the reserve army.

Botwinick's (1993) theory of systematic wage differentials can be extended into the concrete realm through exploring labor market discrimination within the context of capitalist accumulation in general. This second aspect of the theory of the reserve army of labor allows the incorporation of work done on labor market discrimination and segmented labor markets into the analysis. Gender and race discrimination—concrete forms of the general tendency of workers to be differentiated under capitalism—become absorbed and integrated into capitalism's own system of oppression. Competing, privileged workers benefit from these systems of oppression and often work to limit the power and wages of disadvantaged workers.[13]

Political economists Rhonda Williams and Patrick Mason have explored this direction of inquiry. Mason (1993) extends Botwinick's analysis of wage differentials to include the possibility of racial exclusion within competitive capitalism. Access to high-wage jobs is the concrete expression of discrimination based on the abstract understanding of discrimination as a labor allocation device for "determining service in the reserve army" (6). Williams draws on the competition between workers for access to good jobs as it is played out within the constructs of gender and race. She argues that "workers seeking to shelter themselves from bourgeoisie society's most fragile and despised existence—life among the low waged and unemployed—have ample reason to create and wield weapons to shelter themselves from other members of the working class" (Williams 1991, 77). Competition between workers plays out along the lines of gender and race through, among other ways, union exclusion. Williams and Smith (1990) analyze the influence of gender and race in determining salary grade and job assignment in the service and maintenance union at Yale University. Their empirical results suggest that Local 35's wage-setting process reproduces white supremacy within the union. In their sample, white men's jobs receive significant and large wage and grade premiums. White workers employ their power as the dominant union members to maintain their privileges in the labor market.

This analysis suggests that discrimination becomes endemic to the capitalist labor market through a process of accumulation that entails systematic wage differentials. The social structures of insulation help us to determine who is insulated from unemployment and underemployment and who is more or less likely to experience low wages as wage differentials are continually recreated in the labor market. The social structures of insulation also help us to see the linkages between the macroeconomy and microeconomic outcomes. Wage differentials are the result not only of differential human capital, but also of the differential effects of unemployment and access to employment for different groups of workers.

Some Evidence: Wage Curves Disaggregated by Race

We now turn to some empirical tests of the theory that unemployment regulates wages and that workers are differentially insulated from this regulation. The model developed by Blanchflower and Oswald (1994) in *The Wage Curve* is a useful starting point because it tests the extent to which unemployment drives wage changes. Their model makes use of microlevel and macrolevel data. They hypothesize that macroeconomic trends (a measure of unemployment) affect individual earnings. This model can be used to rethink our models of wage determination.

The Model

Blanchflower and Oswald test a model of the form:

$$w_i = \lambda_i \, (U, X_i) \tag{2}$$

where w_j is the wage of person i; X_j is a set of measured characteristics of individual i (such as gender, age, and education); and U is the aggregate unemployment rate.

This model is extended here in two ways. First, we extend the model to an exploration of an alternative measure of unemployment in the economy. Many analysts consider the unemployment rate an overly restrictive measure of "true" unemployment in the economy (Mishel, Bernstein, and Schmitt 1997). The Bureau of Labor Statistics calculates from CPS data the employment status of individuals solely by their work-related and job-search activities during a specific reference week. Employed individuals are those who worked in that week. Unemployed individuals are those who (1) did not work, but who searched for work sometime in the four weeks before the survey, and (2) who are available to work. Individuals are not in the labor force if they meet neither test (Bregger and Haugen 1995). The official calculation of the unemployment rate leaves out workers who do not have a job and would like to work but are "discouraged" by poor labor market prospects, and workers who are underemployed. To capture these dimensions, the Bureau of Labor Statistics recently introduced new, less restrictive measures of underemployment. The underemployment measure includes workers who (1) are working part-time but who want to work full-time, and (2) workers who are discouraged from finding employment. The latter group of workers may not actively search for work because of their malaise, although they would like to work. These underemployment rates are generally just less than twice the unemployment rate for each group of workers (by race, gender, and educational attainment) (Mishel, Bernstein, and Schmitt 1997, 243). To account for the mismeasurement of the official unemployment rate, we calculate a nonemployment rate equal to 1 minus the employment-to-population ratio. This is a measure of all those in the economy who are not employed. Nonemployment is an outer bound to the measurement of true unemployment in the economy.

Second, we extend Blanchflower and Oswald's model by explicitly looking at differences of gender and race. The social-structures-of-insulation model suggests that some workers are less insulated from the effects of unemployment on pay. Given the particular historical configuration of the United States in the late-twentieth century, these workers may be identified by their race or their gender. However, as we have seen above, racial discrimination in the labor market tends to take the form of unequal access to employment, whereas gender discrimination takes the form of occupational segregation. Thus, we would expect that the wage curve is more elastic for workers of color than for white workers, although white women may not have a more elastic wage curve than may white men. To account for these gender and race differences, we test the model for specific gender and race groups.

From these extensions, we develop two testable hypotheses:

$$w_i = \lambda_i\,(U, X_i) \tag{3}$$

$$w_{ij} = \lambda_{ij}\,(U, X_{ij}) \tag{4}$$

where w_{ij} is the wage of person i in the jth group; X_{ij} is a set of measured characteristics of individual i (such as gender, age, and education) in the jth group; and U_j is now a measure of *either* the nonemployment rate or the unemployment rate, depending on the hypothesis tested.

For equation 3, the expectation is that the wage curve will be more elastic when we measure the outer bound of unemployment using the nonemployment rate than when we use the official unemployment rate. For equation 4, the expectation is that groups who are less insulated from unemployment and underemployment will have a higher elasticity of pay with respect to unemployment than will white, male workers.

Data and Method

Following Blanchflower and Oswald (1994),[14] Katz and Krueger (1991), and Freeman (1991), the present study uses data from the CPS Annual Merged File for selected years from 1986 to 1996 for the individual-level employment, earnings, and background data.[15] The CPS Annual Merged File consists of extracts from the Monthly Current Population Survey.[16] The Annual Merged File is a good dataset for weekly and hourly earnings equations. Unlike the March CPS files, the CPS Annual Merged File includes variables for earnings per week and earnings per hour. In the March CPS, analysts must make calculations using three retrospective variables: the annual earnings, weeks worked, and usual weekly hours worked to calculate hourly wages. Although both of these CPS datasets have the advantage of being large enough to generate reliable estimates for different subgroups within the population, they have some well known problems that include the fact that various components of income are underreported. Income at the high end (for confidentiality reasons) is top coded. There is evidence that these caps are not consistent over time: a larger share of incomes are capped over time, and the omission of capital gains created a larger bias over the 1980s.

The sample of the dataset used for this analysis includes only individuals who

- are between 18 and 64 years old,
- are employed in either the private or public sector, excluding those who are self-employed, and
- live in one of the fifty largest Metropolitan Statistical Areas (MSA).[17]

Table 10.1

Mean Earnings per Week by Race and Gender, 1986–1996

	Earnings per Week
Mean earnings per week for all workers	$601.46
by race	
White	622.45
African American	484.73
American Indian	547.82
Asian and Pacific Islander	616.08
Other (including Hispanic)	429.42
By gender	
Male	707.52
Female	481.98

Source: Author's calculation from the CPS Outgoing Rotation Groups, 1986–1996. All values are in 1996 dollars.

Table 10.2

Educational Attainment by Race and Gender, 1986–1996

	African American (%)	White (%)
Some high school	13	11
High school degree	38	32
Some college	31	27
College degree	13	19
Advanced degree	6	12

	Female (%)	Male (%)
Some high school	9	13
High school degree	34	31
Some college	29	26
College degree	18	19
Advanced degree	10	12

Source: Author's calculation from the CPS Outgoing Rotation Groups, 1986–1996. All values are in 1996 dollars.

The CPS Annual Merged File identifies both the individual's MSA and state of residence. There is a degree of sample-selection bias in this analysis because the data only include locations with MSA fips codes and an unemployment rate by gender and race, which is only available for the fifty largest cities.[18] Tables 10.1 and 10.2 show the characteristics of the sample used.

Table 10.3

Unemployment in the 50 Largest Metropolitan Areas in the United States, 1986–1996

Unemployment Rate	1986	1987	1988	1989	1990	1991	1992	1993	1994	1995	1996
Aggregate	6.28	5.77	5.19	4.94	5.34	6.61	7.39	6.81	6.27	5.53	5.14
African American	13.70	12.71	11.30	10.93	11.35	12.57	14.64	12.92	11.83	10.23	10.01
White	5.20	4.74	4.28	4.04	4.43	5.73	6.30	5.82	5.80	4.69	4.32
Female	6.43	5.65	5.28	5.06	5.23	6.35	6.87	6.42	5.96	5.47	5.19
Male	6.15	5.88	5.12	4.84	5.42	6.83	7.85	7.13	6.19	5.61	5.09
African American female	12.84	12.43	11.08	10.08	11.05	12.08	13.38	11.80			
African American male	13.65	11.61	11.78	11.06	11.77	13.17	15.02	13.37			
White female	5.33	4.51	4.26	4.14	4.29	5.37	5.77	5.50			
White male	5.10	4.91	4.35	3.97	4.55	6.03	6.77	6.09			

Source: Bureau of Labor Statistics, *Geographic Profile*, 1986–1996. The BLS stopped tabulating separate unemployment rates for African American women and men and white women and men as of 1994.

Table 10.4

Nonemployment in the 50 Largest Metropolitan Areas in the United States, 1986–1996

Unemployment Rate	1986	1987	1988	1989	1990	1991	1992	1993	1994	1995	1996
Aggregate	37.03	36.44	35.70	35.21	35.63	36.88	37.25	36.92	36.15	35.83	35.27
African American	44.05	42.29	41.14	41.32	42.67	43.70	44.64	43.63	42.81	40.95	40.60
White	36.03	35.53	34.77	34.27	34.44	35.67	36.02	35.60	34.90	34.77	34.31
Female	46.12	45.17	44.30	43.60	43.63	44.49	44.55	44.20	43.36	42.94	42.21
Male	27.03	26.86	26.28	25.99	26.81	28.52	29.28	29.00	28.29	28.10	27.83
African American female	48.60	47.19	45.80	45.14	46.67	48.45	47.55	47.55			
African American male	37.56	34.69	33.71	34.83	37.12	38.59	38.92	39.33			
White female	45.79	44.87	43.91	43.39	43.00	43.67	43.88	43.51			
White male	25.46	25.40	24.90	24.44	25.17	27.06	27.59	27.08			

Source: Bureau of Labor Statistics, *Geographic Profile,* 1986–1996. The BLS stopped tabulating separate unemployment rates for African American women and men and white women and men as of 1994.

For the sample, the mean earnings for men are greater than for women, and mean earnings for whites are greater than for all other racial categories. Whites have a higher degree of educational attainment than other racial groups, being twice as likely as African Americans to have an advanced degree.

The unemployment and nonemployment data come from the *Geographic Profile* (1987). Tables 10.3 and 10.4 show the mean unemployment rate and nonemployment rate, respectively, for the aggregate population and for disaggregated groups from 1986 to 1996.

Results

To test the extent to which the unemployment rate is a poor measure of the true effect of joblessness on wages, we first replicate Blanchflower and Oswald's model using the aggregate unemployment rate for various years. We then estimate the same model, substituting the aggregate nonemployment rate for the unemployment rate.

The model takes the form:

$$\ln w_i = \beta_0 + \beta_1 \ln U + \beta_2 X_i + \beta_3 D_{reg} + \beta_4 D_{indy} + \beta_5 D_{occ} + e_i \qquad (5)$$

where $\ln w$ is the log of earnings per week or the log of the hourly wage (earnings per week over usual hours) for individual i, where the labor market is defined by the MSA an individual lives in; $\ln U$ is the natural log of the unemployment rate or the nonemployment rate defined at the level of the MSA; and X is a vector of characteristics particular to individual i. D_{reg}, D_{indy} and D_{occ} are regional (state), industry, and occupational dummies. The variables in X are dummies for gender, race, marital status, union membership, private sector employee, part-time (less than thirty hours/week), and paid hourly; variables for educational attainment (less than high school, high school graduates, some college, four years of college, and beyond four years of college) and age and its square (to measure for experience). Each specification also includes thirteen dummies for industry classification, fourteen dummies for occupational grouping, and state dummies.

Table 10.5 shows the results from running wage curves with the unemployment rate and Table 10.6 shows the results from estimations with the nonemployment rate. The standard errors on the coefficients have been calculated using robust estimators. The estimates in Table 10.5 are higher than the −0.10 estimates produced by Blanchflower and Oswald (1994). This may be because pay is more elastic in urban areas than in states as a whole, which is how they generally measured unemployment.

A comparison of Tables 10.5 and 10.6 shows that the wage curves with

Table 10.5

Wage Curve with Aggregate Unemployment

	1987	1989	1991	1993	1996
Unemployment rate	−0.15 (.03)***	−0.15 (.03)***	−0.17 (.05)***	−0.10 (.04)**	−0.13 (.03)***

Note: Standard errors in parentheses.
*Significant at the 10% level; **Significant at the 5% level; ***Significant at the 1% level.

Table 10.6

Wage Curve with Aggregate Nonemployment

	1987	1989	1991	1993	1996
Nonemployment rate	−0.29 (.06)***	−0.34 (.07)***	−0.29 (.08)***	−0.24 (.07)***	−0.35 (.10)***

Note: Standard errors in parentheses.
*Significant at the 10% level; **Significant at the 5% level; ***Significant at the 1% level.

Figure 10.3 **Wage Curves: Aggregate Nonemployment Elasticities, by Race**

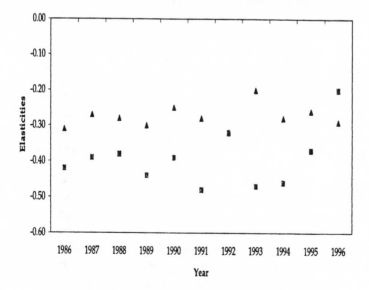

■ African American ▲ White

the unemployment rate have lower elasticities than the wage curves with the nonemployment rate. The trends over the business cycle are largely similar across the two sets of estimations, although the wage curves with the non-employment rate show somewhat greater fluctuations.

The Effect of Discrimination on Wages

To test to what extent the lack of full employment perpetuates wage inequality between African American and white workers, we estimate the following specification of the wage curve:

$$\ln w_{ij} = \gamma_0 + \gamma_1 \ln U + \gamma_2 X_{ij} + \gamma_3 D_{reg} + \gamma_4 D_{indy} + \gamma_5 D_{occ} + e_{ij} \qquad (6)$$

where ln w is the log of earnings per week or the log of the hourly wage (earnings per week over usual hours) for individual i in group j (African American or white); and ln U is the natural log of the unemployment rate or the nonemployment rate defined at the level of the MSA.

Tables 10.7 and 10.8 show the results of the estimates for the two sets of specifications for 1987, 1989, 1991, 1993, and 1996, using the unemployment and nonemployment rates. For each demographic group, the table shows only the estimated coefficient on the aggregate MSA unemployment or nonemployment rate. These tables show that the wage curve varies over the business cycle, and that African American wages are more sensitive to the business cycle than are the wages of any other group. The elasticity of African American pay is generally higher than for other groups of workers, except for 1996, when African American female pay becomes less elastic than for other groups. Figure 10.3 shows a plot of the coefficients using the nonemployment rate, where we can clearly see that, except for 1992, African American pay is more elastic with respect to the nonemployment rate than is white pay.[19] The recession year of 1991 shows the most elastic wage curves when testing the model with the unemployment rate, but 1989 and 1996 show the most elastic curves when testing with the nonemployment rate. The more elastic wage curves with the nonemployment rate indicate that the nonemployed cause a stronger downward pull on wages in tight labor markets than in weak labor markets.

These results demonstrate that the pay of those workers who are most likely to experience employment discrimination is more elastic with respect to unemployment and nonemployment than is the pay of non–discriminated-against workers. This fits with the theory of the social structures of insulation, in that workers who are less insulated from unemployment and underemployment will be more vulnerable to lower wages.

Table 10.7

Wage Curves with Aggregate Unemployment, by Group

	1987	1989	1991	1993	1996
African American	−0.18 (.07)***	−0.16 (.04)***	−0.33 (.10)***	−0.29 (.09)***	−0.10 (.04)**
Female	−0.19 (.08)***	−0.14 (.05)***	−0.30 (.10)***	−0.23 (.11)**	−0.03 (.05)
Male	−0.18 (.06)***	−0.21 (.03)***	−0.35 (.12)***	−0.34 (.08)***	−0.18 (.05)***
White	−0.14 (.03)***	−0.14 (.04)***	−0.16 (.06)***	−0.07 (.05)***	−0.15 (.03)***
Female	−0.12 (.04)***	−0.13 (.06)***	−0.17 (.07)***	−0.07 (.07)	−0.11 (.04)***
Male	−0.17 (.03)***	−0.15 (.04)***	−0.15 (.07)***	−0.07 (.05)	−0.18 (.04)***

Note: Standard errors in parentheses.
*Significant at the 10% level;**Significant at the 5% level;***Significant at the 1% level.

Table 10.8

Wage Curves with Aggregate Nonemployment, by Group

	1987	1989	1991	1993	1996
African American	−0.39 (.06)***	−0.44 (.07)***	−0.48 (.13)***	−0.47 (.14)***	−0.20 (.11)*
Female	−0.37 (.10)***	−0.40 (.09)***	−0.47 (.11)***	−0.46 (.16)***	−0.13 (.17)***
Male	−0.42 (.07)***	−0.51 (.08)***	−0.48 (.16)***	−0.46 (.17)***	−0.32 (.13)**
White	−0.27 (.06)***	−0.30 (.09)***	−0.28 (.10)***	−0.20 (.08)**	−0.29 (.12)***
Female	−0.23 (.07)***	−0.30 (.11)***	−0.26 (.11)**	−0.14 (.09)***	−0.28 (.13)**
Male	−0.31 (.07)***	−0.31 (.08)***	−0.29 (.11)***	−0.27 (.09)***	−0.49 (.12)***

Note: Standard errors in parentheses.
*Significant at the 10% level;**Significant at the 5% level;***Significant at the 1% level.

Conclusions

The empirical results provide evidence that discrimination broadly affects the relationship between unemployment and pay. Discrimination against African American workers serves to lower their pay while not affecting the pay of white workers to a great degree. The relationship between unemployment and pay is mediated by discrimination; it is stronger for those who are discriminated against in the labor market. Most importantly, the current systemic discrimination against African American workers leads to lower employment rates and, as a result, lower pay.

The theory of the social structures of insulation allows us to see how the negative relationship between unemployment and pay is mediated through social processes, primarily through discrimination in the labor market. The process of accumulation creates unemployment and inequality. Labor-market discrimination allocates workers to places in the employment/unemployment hierarchy.

As we see the links between full employment and discrimination, we also see that to move to full employment we must end discrimination. Understanding the macroeconomic mechanisms that engender discrimination as a result of inequality leads us to a different path to full employment. It is not merely enough to think about low, aggregate unemployment rates. We must think about full employment in terms of both employment and its effects on wage determination. We should think of full employment in terms of the employment of all. Through the lens of the social structures of insulation, a full employment program simultaneously becomes a program for reducing income inequality in general and, more specifically, between discriminated- and non–discriminated-against groups.

Our commitment to full employment must be made with our eyes open, and with full cognizance of the role that discrimination plays in the allocation of workers to unemployment and, subsequently, wage determination. A commitment to full employment means making a commitment to treat workers equally and fairly in the labor market by equalizing the relative degrees of insulation from unemployment workers now have. To do this, discrimination's role in creating disparity in relative degrees of insulation must end.

Notes

1. The Bureau of Labor Statistics has published a series of new unemployment indicators that address some of these issues (Bregger and Haugen 1995).

2. There are two other points of departure: (1) a clear analysis of the relationship between social policy, labor markets, and the macroeconomy (Boushey 1997); and

(2) an understanding of the way that these processes are contingent and specific in and across space. Neither of these issues will be addressed in this paper.

3. See Blanchflower and Oswald (1994); Schor (1987); Schor and Bowles (1987); Rebitzer (1988); Weisskopf, Bowles, and Gordon (1983).

4. The reserve army of labor can be derived from Marx's labor theory of value. Marx (1986 [1887]) argues that firms are only able to increase their rate of profit through increasing the surplus value extracted from the workers. Machinery and raw materials cannot produce a surplus because, in general, constant capital must be purchased at a price equal to its cost of reproduction. Labor, on the other hand, can be purchased for less than the costs of reproducing itself. Therefore, a surplus can be extracted from labor, which is from where profits on production come from. Firms then constantly search for cheaper production methods, struggling to increase the relative or absolute surplus value from workers.

5. Blanchflower and Oswald are not the only mainstream economists whose empirical findings go beyond the boundaries of neoclassical theory. Card and Krueger's (1995) work on the minimum wage also offers empirical evidence that extends beyond the confines of textbook predictions of the labor market. They find that raising the minimum wage does not necessarily lead to lower employment but, in certain cases, actually leads to higher employment.

6. Skilled labor will receive higher wage rates than unskilled because of the extra costs of training skilled labor (Marx 1986, 172). This does not suggest, however, that all workers with similar skills will receive a uniform wage.

7. There are still many cases where capitalism works to increase absolute surplus value in the modern era. For example, the rise in the number of sweatshops in places like New York City, and recent strikes, such as the Staley workers' battle in Illinois over the length of the working day, are examples of capitalism increasing absolute surplus value, rather than relative surplus value.

8. Marx (1986) developed the idea that the pool of unemployed workers (the reserve army) is composed of groups of workers with different relationships to the capitalist economy. He divides the reserve army of labor into four specific types: the floating, the latent, the stagnant, and paupers. The floating reserve is those workers who are mainly attached to the centers of modern industry. Their employment is characterized by constantly interrupted periods of employment as they are continually repelled and attracted to the paid labor market. The latent reserve are those workers who are continually on the point of passing over into a proletariat, such as early agricultural workers who moved into the urban centers to seek stable employment, or women as they move from housework to paid work. The stagnant reserve is those workers who are not on the verge of entering (or reentering) the labor force. These workers are less advantaged than the floating. Finally, there are the paupers. Race-ethnicity, gender, age, and disability all affect an individual's place in the spectrum of the reserve army of labor. Differences in unemployment across groups of workers lead to differences in pay across these groups.

9. Losses are relative to males of other racial/ethnic backgrounds.

10. For example, women are more likely to be in the relatively low-paying medical specialties of pediatrics and primary medicine than in the higher-paying specialties.

11. Although men and women who work together in the same job cell earn similar wages, this type of integration is quite rare. Across the five industries Groshen surveyed (plastics products, life insurance, nonelectrical machinery, banking, and computer and data processing), 83 percent of the workers work in job cells with an absolute male/female gap of 5 percent or where there are no workers of the opposite sex.

12. It has been argued that the segmented labor-market approach may be well suited to addressing occupation segregation as a form of discrimination. Segmented labor-market theorists argue that workers do not compete in one labor market but actually are competing in different labor-market segments. The most influential subdivision of labor markets has been into primary and secondary jobs (Doeringer and Piore 1971; Gordon, Edwards, and Reich 1982). Primary jobs generally require a high level of skills, offer room for occupational advancement, and, hence, a degree of economic security. Secondary jobs do not offer a great deal of occupational advancement, may not require a high degree of skill, and are at the lower end of the pay spectrum. In the early segmented labor-market models, segmentation patterns are not primarily affected by the history of race relations and gender roles, although historically women and racial minorities have dominated the secondary job segments. The early segmentation theorists looked at the labor market in terms of productivity: The labor market is segmented in terms of the characteristics of jobs. Later authors of theories on segmented labor markets have, however, argued that the dynamics of race or gender (but not usually both) have greatly affected the process of segmentation. Some labor-market segmentation theorists argue that gender and race are primary determinants of reasons for particular jobs being in the secondary labor market (Albelda 1985). Feminist and antiracist authors argue that gender and race do the assignment to the secondary labor market. Further, jobs are defined as "unskilled" if they are dominated by women or minorities.

13. The particular forms of discrimination in the United States are peculiar to our historical development, and the discrimination experienced by any particular minority does not necessarily transcend those borders. This theory is cognizant of this fact. It begins from the abstract and allows concrete, historical circumstances to dictate which particular groups of people experience discrimination in the United States while reciprocally allowing this process to then inform the abstract theory.

14. Blanchflower and Oswald use the Current Population Survey (CPS) Files for most of their analysis. They use the CPS Annual Merge Files for their analysis, using Metropolitan Statistical Area (MSA) level unemployment for 1987.

15. This analysis uses separate years rather than pooling the data, as Blanchflower and Oswald do, because there are problems with some years. For example, in 1995, MSA standardized codes for geographical locations from the Federal Information Processing Service (fips) are not available for a full quarter and the BLS further cautions that all MSA fips codes are suspect for that year (A fips code is a standardized code for geographical locations in the United States from the Federal Information Processing Service). There also appear to be problems with the 1992 data.

16. Each household entering the CPS is administered four monthly interviews, then ignored for eight months, then interviewed again for four more months. Since 1979, only households in months four and eight have been asked their usual weekly earnings and usual weekly hours of work. These are the outgoing rotation groups and each year the (BLS) gathers all these interviews together into a single *Annual Merged File*. The National Bureau of Economic Research prepares *CPS Labor Extracts (3rd Edition) NBER 50 Variable Uniform Extract* with information appropriate for analysis of labor market issues from the monthly outgoing rotation group files.

17. The Census Bureau defines an MSA as "an urban area that meets specified size criteria—either it has a city of at least 50,000 inhabitants . . . or it contains an urbanized area of at least 50,000 inhabitants and has a total population of at least 100,000." Primary and consolidated MSAs are larger urban metropolitan areas (1995).

18. There are actually two issues of sample-selection bias. The first occurs when choosing individuals who are working, excluding those who may have higher reservation wages and therefore may be unemployed. The second bias occurs when choosing only individuals who live in the fifty largest cities.

19. The coefficient for 1995 must be interpreted with care because it covers only three-quarters of the year. For three months, the CPS does not provide MSA fips codes.

Bibliography

Albelda, Randy. 1985. "'Nice Work If You Can Get It': Segmentation of White and Black Women Workers in the Post-War Period." *Review of Radical Political Economics* 17, no. 3: 72–85.

Albelda, Randy, and Chris Tilly. 1997. *Glass Ceilings and Bottomless Pits: Women's Work, Women's Poverty*. Boston: South End.

Bergmann, Barbara. 1989. "Does the Market for Women's Labor Need Fixing?" *Journal of Economic Perspectives* 3, no. 1 (winter).

Bernstein, Jared, and Lawrence Mishel. 1998. "Jobs Picture: Wage Gains, More Hours Lift Family Income Above Pre-Recession Level." Economic Policy Institute, September. http://www.epn.org

Bielby, William, and James Baron. 1984. "A Woman's Place Is with Other Women: Sex Segregation Within Organizations." In *Sex Segregation in the Workplace: Trends, Explanations, Remedies*, ed. Barbara Reskin. Washington, DC: National Academy Press, 27–55.

Blanchflower, David G., and Andrew J. Oswald. 1994. *The Wage Curve*. Cambridge: MIT Press.

Blank, Rebecca, and David Card. 1993. "Poverty, Income Distribution, and Growth: Are They Still Connected?" *Brookings Papers on Economic Activity* 2: 285–339.

Bluestone, Barry, and Bennett Harrison. 1982. *The Deindustrialization of America: Plant Closings, Community Abandonment, and the Dismantling of Basic Industry*. New York: Basic Books.

Boston, Thomas. 1988. *Race, Class, and Conservatism*. Boston: Unwin Hyman.

Botwinick, Howard. 1993. *Persistent Inequalities: Wage Disparity Under Capitalist Competition*. Princeton: Princeton University Press.

Bound, John, and Richard Freeman. 1992. "What Went Wrong? The Erosion of Relative Earnings and Employment Among Young Black Men in the 1980s." *Quarterly Journal of Economics* 107: 201–232.

Boushey, Heather. 1997. "Embracing Discrimination? The Relationship Between Low-Wage Labor Markets and Policies in Aid of the Poor." In *Gender and Political Economy: Incorporating Diversity into Theory and Policy*, ed. Ellen Mutari, Heather Boushey, and William Fraher. Armonk, NY: M.E. Sharpe.

Boushey, Heather, and Robert Cherry. (Forthcoming). "The Impact of Discrimination and Labor Market Tightness on Regional Employment Rate Differences." In *The Impact of a Tight Labor Market on Black Employment Problems*, ed. Robert Cherry and William Rogers. New York: Russell Sage.

Braverman, Harry. 1974. *Labor and Monopoly Capital*. New York: Monthly Review Press.

Bregger, John E., and Steven E. Haugen. 1995. "BLS Introduces a New Range of Alternative Unemployment Measures." *Monthly Labor Review* (October): 19–26.

Bureau of Labor Statistics. 1987. In *Geographic Profile of Employment and Unemployment*, Appendix C, bulletin no. 2305. Washington, DC: U.S. Department of Labor.

Card, David. 1995. "*The Wage Curve*: A Review." *Journal of Economic Literature* 33 (June): 785–799.

Card, David, and Alan Krueger. 1995. *Myth and Measurement: The New Economics of the Minimum Wage*. Princeton: Princeton University Press.

Darity, William, Jr., Jason Dietrich, and David K. Guilkey. 1997. "Racial and Ethnic Inequality in the United States: A Secular Perspective." *American Economic Review* 87, no. 2: 301–305.

Doeringer, Peter, and Michael Piore. 1971. *Internal Labor Markets and Manpower Analysis*. Lexington, MA: Heath.

Fix, Michael, George C. Galster, and Raymond J. Struyk. 1982. "An Overview of Auditing for Discrimination." In *Clear and Convincing Evidence: Measurement of Discrimination in America*, ed. Michael Fix and Raymond J. Struyk. Washington, DC: Urban Institute.

Foley, Duncan, and Adalmir Marquetti. 1997. "Economic Growth from a Classical Perspective." Paper for the International Colloquium at the University of Brasília, April.

Freeman, Richard. 1991. "Employment and Earnings of Disadvantaged Young Men in a Labor Shortage Economy." In *The Urban Underclass*, ed. Christopher Jencks and Paul E. Peterson. Washington, DC: Brookings Institution.

Fuchs, Victor. 1988. *Women's Quest for Economic Equality*. Boston: Harvard University Press.

Galbraith, James K. 1998. *Created Unequal: The Crisis in American Pay*. New York: Free Press.

Goodwin, R.M. 1972. "A Growth Cycle." In *A Critique of Economic Theory*, ed. E.K. Hunt, and J.G. Schwartz. London: Penguin.

Gordon, David M., Richard Edwards, and Michael Reich. 1982. *Segmented Work, Divided Workers: The Historical Transformation of Labor in the United States*. New York: Cambridge University Press.

Groshen, Erica L. 1991. "The Structure of the Female/Male Wage Differential." *The Journal of Human Resources* 26 (summer): 457–452.

Howell, David, and Maury Gittleman. 1994. "Changes in the Structure and Quality of Jobs in the U.S.: Effects by Race and Gender, 1973–90." Working paper, New School for Social Research, July.

Juhn, Chinhui. (Forthcoming). "Black-White Employment Differential in a Tight Labor Market." Paper presented at Conference on Unemployment and Race, October 1998. In *The Impact of a Tight Labor Market on Black Employment Problems*, ed. Robert Cherry and William Rogers. New York: Russell Sage.

Kalecki, Michel. 1971 [1943]. "Political Aspects of Full Employment." In Michel Kalecki, *Selected Essays on the Dynamics of the Capitalist Economy, 1933–1970*. Cambridge: Cambridge University Press.

Katz, Lawrence, and Alan B. Krueger. 1991. "Changes in the Structure of Wages in the Public and Private Sectors." In *Research in Labor Economics*, Vol. 12, ed. Ronald G. Ehrenberg. Greenwich, CT: JAI Press, 137–72.

Keynes, John Maynard. 1937. *The General Theory of Employment, Interest, and Money*. New York: Harcourt Brace Jovanovich

King, Mary. 1992. "Occupational Segregation by Sex and Race, 1940–1988." *Monthly Labor Review* 115, no. 4: 30–36.

Kirschenman, Joleen, and Kathryn M. Neckerman. 1991. "'We'd Love to Hire Them, but . . .' The Meaning of Race for Employers." In *The Urban Underclass*, ed. Christopher Jencks and Paul Peterson. Washington, DC: Brookings Institution.
Lemann, Nicholas. 1992. *The Promised Land: The Great Black Migration and How It Changed America*. New York: Vintage Books.
Marx, Karl. 1986 [1887]. *Capital: A Critique of Political Economy*. Vol. I. Moscow: Progress Publishers.
Mason, Patrick L. 1993. "Accumulation, Segmentation and the Discriminatory Process in the Market for Labor Power." *Review of Radical Political Economics* 25, no. 2: 1–25.
Mishel, Lawrence, Jared Bernstein, and John Schmitt. 1997. *The State of Working America: 1996–97*. Armonk, NY: M.E. Sharpe.
Murphy, Kevin M., and Robert Topel. 1997. "Unemployment and Nonemployment." *American Economic Review* 87, no. 2 (May): 295–300.
Rebitzer, James B. 1988. "Unemployment, Labor Relations, and Unit Labor Costs." *American Economic Review* 78, no. 2 (May): 389–394.
Reich, Michael. 1982. *Racial Inequality: A Political-Economic Analysis*. Princeton: Princeton University Press.
Reskin, Barbara, and Heidi I. Hartmann, eds. 1986. *Women's Work, Men's Work: Sex Segregation on the Job*. Washington, DC: National Academy Press.
Schor, Juliet. 1987. "Does Work Intensity Respond to Macroeconomic Variables? Evidence from British Manufacturing, 1970–1986." Working paper, Harvard University.
Schor, Juliet, and Samuel Bowles. 1987. "Employment, Rents, and the Incidence of Strikes." *Review of Economics and Statistics* (November): 584–592.
Seitchik, Adam. 1989. "Who Are the Displaced Workers?" In *From One Job to the Next: Worker Adjustment in a Changing Labor Market*, ed. Adam Seitchik and Jeffrey Zornitsky. Kalamazoo, MI: W.E. Upjohn Institute for Employment Research.
Shaikh, Anwar. 1980. "Marxian Competition Versus Perfect Competition: Further Comments on the So-called Choice of Technique." *Cambridge Journal of Economics* 4: 75–83.
Spriggs, William, and Rhonda Williams. (Forthcoming). "What Do We Need to Explain About African American Unemployment?" Paper presented at Conference on Unemployment and Race, October 1998. In *The Impact of a Tight Labor Market on Black Employment Problems*, ed. Robert Cherry and William Rogers. New York: Russell Sage.
Weisskopf, Thomas, Samuel Bowles, and David Gordon. 1983. "Hearts and Minds: A Social Model of Aggregate Productivity Growth in the United States, 1948–79." *Brookings Papers on Economic Activity* 2: 381–441.
Williams, Rhonda. 1991. "Competition, Discrimination, and Differential Wage Rates: On the Continued Relevance of Marxian Theory to the Analysis of Earnings and Employment Inequality." In *New Approaches to Economic and Social Analyses of Discrimination*, ed. Richard Cornwall and Phanindra Wunnava. New York: Praeger.
Williams, Rhonda, and Peggie R. Smith. 1990. "What Else Do Unions Do? Race and Gender in Local 35." *Review of African American Political Economy* 18, no. 3: 59–77.

11

Commitment to Full Employment in a Global Economy

On October 8, 1996, the world awoke to learn that Columbia University economist William Vickrey had been named a co-winner of the Nobel Prize in economics. On October 11, Bill Vickrey was dead.

In a spate of interviews between 8 and 11 October, Vickrey noted that he was pleased to be a Nobel laureate, not for the money he would personally receive, but rather for the public platform it would give him to explain how "the insane pursuit of the holy grail of a balanced budget in the end is going to drive the economy into a depression." Here, finally, was a voice that could attract attention to the Keynesian verity that there was an important need for government "to exercise a guiding influence" to ensure that effective demand is maintained at its full-employment level. There is no doubt in my mind that his Nobel Prize acceptance speech would have developed this theme. But before Vickrey could reiterate this message sufficiently to offset the conventional wisdom of mainstream economists who emphasize the need to maintain a natural rate of unemployment, his voice was silenced.

I first met Bill Vickrey in the 1960s when he and I were "expert witnesses" (usually on opposite sides) on a number of Federal Communications Commission cases involving the regulation of telecommunication services and pricing policy. Though we did not see eye-to-eye in our testimonies on the microeconomics of public utility regulation, we did find an easy compatibility on macroeconomic issues whenever we discussed these in a more informal setting.

Vickrey attended the first four of the Post Keynesian Workshops that I organized in Tennessee beginning in 1986. Typically, Vickrey would arrive at the conference hotel without informing us that he planned to attend. Accordingly, his role was to raise substantive issues as an audience member.

As usual, Vickrey made a last-minute appearance just before the start of the June 1996 Post Keynesian Conference in Knoxville. This time, however, he gave me a draft of a paper entitled "A Trans-Keynesian Manifesto" that he wanted to present to the Post Keynesian Workshop. I was truly impressed by the paper and, despite an already overloaded program, shifted sessions and papers around to make room for a Vickrey presentation. The paper created some very heated discussions. At the end of the workshop, I indicated to Bill that I would be pleased to publish a version of the paper after he revised it to include some of the many valid responses his presentation had provoked. Less than a month before he was named a Nobel Prize recipient, Vickrey sent me a revised version of his "Trans-Keynesian Manifesto."

I published Vickrey's paper in the summer 1997 issue of the *Journal of Post Keynesian Economics*. I believe this manifesto would have been the backbone of Vickrey's Nobel Prize acceptance speech. So while death may have denied Vickrey the bully pulpit that he so desired to educate policymakers to the follies of budget-balancing mania, I am pleased that the Post Keynesians gave him a public platform.

Vickrey's Trans-Keynesian Manifesto

Vickrey preferred the term "trans-Keynesian" to post Keynesian. The latter, Vickrey claimed, implied that Keynes was being left behind. Trans-Keynesian, on the other hand, connoted "the building on or going beyond Keynes" to deal with the economic environment of the twenty-first century (Vickrey 1997, 495).

Vickrey's manifesto involved seventeen propositions. The four most important propositions are:

Proposition 5. Full employment requires large government deficits.
Proposition 6. Monetary policy cannot fill the gap.
Proposition 7. Policies encouraging individual saving produce exactly the opposite of intended results, that is, Solow-type growth models are not applicable to monetary economies.
Proposition 10. Privatization of the Social Security system can be disastrous.
Proposition 14. Unemployment is not needed to control inflation.

In discussing these seventeen propositions, Vickrey was more radical in his proposals than most "Keynesians," including myself. For example, Vickrey proposed that the measured unemployment rate should be pushed down "to below 2 percent" (ibid. 504). He even went so far as to declare "[a]n economy with ten percent inflation and two percent unemployment would be far healthier in human terms" (ibid. 505). This statement would be anathema to the economic policymakers in Washington and even to some of his professional colleagues at Columbia University. In this essay, I want to focus on only one proposition of Vickrey's trans-Keynesian manifesto where, in my opinion, this radical reformer was too conservative or still too wedded to the classical model that he used so brilliantly in his microeconomic analysis.

The Open Economy Sector

Vickrey's Proposition 9 states, "Full employment in open economies requires floating exchange rates."[1] Vickrey did caution, however, that in a flexible-exchange-rate system there is "some danger of speculative gyrations in the foreign exchange markets," but he argued that these gyrations would be most important only "at the time of inauguration of the new [trans-Keynesian] policy." Moreover, Vickrey (ibid. 501) believed that the "costs [of speculative gyrations] would be of little moment." The evidence since the East Asian currency crisis of 1997 involving the market gyrations of market-determined flexible exchange rates, however, casts doubt on these claims.

In these days when Asian tigers collapse and Russian bears menace our global economy, we are being haunted by the question, "Can it happen again?" Can we have another Great Depression at the end of the twentieth century? In today's circumstances, it appears that speculative gyrations in international capital markets can inflict long-run permanent and severe damages. Southeast Asia is already in the grip of a Great Depression and Japan, after having almost a decade of stagnation, is falling into a great recession.

Writing in 1936, Keynes noted, "It is enterprise which builds and improves the world's possessions. . . . Speculators may do no harm as bubbles on the steady stream of enterprise. But the position is serious when enterprise becomes the bubbles on a whirlpool of speculation." Comparing the pre-1973 economic record with the post-1973 period indicates that, since 1973, enterprise has slowly become enmeshed in an ever-increasing whirlpool of speculation. The Bretton Woods years of 1950 to 1973 were an era of unsurpassed economic global prosperity. Irma Adelman (1991) has characterized this Bretton Woods period as a "Golden Age of Economic Development . . . an era of unprecedented sustained economic growth in both developed and developing countries."

Table 11.1 provides the statistical evidence (augmented by more recent data) that Adelman used in reaching her conclusion about our economic golden age.

The average annual growth rate of Organization for Economic Cooperation and Development (OECD) countries' real gross domestic product (GDP) per capita from 1950 to 1973 was almost double the peak annual growth rate of industrializing nations during the Industrial Revolution, while labor's pro-

Table 11.1

Real GDP (annualized growth rate, %)

| | | Real GDP per capita | |
Year	World	OECD nations	Developing nations
1700–1820	na	0.2	na
1820–1913	na	1.2	na
1919–1940	na	1.9	na
1950–1973	na	4.9	3.3
1973–1981	na	1.3	na
1981–1990	1.2	2.2	1.2
1991–1993	−0.4	0.6	2.6
1994–1995	1.3	2.3	2.9

| | | Total Real GDP | |
	World	OECD nations	Developing nations*
1950–1973	na	5.9	5.5
1966–1973	5.1	4.8	6.9
1974–1980	3.4	2.9	5.0
1981–1990	3.2	3.1	3.3
1991–1993	1.2	1.2	4.6
1994–1995	2.8	2.6	4.7

*Excluding Eastern and Central Europe and former Soviet Union.

ductivity growth rate was almost triple that of the Industrial Revolution. The resulting prosperity of the industrialized world was transmitted to the less developed nations through world trade, aid, and direct foreign investment. From 1950 to 1973, average growth rate in per capita GDP for less developed countries (LDCs) was 3.3 percent, almost triple the average growth rate experienced by the industrializing nations during the Industrial Revolution. Aggregate GDP of the LDCs increased at almost the same rate as that of the developed nations, 5.5 percent and 5.9 percent, respectively. The higher population growth of the LDCs caused the lower per capita income growth.

Since 1973, OECD economic growth has been approximately half of what it was during the Bretton Woods golden age and not much better than the experience of the nineteenth- and early twentieth-century industrialized nations. Today's world unemployment situation is very grim. Although the average unemployment rate in the European Union has declined from 11.3

percent in July 1996 to 10.2 percent in May 1998, global unemployment, according to the International Labor Organization (ILO), will increase to 15 percent by the end of 1998, with 150 million unemployed (compared to 130 million in 1996). With the exception of the United States, unemployment rates in OECD nations have reached or remained close to historical highs not seen since before World War II. With the Asian contagion and Russian financial crisis threatening to infect Latin America, higher global unemployment seems inevitable. Even Federal Reserve Board Chairman Alan Greenspan has indicated that the United States cannot remain an island of prosperity in the global sea of recession and depression.

The Lesson that Should Have Been Learned

What can we conclude from these facts? During the postwar period until 1973, global economic performance was nothing short of spectacular, despite fixed exchange rates, increasing rigidities in national labor markets, and widespread capital controls throughout the industrialized world, including the United States. Since 1973, global economic performance has been much worse than that experienced during Adelman's golden age of economic development.

Until 1973, the international payments system was, in large measure, shaped by Keynes's thesis that flexible exchange rates and free international capital mobility are incompatible with global full employment and rapid economic growth in an era of multilateral free trade (Felix 1997–1998). Operating until 1973 under an international payments system that accommodated Keynes's "incompatibility thesis," the global economy experienced unparalleled economic growth and prosperity. This accommodation occurred when a fixed-exchange-rate and capital controls system was combined with a civilizing economic principle that had emphasized, namely that creditor nations must accept a major share of the responsibility for solving persistent international payments imbalances.

In the 1960s, mainstream classical economists developed open economy models based on three classical axioms that Keynes has overthrown.[2] These axioms are the foundation of the classical (supply side) models that were propagated to "demonstrate" that Keynes's incompatibility thesis was wrong. Instead these classical models "proved" that free trade and optimum global economic growth required a laissez-faire approach with flexible exchange rates, free international capital mobility, and flexible domestic labor markets where those who experienced long-term employment were naturally slated for the Darwinian dustbin.

The worldly wisdom of our economics profession became that any regulation of financial markets and any policy of labor market intervention, in terms of minimum wages, occupational safety requirements, or labor unions' support, imposed huge costs on society. Free markets from "onerous" government oversight and regulation and, policymakers were confident, a world of heavenly economic bliss would envelop the planet.

Those economists who called themselves Neoclassical Synthesis Keynesians had already adopted microfoundations that required the three (neo)classical axioms for their closed economy models (Davidson 1984). Consequently, these Old Keynesians were easy prey for the classical counterrevolution analysis of closed and open economies. Nevertheless, this successful academic resurrection of the classical system would have not been sufficient to alter the policy mix if it were not for events of the 1970s.

The 1973 oil price shock created huge international payments imbalances and unleashed inflationary forces in oil-consuming nations. The resulting economic dislocation placed policymakers in a difficult position. Consequently, they found irresistible the allure of the Panglossian siren song that "all is for the best in the best of all possible worlds provided we let well enough alone." Without having to admit that they did not know what to do, policymakers used the conclusions of the 1960s classical counterrevolutionary theories to justify their abandonment of (1) policies to protect workers in the marketplace, and (2) Keynes's international policy prescriptions to constrain "hot money" international capital flows, and to maintain fixed, but adjustable, exchange rates. Instead, a "leave it to the efficient marketplace" philosophy was adopted. Then if anything went wrong, policymakers could argue that they could not be blamed for it; after all, our efficient markets "know" best, as Nobel Prize-winning economists Friedman, Lucas, Merton, and Scholes continually assured us.

Since the 1973 breakdown of Bretton Woods's fixed-exchange-rate international-payments system, the global economy has stumbled from one global economic crisis to another; for example, stagflation in the 1970s, the Latin American and African debt problems of the 1980s, and the international financial market crises of the 1990s. Global economic growth has slowed significantly while the growing global population threatens to reduce standards of living. Economics has once more become the dismal science with the potential for Malthusian overtones.

The post-1973 abandonment of a fixed-exchange-rate system changed the international world of finance by making the exchange rate itself an object of speculation. Utilizing new computer technology, financial capital could race around the globe at the speed of light. Since the mid-1970s, international financial transactions have grown thirty times as fast as the growth in international trade (Felix 1997–1998). International financial flows now dominate trade payments. Exchange-rate movements reflect changes in speculative positions rather than changes in patterns of trade.

Significant exchange-rate movements affect the international competitive position of domestic vis-à-vis foreign industries and therefore tend to depress the inducement to invest in large projects with irreversible sunk costs. In an uncertain (nonergodic) world, where the future cannot be reliably predicted from past and present price signals, volatile exchange rates undermine entrepreneurs' confidence in their ability to appraise the potential profitability of any large investment project. Every exchange rate increase threatens not only domestic industries with significant loss of export-market share, but also home-market share loss as imports become less expensive. Managers realize that any unexpected upward blip in the exchange rate during the lifetime of any contemplated investment project can saddle their enterprises with irreversible costly idle capacity. Consequently, the marginal efficiency of investment is reduced. The greater the uncertainty regarding future exchange rates, the less investment globally, just as Keynes's (1936, chap. 17) analysis of liquidity preference and investment predicted. As a result, trade and real investment spending in open economies have become tail wagged by the international speculative exchange-rate dog.

It is not surprising, therefore, that when the free world changed from a fixed- to a flexible-exchange-rate system, the annual growth rate in investment in plant and equipment in OECD nations fell from 6 percent (before 1973) to less than 3 percent (since 1973). Less investment growth meant a slower economic growth rate in OECD nations (from 5.9 percent to 2.8 percent), while labor productivity growth declined even more dramatically (from 4.6 percent to 1.6 percent).

For more than a quarter century, the mantra of professional economists' conventional wisdom has been "deregulate markets and reduce the role of government and thou shalt enter the kingdom of economic bliss." Instead of bringing the utopian benefits promised, the post–Bretton Woods system of flexible-exchange-rates combined with financial and labor market deregulation has generated a growing international monetary crisis as well as global unemployment on a grand scale. As early as 1986, *New York Times* columnist Flora Lewis noted that government and business leaders recognize that "the issues of trade, debt, and currency exchange rates are intertwined." Lewis warned that the world is on a course leading to an economic calamity, yet "nobody wants to speak out and be accused of setting off a panic. . . . [T]he most sober judgment is that the best thing that can be done now is to buy more time for adjustments to head off a crash. . . . [D]ecision makers aren't going to take sensible measures until they are forced to by crisis." Is the Asian financial crisis the event that will finally galvanize public opinion to the need for major international monetary institutional reforms?

Or will Keynes's (ibid. 158) aphorism—"Worldly wisdom teaches that it is better to fail conventionally than succeed unconventionally"—rule the day? I do not see any national leader willing to challenge conventional economic analysis and call for a complete and thorough overhaul of an international payments system that is far worse than the one we abandoned in 1973. Instead, at best, there are calls for patches on the current payments system in terms of a marginal transactions tax here or a marginally larger lender of last resort, or even inconsistent calls for Keynesian spending in Japan while lauding budget surpluses in the United States and reduced budget deficits in the European Union. With Vickrey's death, there is no one with significant media visibility who has the courage to speak out in public forums and suggest that the classical economic philosophy that has rationalized our macroeconomic affairs in recent decades is a formula for potential economic disaster at worst, and modest global economic growth at best.

Only by a thorough reforming of the world's international payments system can we prime our entrepreneurial, money-using, market-oriented economy to permit Vickrey's manifesto of national macropolicies to expand aggregate demand internally without fear of a balance-of-payments constraint. This is the only possible route to providing a golden age of economic growth for the twenty-first century similar to what the global economy experienced between 1950 and 1973.

This post-trans-Keynesian message, however, is contrary to the conventional wisdom of mainstream economic theory that attributes the cause of persistently high unemployment to labor-market rigidities (in closed economic models). In an open economy context, the conventional wisdom is that high unemployment is due to the national government's attempting to pursue expansionary monetary and fiscal policy while trying to maintain a fixed-exchange-rate in an era of free international capital mobility. Since the late 1960s, the conventional wisdom of economists has been to advocate micropolicies to free up both labor and capital mobility.[3] This belief in a policy to loosen labor and capital movements I call "the laxative theory of economic bliss." If such purgative capital- and labor-market medicine succeeds in increasing employment growth in any one country, it does so only by exporting some of its unemployment to its trading partners. The pursuit of these purgative prescriptions in many nations simultaneously invokes a negative sum game that unleashes deflationary forces around the globe.

Proposed Solutions that Cannot Succeed

Are the major economies doomed by the free market to endure another Great Depression? Or are there other alternatives that can restore the golden age we experienced in midcentury?

Since 1974, Nobel Prize winner James Tobin has been almost the only voice with significant visibility in the economics profession warning that free international financial markets with flexible exchange rates create volatile international financial markets that can have a "devastating impact on specific industries and whole economies." Tobin advocates that governments limit market volatility by increasing the transactions costs on all international payments via a small "Tobin tax." Unfortunately, though Tobin's assessment of the problem is correct, his proposal cannot do what he claims it will. The empirical evidence is that any increase in the transactions costs significantly increases measured market volatility (Davidson 1998) and, more importantly, that the Tobin tax has a greater impact on international trade than any alleged impact on speculation (Davidson 1997). The "Tobin tax" solution is the wrong tool to solve the growing international financial speculative market problem.

Since the Mexican peso crisis of 1994, pragmatic policymakers have advocated a lender-of-last resort (LOLR) to stop the hemorrhaging of international financial market liquidity and to "bail out" international investors. In 1994, U.S. Treasury Secretary Robert Rubin encouraged President Clinton to play this LOLR role. With Clinton's liquidity facilities exhausted, the International Monetary Fund (IMF) stepped into this lender role when the Asian crisis of 1997 and the Russian bear emerged in 1998. When the IMF recently reached the end of its liquidity rope, Director Stanley Fisher suggested that the Group of Seven (G-7) nations take over the LOLR function. Fisher's cry for a G-7 LOLR collaboration is equivalent to recruiting a volunteer fire department to douse the flames after someone has cried "Fire!" in a crowded theater. Even if the fire is ultimately extinguished, there will be a lot of innocent casualties. Moreover, every new currency fire requires the LOLR to pour more liquidity into the market to put out the flames. The goal should be to produce a permanent fire prevention solution, not to rely on organizing larger and larger volunteer fire fighting companies after each new currency fire breakout.

Finally, the man who "broke the bank of England," George Soros, recommended a currency board solution for the Russian ruble. A currency board fixes the exchange rate so that the domestic money supply does not exceed the amount of foreign reserves a nation possesses. Thus, if and when investors panic and rush to exit from a nation, the currency board maintains the exchange rate by selling foreign reserves and reducing the domestic money supply by an equivalent sum. A currency board solution, therefore, is equivalent to the bloodletting prescribed by seventeenth-century doctors to cure a fever. Enough blood loss can, of course, always reduce a fever but often at a terrible cost to the body of the patient. Similarly, a currency board's dousing of the flames of a currency crisis will result in a moribund economy.

What Can We Do?

As the international payments system has become more stable, financial markets around the world have become more volatile. The classical economic prescription of leaving it to the market is finally being recognized for what it is: a snake oil medicinal that separates fools (even those who win the Nobel Prize) from their money.

If we reject conventional wisdom and instead adopt the innovative principles that Keynes recommended for the postwar international monetary system, we can design a system that will prevent currency fires while promoting global prosperity. Keynes recommended the simultaneous institution of three conditions: (1) a fixed, but adjustable, exchange-rate system; (2) a built-in apparatus that prevents rapid international movements of liquid portfolio funds, that is, international capital movement regulations; and (3) a mechanism that requires any nation experiencing persistent current account surpluses to accept the major burden of refluxing the resulting excessive foreign reserve credits back to other nations.

Since 1992, I have been urging a clearing union proposal explicitly designed to (1) prevent a lack of global effective demand due to any nation's holding excessive foreign reserves or draining reserves from the system; (2) provide an automatic mechanism for placing a major burden of payments adjustments on those nations who persistently amass excessive foreign reserves; (3) provide each nation with the ability to monitor and, when necessary, to control movements of flights of capital that can destabilize financial markets; and (4) permit each nation to pursue full employment unhampered by international-payments-imbalances problems. And this proposal will never require a LOLR "bailout" financed by taxpayer dollars.

Too often, economic discussions on the requirements for a good international payments system have been limited to the question of the advantages and disadvantages of fixed- versus flexible-exchange rates. Vickrey's Proposition 9 falls into this category. Although this issue is very important, the facts of experience, plus Keynes's revolutionary analysis, indicate that more is required than simply choosing between fixed- and flexible-exchange rates if a mechanism is to be designed to (a) prevent the inevitable international liquidity crisis caused by a persistent international payments imbalance, and (b) promote a long-run stable international standard of value.

To reduce entrepreneurial uncertainties and the possibility of massive currency misalignments, Keynes recommended the adoption of a fixed, but adjustable, exchange rate system. More importantly, Keynes argued that the "main cause of failure" of any traditional payments system, whether based on fixed or flexible rates, was its inability to actively foster continuous global economic expansion in the face of persistent current-account imbalances. An essential characteristic of the design of any international payments system requires transferring "the onus of adjustment from the debtor to the creditor position," and thereby aiming "at the substitution of an expansionist, in place of a contractionist, pressure on world trade" without removing all discipline from the deficit trading partner (1980, 176).

This transfer of the onus of adjustment occurred after World War II. In the immediate postwar period, economic recovery of the free capitalist world required the European nations to run huge import surpluses to feed their populations and rebuild their war-devastated plant and equipment. This implied that the United States would have to provide enormous credits to finance the required export surplus to Europe. The resulting European indebtedness would be so burdensome that it was unlikely that, even in the long run, the European nations could ever service this debt. Moreover, American policymakers were mindful that reparation payments after World War I were financed by American investors lending Germany foreign exchange, and that Germany never repaid these loans. Given this history and existing circumstances, it was obvious that private lending facilities could not be expected to provide the credits necessary for European recovery.

Under the Bretton Woods system designed by Harry Dexter White, the main mechanism available for redressing this potentially lopsided global import-export trade flow was for the debtors to accept the entire burden of adjustment by "tightening their belts" and reducing their demand for imports to what they could earn from exports.[4] The result would have been to depress further the standard of living of Western Europe.

Instead the United States produced the Marshall Plan and other foreign grants and aid programs. The Marshall Plan provided $5 billion in aid in eighteen months and a total of $13 billion in four years. (In 1997 dollars this is equivalent to almost $150 billion.) The Marshall Plan transfers represented approximately 2 percent per annum of the gross national product (GNP) of the United States. Yet no United States resident felt deprived of goods and services. Real GNP per capita in the United States during the first year of the Marshall Plan was still 25 percent larger than in the last peacetime year of 1940. Per capita GNP continued to grow throughout the 1950s.[5] There was no real sacrifice associated with the American government's unilateral transfer. The resulting exports were produced by employing what otherwise would have been idle resources. For the first time in its history, the United States did not suffer from a severe recession immediately after the cessation of a major war. The world experienced an economic "free lunch" as both the potential debtors and the creditor nation gained from this "giveaway."

The United States maintained a positive merchandise trade balance until the first oil price shock in 1973. More than offsetting this trade surplus during most of the 1960s, however, were foreign and military unilateral transfers plus net capital outflows. The Bretton Woods system had no way of automatically forcing the emerging current account surplus nations to step into the adjustment role that the United States had been playing since 1947. Instead, these surplus nations continued to convert some portion of their annual dollar surpluses into calls on U.S. gold reserves. The seeds of the destruction of the Bretton Woods system and the golden age of economic development were sown as surplus nations drained gold reserves from the United States.

When the United States closed the gold window and unilaterally withdrew from a Bretton Woods system that could accommodate Keynes's incompatibility thesis, the last vestige of Keynes's enlightened international monetary approach was lost, apparently without regret or regard as to how well it had served the global economy.

A Post Keynesian International Payments System

The following proposal for an international payments system builds on Keynes's incompatibility thesis to create a permanent expansionist pressure on world trade and development similar to what we experienced during the 1947–1973 period. In an interdependent world economy, some degree of economic cooperation among trading partners is necessary. Our proposal, however, does not require the establishment of a supranational central bank to create a Unionized Monetary System (UMS) as Keynes suggested in his Bancor Plan—even if this is believed desirable on other grounds. At this stage in the evolution of world politics, a global supranational central bank is not feasible.[6] Our suggestion is a more modest one aimed at obtaining an international agreement that does not require the surrendering of either national control of local banking systems or independent national fiscal policies.

What is required is a *closed* double-entry bookkeeping clearing institution to keep the payments score among the various trading regions, plus some mutually agreed-upon rules to create and reflux liquidity while maintaining the international purchasing power of the international currency. There are eight provisions necessary for my clearing union proposal to meet the criteria laid down by Keynes. These are:

1. The unit account and ultimate reserve asset for international liquidity is the International Money Clearing Unit (IMCU). All IMCUs are held only by central banks, not by the public.
2. Each nation's or UMS's central bank is committed to guarantee one-

way convertibility from IMCU deposits at the clearing union to its domestic money. Each central bank will set its own rules regarding making available foreign monies (through IMCU clearing transactions) to its own bankers and private-sector residents.[7]

Since central banks agree to sell their own liabilities (one-way convertibility) against the IMCU only to other central bankers and the international clearing agency while they simultaneously hold only IMCUs as liquid reserve assets for international financial transactions, there can be no draining of reserves from the system. All major private international transactions ultimately clear between central banks on their own account within the international clearing institution.

3. The exchange rate between the domestic currency and the IMCU is set *initially* by each nation—just as it would be if one instituted an international gold standard. Provisions 7 and 8 infra indicate when and how this nominal exchange rate between the national currency and the IMCU would change in the future.

4. Contracts between private individuals will continue to be denominated into whatever domestic currency permitted by local laws and agreed upon by the contracting parties. Contracts to be settled in terms of a foreign currency will therefore require some announced commitment from the central bank (through private-sector bankers) of the availability of foreign funds to meet such private contractual obligations.

5. An overdraft system to be used to make available short-term unused creditor balances at the clearinghouse will finance the productive international transactions of others who need short-term credit. The terms will be determined by the pro bono publico clearing managers.

6. A trigger mechanism to encourage any creditor nation to spend what is deemed (in advance) by agreement of the international community to be *"excessive"* credit balances. These excessive credits can be spent in three ways: (1) on the products of any other member of the clearing union; (2) on new direct foreign investment projects; and (3) to provide unilateral transfers (foreign aid) to deficit members. Spending via (1) forces the surplus nation to make the adjustment directly by way of the balance on goods and services. Spending by way of (3) permits adjustment directly by the current account balance, while (2) provides adjustment by the capital accounts (without setting up a contractual debt that will *require* reverse current account flows in the future).

Consequently, provision 6 provides the surplus country with considerable discretion in deciding how to accept the "onus" of adjustment in what it believes to be its residents' best interests. It does not, however, permit the surplus nation to shift the burden to the deficit nation(s) via contractual requirements for debt service charges independent of what the deficit nation can afford.[8] The important thing is to make sure that continual oversaving[9] by surplus nations cannot unleash depressionary forces or a building up of international debts so encumbering as to impoverish the global economy of the twenty-first century.

In the unlikely event that the surplus nation does not spend or give away these credits within a specified time, the clearing agency would confiscate (and redistribute to debtor members) the portion of credits deemed excess.[10] This last-resort confiscatory action by the managers of the clearing agency would make a payments adjustment via unilateral transfer payments in the current accounts.

Under either a fixed- or flexible-rate system, nations may experience persistent trade deficits merely because their trading partners are not living up to their means, that is, because other nations are continually hoarding a portion of their foreign export earnings (plus net unilateral transfers). By so doing, these oversavers are creating a lack of global effective demand. Under provision 6, deficit countries would no longer have to deflate their real economy merely to adjust their payment imbalance because others are oversaving. Instead, the system would seek to remedy the payment deficit by increasing opportunities for deficit nations to work their way out of deficits by selling more abroad.

A system to stabilize the long-term purchasing power of the IMCU (in terms of each member nation's domestically produced market basket of goods) can be developed. This requires a system of fixed exchange rates between the local currency and the IMCU that changes only to reflect permanent increases in efficiency wages.[11] This assures each central bank that its holdings of IMCUs as the nation's foreign reserves will never lose purchasing power in terms of foreign produced goods, even if a foreign government permits wage-price inflation to occur within its borders. Consequently, the rate between the local currency and the IMCU would change with inflation in the local money price of the domestic commodity basket.

7. A provision to produce a system designed to maintain the relative efficiency wage parities among nations. In such a system, the adjustability of nominal exchange rates will be primarily (but not always, see provision 8) to offset changes in efficiency wages among trading partners. A beneficial effect that follows from this provision is that it eliminates the possibility that a specific industry in any nation can be put at a competitive disadvantage (or secure a competitive advantage) against foreign producers solely because the nominal exchange rate changed independently of changes in efficiency wages and the real costs of production in each nation.

Consequently, nominal exchange rate variability can no longer create the problem of a loss of competitiveness due solely to the overvaluing of a currency, as, for example, experienced by the industries in the American "rust belt" during the period 1982 to 1985. Even if temporary, currency appreciation independent of changes in efficiency wages can have significant permanent real costs as industries abandon export markets, and existing plant and equipment is cast aside as too costly to maintain.

Provision 7 also prevents any nation from engaging in a beggar-thy-neighbor, export-thy-unemployment policy by pursuing an exchange-rate devaluation that does not reflect changes in efficiency wages. Once the initial exchange rates are chosen and relative efficiency wages are locked in, reductions in real production costs associated with a relative decline in efficiency wages due to relatively greater improvements in productivity will be the main factor (with the exception of provision 8), justifying an adjustment in the exchange rate.

Although provision 6 prevents any country from piling up persistent excessive surpluses, this does not mean that it is impossible for one or more nations to run persistent deficits. Consequently, proposal 8 infra provides a program for addressing the problem of persistent export-import deficits in any one nation.

8. If a country is at *full employment* and still has a tendency toward persistent international deficits on its current account, then this is prima facie evidence that it does not possess the productive capacity to maintain its current standard of living. If the deficit nation is a poor one, then surely there is a case for the richer nations who are in surplus to transfer some of their excess credit balances to support the poor nation.[12] If it is a relatively rich country, then the deficit nation must alter its standard of living by reducing its relative terms of trade with its major trading partners. Rules, agreed upon in advance, would require the trade-deficit-rich nation to devalue its exchange rate by stipulated increments per period until evidence becomes available to indicate that the export-import imbalance is eliminated without unleashing significant recessionary forces.

If, on the other hand, the payment deficit persists despite a continuous positive balance of trade in goods and services, then there is evidence that the deficit nation might be carrying too heavy an international debt service obligation. The pro bono officials of the clearing union should bring the debtor and creditors into negotiations to reduce annual debt service payments by (1) lengthening the payments period, (2) reducing the interest charges, or (3) debt forgiveness.[13]

If any government objects to the idea that IMCU provisions provide governments with the ability to limit the free movement of "capital" funds, then this nation is free to join other nations of similar attitude in forming a regional currency union (UMS) and thereby ensuring a free flow of funds among the residents of the currency union.

Conclusion

Some believe my clearing union plan is utopian. If we start with the defeatist attitude that it is too difficult to change the awkward system in which we are enmeshed, then no progress will be made. We must reject such defeatism at this exploratory stage and merely ask whether these particular proposals for improving the operations of the international payments system to promote global growth will create more difficulties than other proposed innovations. The health of the world economic system will not permit us to muddle through!

Once we have reformed the international monetary payments system so that nations do not have to fear balance-of-payments problems, then the leaders of the major nations of the world can take steps to stimulate domestic aggregate demand in line with Vickrey's trans-Keynesian manifesto without having to fear adverse economic consequences for their own nation. Then, and only then, we may restore a golden age of economic development to our planet.

Notes

1. Vickrey argues that "for *small open economies*, combining free trade with fixed or narrowly constrained exchange rates would make it possible for any one of them to pursue a full employment policy independently" (Vickrey 1997, 500, emphasis added).

2. These classical axioms are the neutrality of money axiom, the gross substitution axiom, and the ergodic axiom (see Davidson 1984).

3. I take up the question of capital controls in more detail in a forthcoming paper titled, "The Case for Regulating International Capital Flows," sponsored by the Social Market Foundation, London, November 17, 1998.

4. The "scarce currency" clause of the Bretton Woods Agreement would permit European nations to discriminate against American imports. But this would not resolve the problem since there was no other major source of goods necessary to feed and rebuild Europe.

5. Only in the small recessions of 1949 and 1957 did per capita GNP stop growing. But even during these brief periods, GNP never declined.

6. This does not deny that some groups of trading partners may wish to integrate their central banks and banking systems into a regional UMS common market. The Maastricht Treaty implies that ultimately there will be a single currency among all the European Community of Nations governed by a single supranational central bank. If some nations were willing to develop an inter-regional UMS, they would be free to

develop their own UMS clearing mechanism that would operate as a single unit in the larger global clearing union proposed below.

7. Correspondent banking will have to operate through the International Clearing Agency, with each central bank regulating the international relations and operations of its domestic banking firms.

8. Small-scale smuggling of currency across borders, etc., can never be completely eliminated. But such movements are merely a flea on a dog's back—a minor, but not debilitating, irritation. If, however, most of the residents of a nation hold and use (in violation of legal tender laws) a foreign currency for domestic transactions and as a store of value (for example, as in Russia), this is evidence of a lack of confidence in the government and its monetary authority. Unless confidence is restored, all attempts to restore economic prosperity will fail. Some may fear that if a surplus nation is close to the trigger point it could short-circuit the system by making loans to reduce its credit balance *prior* to setting off the trigger. Since preventing unreasonable debt service obligations is an important objective of this proposal, a mechanism that monitors and can restrict such pretrigger lending activities may be required.

One possible way of eliminating this trigger-avoidance lending loophole is as follows: An initial agreement as to what constitutes sensible and flexible criteria for judging when debt-servicing burdens become unreasonable is established. Given these criteria, the clearing union managers would have the responsibility for preventing additional loans that push debt burdens beyond reasonable servicing levels. In other words, loans that push debt burdens too far could not be cleared though the clearing union, that is, the managers would refuse to release the IMCUs for loan purposes from the surplus country's account. (I am indebted to Robert Blecker for suggesting this point.)

The managers would also be required to make periodic public reports on the level of credits being accumulated by surplus nations and to indicate how close these surpluses are to the trigger point. Such reports would provide an informational edge for debtor nations permitting them to bargain more successively regarding the terms of refinancing existing loans or new loans. All loans would still have to meet the clearing union's guidelines for reasonableness.

I do not discount the difficulties involved in setting up and getting agreement on criteria for establishing unreasonable debt service burdens. (For some suggestions, however, see the second paragraph of provision 8.) In the absence of cooperation and a spirit of good will that is necessary for the clearing union to provide a mechanism assuring the economic prosperity of all members, however, no progress can ever be made.

Moreover, as the 1980s and 1990s international debt problems of African and Latin American nations clearly demonstrate, creditors ultimately have to forgive some debt when they have previously encouraged excessive debt burdens. Under the current system, however, debt forgiveness is a last-resort solution acceptable only after both debtor and creditor nations suffer from faltering economic growth. Surely a more intelligent option is to develop an institutional arrangement that prevents excessive debt-servicing burdens from ever occurring.

9. Oversaving is defined as a nation persistently spending less on imports plus direct equity foreign investment than on the nation's export earnings plus net unilateral transfers.

10. Whatever "excessive" credit balances are redistributed shall be apportioned among the debtor nations (perhaps based on a formula that is inversely related to each debtor's per capita income and directly related to the size of its international debt) to be used to reduce debit balances at the clearing union.

11. The efficiency wage is related to the money wage divided by the average product of labor. It is the unit labor cost modified by the profit markup in domestic money terms of domestically produced GNP. At this preliminary stage of this proposal, it would serve no useful purpose to decide whether the domestic market basket should include both tradable and nontradable goods and services. (With the growth of tourism, increasingly more nontradable goods become potentially tradable.) I personally prefer the wider concept of the domestic market basket, but it is not obvious that any essential principle is lost if a tradable-only concept is used, or if some nations use the wider concept while others the narrower one.

12. This is equivalent to a negative income tax for poor fully employed families within a nation. (See Davidson, 1987–1988 for further development of this argument.)

13. The actual program adopted for debt service reduction will depend on many parameters, including the relative income and wealth of the debtor vis-à-vis the creditor, the ability of the debtor to increase its per capita real income, and so on.

References

Adelman, Irma. 1991. "Long-Term Economic Development." Working paper no. 589, California Agricultural Experiment Station, Berkeley, March.

Davidson, Paul. 1984. "Reviving Keynes's Revolution." *Journal of Post Keynesian Economics* 6, no. 4:561–583.

———. 1987–1988. "A Modest Set of Proposals for Solving the International Debt Crisis." *Journal of Post Keynesian Economics* 10, no. 2:323–338.

———. 1992–1993. "Reforming the World's Money." *Journal of Post Keynesian Economics* 15, no. 2:153–180.

———. 1997. "Are Grains of Sand in the Wheels of International Finance Sufficient to Do the Job When Boulders Are Often Required?" *Economic Journal* 107 (May): 671–686.

———. 1998. "Volatile Financial Markets and the Speculator." *Economic Issues* 3.

Felix, D. 1997–1998. "On Drawing Policy Lessons from Recent Latin American Currency Crises." *Journal of Post Keynesian Economics* 20, no. 2:191–222.

Keynes, J.M. 1936. *The General Theory of Employment, Interest, and Money.* New York: Harcourt, Brace.

———. 1980. *The Collected Writings of John Maynard Keynes,* 23, ed. D. Moggridge. London: Macmillan.

Tobin, James. 1974. *The New Economics One Decade Older.* Princeton: Princeton University Press.

Vickrey, William. 1997. "A Trans-Keynesian Manifesto (Thoughts About an Asset-Based Macroeconomics." *Journal of Post Keynesian Economics* 19, no. 495–510.

12

THOMAS I. PALLEY

Why a Global Clearing Union Based on Fixed Exchange Rates Won't Work

A Response to Paul Davidson

William Vickrey would likely have approved of Paul Davidson's paper as an example of thought-provoking economic analysis used to imagine new mechanisms for dealing with a serious economic problem. These were the hallmarks of Vickrey's own work on auctions and congestion pricing, and they won him the Nobel Prize in economics. However, approval does not equal agreement.

Davidson begins his paper by identifying the dramatically changed growth performance marking the years since 1973, but then leaps to attribute the earlier, better global economic performance, in the period 1950 to 1973, to an international system based on fixed exchange rates and capital controls. Underpinning this claim is an elevation of the virtues of fixed exchange rates, and an assertion about the negative effects of flexible exchange rates that I find problematic.

The "fixed-versus-flexible exchange rate" issue cannot be considered independently of the regime governing capital mobility. How effectively the system of exchange rates functions depends critically on the nature of capital mobility. Flexible exchange rates are accused of doing much damage, but the reality is that the damage has largely been done by excessive capital mobility.

There is much evidence to support this claim. For instance, in the early 1980s, the United States and Great Britain both suffered massive deindustrialization as capital inflows bid up the exchange rate in response to high interest rates. Jobs were lost and the economy permanently changed, not because of productivity problems but because of financial inflows driven by interest-rate differentials. A second example comes from France where, in 1983, the Mitterand government was forced to abandon its Keynesian reflation as capital exited France in response to policies it disliked, and created a franc crisis. Finally, the negative effects of inappropriate capital mobility have been clearly visible in East Asia's recent economic collapse. Driven by herd behavior, hot money rushed in, seeking high returns without regard to risk. When these flows reversed, they caused a financial panic and a collapse in currency value; this triggered a deep recession in East Asia that spread tremors through the wider global economy. Once again, it was capital flows rather than flexible exchange rates that were the precipitating factor.

Davidson makes much of the contribution of fixed exchange rates to the prosperity of the 1950s and 1960s, yet it is not at all that clear that fixed exchange rates had much to do with this success. First, immediately after World War II, Europe needed to run deficits in order to rebuild, and this rebuilding was financed by the Marshall Plan. Thereafter, Europe's dollar shortage was financed by U.S. military transfers, U.S. portfolio investment, and U.S. multinational foreign direct investment. Thus, it was the system of funding that was important, not the exchange-rate regime. Second, until 1958, nearly all European countries had extremely strict capital controls, and this promoted financial stability. Third, and most importantly, the period 1945 to 1973 was one of rising productive capacity owing to high levels of investment and rapid productivity gains. The additional supply generated by this expansion was absorbed by growing domestic demand in both the United States and Europe. International trade absorbed only a small fraction of this as countries were much less integrated. Instead, domestic consumption and investment both grew rapidly. The reason was expansionary monetary policy pursued by national monetary authorities, combined with rising wages driven by bargaining conditions favorable to working people. In particular, unemployment rates were low, unions were stronger, and business had not yet devised the technologies and organizational structure enabling it to roam the globe in search of the cheapest, most exploitable labor. Fixed exchange rates were not the cause of prosperity: instead, success was the result of Keynesian macroeconomic policy combined with the right structural conditions (Palley 1998a).

Moreover, it is possible that not only did fixed exchange rates not help, they may actually have hindered. This is illustrated by considering the plight of the British economy. It was persistently troubled by having an overvalued exchange rate, and faced continual speculative pressures that forced the adoption of stop-go economic policies that disrupted growth. Ultimately, the United Kingdom was forced into a full-scale devaluation of sterling in 1967. Had Britain had flexible exchange rates combined with capital controls, it is possible that it would have enjoyed faster growth and diminished cyclical fluctuations.

Davidson advocates fixed exchange rates, but the fact is that countries have different underlying rates of productivity growth and different rates of inflation. This, in turn, forces periodic adjustment that opens the door to speculation. In effect, speculators are offered a "one-way option." The weak currencies are easily identifiable on the basis of economic fundamentals. Consequently there is an incentive to sell these currencies and buy them back after devaluation. If a devaluation occurs, speculators win big; if it does not happen, all they have lost are the transaction costs that are increasingly negligible owing to financial innovation. This one-way option is exactly what George Soros took advantage of in 1992.

A final point on the exchange-rate question addresses Davidson's claim that flexible exchange rates have reduced investment. In fact, there are grounds for claiming that they may have increased investment since firms have built production facilities in many countries to hedge against currency fluctuations. There is certainly a negative dimension to this transformation of corporations into footloose organizations with increased bargaining power vis-à-vis workers. However, it has not lowered investment. To the extent that investment has been lower, flexible exchange rates are not to blame; instead, it is because policymakers have been prompted by the theory of the natural rate of unemployment to run economies with much slacker demand conditions and much higher rates of unemployment.

A call for fixed exchange rates is one part of Davidson's program. The second part is the establishment of an international clearing union. This union would have countries clear their payment deficits at the fixed exchange rate with the official clearinghouse. The motivation for this arrangement is absolutely correct, as today's global economy is suffering from a deflationary bias owing to reliance on export-led growth. Davidson aims to end this deflationary bias by forcing countries to spend their trade surpluses.

That said, there are many problems with this scheme. First, there is the reliance on fixed exchange rates that I have already criticized. Second, Davidson seeks to sell his suggestion as a clearinghouse when in fact it is a global central bank. The clearinghouse has power to decide exchange rate settings; it has the power to determine global interest rates since it determines the rate at which deficit countries can borrow from the clearing union. This rate will determine national interest rates that will then be arbitraged across countries by international money markets. Finally, the only way the system can accommodate global economic growth is to have the supply of International Money Clearing Units (ICMUs) grow, and the clearinghouse will therefore determine the growth of world liquidity. Thus it is a de facto global central bank. Since the world economy is not an optimal currency area, there are good economic reasons why countries do not want to give up sovereign monetary policy, and there are good political reasons why they will not.

There are other significant problems with the proposed arrangement. The balances with the clearing union are official settlement balances, and Davidson advocates that surplus countries be forced to spend the balances they accumulate. On one level, this is a very sensible proposition. In effect, it forces surplus countries, rather than deficit countries, to adjust to balance-of-payments imbalances. This gives the global economy an expansionary tilt, replacing the current deflationary tilt that exists under today's system that requires that deficit countries contract to correct their trade deficits.

However, though the intention is sound, the scheme has implementation problems. Davidson's scheme requires surplus countries to spend their foreign trade surpluses, which accumulate as official settlements balances, or lose them. How is this to be accomplished? Are governments or individuals to spend them? If individuals, how are these balances to find their way into the hands of individual agents, and how are those agents to be given the incentive to spend them on foreign goods and services? It begins to look as if the clearinghouse will not only run monetary policy, but will also end up running fiscal policy by dishing out tax credits.

Another problem is that countries may need to run structural surpluses and accumulate foreign financial assets. Here, one thinks of the OPEC countries that suddenly found themselves with massive trade surpluses in the 1970s. Forcing them to immediately consume these surpluses would have been well-nigh impossible, as they simply did not have the capacity to do so.

A final problem concerns the place of portfolio investment in the new scheme. Portfolio investment can serve a valuable purpose in promoting global growth. Investors are able to get higher rates of return, while developing countries get access to capital at cheaper rates. To the extent that they borrow, they also retain the benefit of being the residual claimants (that is, the equity holders). Yet, there appears no place for this type of mutually beneficial transaction in Davidson's scheme and, once allowed, the speculative genie is let back out of the bottle. This consideration reveals how Davidson's proposal underestimates the productive contribution that international financial markets can make to allocating resources and pricing goods and services. The challenge is not to get rid of international financial markets, but rather to take the instability out by putting in place rules that provide the right incentives.

Finally, we come to the most important point of all. Redesigning the international financial architecture to eliminate instability and deflationary tendencies is surely necessary, but it is only a part of the solution. Restoring the equitable pro-growth environment that marked the golden age between 1950 and 1973 requires the restoration of expansionary domestic monetary and fiscal policies, and, most important, it requires the restoration of the balance of power between capital and labor (Palley 1998a; 1998b). Only then will generalized wage growth be restored.

References

Palley, Thomas I. 1998a. *Plenty of Nothing: The Downsizing of the American Dream and the Case for Structural Keynesianism*. Princeton: Princeton University Press.

———. 1998b. "International Finance and the Problem of Capital Account Governance: A Blueprint for Reform." AFL-CIO Public Policy Department, Economic Policy Paper E017.

———. 1999. "Goodbye Washington Consensus, Hello Main Street Alternative." *Dissent* (spring): 48–52.

13

JOHN LANGMORE

Employment and International Financial Markets

William Vickrey was a particularly important contributor to what is currently the most significant focus for innovative work by economists: full employment. Growth of employment has become the highest priority for national and international economic and social policy; it will contribute more to increasing personal and national economic security, to reducing waste, increasing efficiency, improving equity, reducing poverty, and strengthening social integration than any other economic or social achievement. Yet, in most countries, unemployment and underemployment are disastrously high.

Vickrey was an intellectually powerful innovator and analyst in both theory and policy, and an advocate of full employment. Many of us were stimulated and inspired by him. His presidential address to the American Economic Association in 1993 was a personal encouragement to me as I struggled for changes in Australian economic policy to make employment growth a central goal. I often quoted his comment that "the natural rate of unemployment . . . is one of the most vicious euphemisms ever coined."

Vickrey's "Trans-Keynesian Manifesto" is in this mold, though some of its propositions are certainly debatable, for example, that full employment requires large government deficits. Surely full employment can be achieved with a more complex strategy that allows budgets to be balanced over a full business cycle and concentrates outlays on programs that maximize employment, such as the full range of labor-intensive social services. Another key to full employment is the adoption of additional instruments that contribute to simultaneous reduction of unemployment and inflation, such as a comprehensive, equitable prices-and-incomes policy or social pact.

Paul Davidson's essay, "Commitment to Full Employment in a Global Economy," focuses on the important issues. His initial focus on the contrast between the decades before and after 1973 is vitally important, and his critique of the market fundamentalist mantras of the last quarter century is very effective. He is clear about goals and avoids the confusion of means with ends that bedevils the economics profession.

One factor behind the slower global growth of the last twenty-five years, which Davidson could perhaps have emphasized more, is high average real interest rates. In major industrial countries, long-term real interest rates averaged 1.7 percent between 1956 and 1973, zero for the rest of the 1970s, and 5.9 percent between 1981 and 1993, more than 4 percent above the average for the "golden age." This must have retarded investment and employment growth, in both developed and developing countries. It is possible to argue that the higher rates in the latter period are one result of liberalization, as countries have struggled to influence their exchange rates, to offset turbulence, and to win the confidence of financial markets.

That anarchic international financial markets can cause massive destruction and be a major impediment to economic and social development is now much more widely recognized, which would delight Vickrey. International financial markets can undermine economies both through turbulence and through their dominance of national policy. Speaking at the International Monetary Fund/ World Bank annual meetings in Washington in October 1998, Paul Krugman rightly pointed to the extraordinary contradiction of countries being forced to adopt contractionary macroeconomic policies in order to attempt to obtain the confidence of financial markets when their central problems are recession, unemployment, and poverty. This is recognition from the more cautious wing of the economics profession of what the United Nations Conference on Trade and Development (UNCTAD) and John Eatwell noted several years ago: that financial market liberalization seems to have been associated with higher average global real interest rates, greater macroeconomic restraint, and therefore, higher unemployment.

The recent recognition by the G7 finance ministers and European Union heads of government that growth, not stabilization, must be the central concern of macro policy is a vital step along the way, but it could be completely transitory. The first and most important requirement for full employment is to put full employment at the center of national policy and keep it there.

The second requirement is to make financial markets the servant of economies and societies rather than the dominant determinant of the parameters of public policy. Davidson makes an interesting proposal for achieving this. He begins, however, with an unnecessary and misjudged dismissal of the Tobin tax. He says in effect that, because the Tobin tax could not solve all problems, it cannot solve any of them. Yet neither Tobin nor others who have written about his proposal have claimed that it would solve all of the problems of financial markets. Tobin's claim was always modest: A small transaction tax would reduce the quantity of short-term international financial transactions by putting "sand in the wheels," making domestic monetary management less difficult. The advocates have always argued that it should be part of a larger package of measures. The Tobin tax would reduce the excessive variability in the quantity of short-term international financial flows. That alone is a sufficiently desirable outcome to justify its introduction.

Further, the Tobin tax's impact on the volatility of exchange rates is not as clear as Davidson describes. After a review, Barry Eichengreen has described the empirical evidence on the impact of transaction taxes on market volatility as weak, and notes that, with certain reasonable assumptions, a Tobin tax would reduce exchange-rate volatility. Recognizing that foreign exchange markets have different characteristics from those where transactions taxes have previously been used and the results assessed, the effect of the tax on price can be regarded as uncertain. The impact of the Tobin tax on trade would be slight at the modest rates that are normally discussed.

The benefits of the Tobin tax for stability of short-term financial flows, for economic management, and for revenue—which would be substantial in many countries—justify attempting the international negotiations that would be necessary for its introduction. The Tobin tax is both feasible and desirable, though alone it would not be sufficient to stabilize international financial markets. Davidson does not need to demolish that proposal in order to justify his own.

It is now clear, however, that strengthening the international financial institutional structure is essential. Davidson's proposal is one of a number of suggestions that should be seriously evaluated, and that of Eatwell and Lance Taylor is another.

An open, accountable process—one that is not, by the way, currently in place—is essential for such an evaluation to have credibility. The reforms announced by the G7 in October of 1998 were prepared entirely outside of public scrutiny and without any exposure to public or parliamentary discussion. The so called "Willard Group," twenty-two countries that were unilaterally invited by the United States to the Willard Hotel in Washington in the fall of 1997, was outside any of the existing international institutions, an example of more of the same hegemonic superpower management of global affairs. Usually, the hegemon is the United States; in this case, it was the United States and Britain together, no doubt because of British dominance of international financial markets. The value of international financial transactions in London is still twice that in New York. Yet these arrangements have profound implications for all countries and so should be discussed openly and inclusively.

A global conference on international financial reform might be the focus for the required discussions and for the agreement necessary to ratify them. Such reform is a requirement for the achievement of full employment sought by Vickrey with such high intelligence.

14

James K. Galbraith

The Keynesian Economics of Unemployment and Inequality

William Vickrey believed in the cause of full employment not just as a political matter, but with tenacious insistence that the laws of economics do not preclude the achievement and maintenance of full employment over time. This is the principle that Vickrey argued and that I wish also to argue.

Rarely have so many economists of prominence and influence been as united as they were three years ago around the idea of the non-accelerating inflation rate of unemployment (NAIRU), the proposition that an unemployment rate below 6 percent was a dangerous thing. Those of us who advocated lower unemployment rates were a cranky fringe, not admitted to serious policy discussions and carefully excluded from the higher circles of the academy. But three ensuing years of unemployment far below 6 percent, without rising inflation, have left no doubt, even in the most skeptical minds, as to who was right and who was wrong in that discussion.

This is one explanation for the collapse of NAIRU, but it is not an entirely complete explanation. Further explanation includes the fact that, as unemployment fell, so too did many econometric estimates of the NAIRU, leaving us to ask: Why didn't these estimates maintain the credibility and persuasive power of that original rock-solid 6 percent? The answer has to do with the more profound connection between economics and policy. Whatever the deep logic of a hysteric NAIRU, or a TV NAIRU (that time-varying NAIRU that I once described as a small-screen, moving-image, black-box NAIRU), it is very clear that if the NAIRU follows a random walk, then it has lost the capacity to be useful, even to those who would otherwise like to use it as a concept for setting policy.

Joe Stiglitz (1993), in his recent, last-gasp defenses of the *idea* of the NAIRU, offered ringing affirmations of the statistical significance of the NAIRU equations and their important role in the econometric research of the Council of Economic Advisors. But when pressed, he declined to reveal the exact estimate, or even the range of estimates, of the NAIRU at that moment. He went on to deny that these highly useful constructs were actually being used for any practical purpose in the setting of public policy. I have to admit that, at that point, I threw up my hands and, considering the argument to be over, said that the only real difference between Stiglitz and me on this point is that I am not a church-going man.

But the coup de grace came from a man I often find entering my thoughts who is a great figure in our popular culture by any standard: Alan Greenspan. One of the regular features of the NAIRU period was an adverse reaction from the stock market to any progress against unemployment. The jobless rate might fall; stocks would drop on the news; and the press would write, with a reflexive instinct that never varied, that investors were showing their fear of inflation. This was the practical influence of the NAIRU model at work when coupled to that other great contribution of your local economists, the efficient-markets hypothesis.

In fact, of course, stock values drop when investors decide that interest rates are likely to rise. And the fear of rising interest rates came to be associated with falling unemployment, not because investors believe in NAIRU, but because they believed the Federal Reserve believed in NAIRU and that, therefore, Chairman Greenspan might react to the drop in the unemployment rate by agreeing, no doubt under pressure from that coterie of bank-influenced regional Federal Reserve Bank presidents who always want higher interest rates no matter what the economic conditions, that Mr. Greenspan might, under pressure from them, acquiesce to higher interest rates in the wake of a fallen unemployment rate.

In other words, investors feared not NAIRU, but belief in NAIRU, which gave us a little situation not altogether unlike the experience of the Mexicans who have a monetary crisis once every six years when they have a change of government. In our case, we found ourselves with a monetary crisis once every six weeks, whenever the Federal Open Market Committee met. And the only difference between our situation and Mexico's was that ours occurred with fifty-two times greater frequency. But thus it was that Alan Greenspan was in position to land the decisive blow. Simply by letting it be known that monetary policy did not, and was not going to, follow a NAIRU model, he destroyed the ostensible link between low unemployment and rising inflation expectations. Wall Street stopped reacting to the unemployment numbers. And NAIRU, which came to the larger public through a financial press that is geared to what goes on on Wall Street, simply evanesced, like the Cheshire Cat, leaving nothing behind but a smile.

This result, I need not point out, is entirely consistent with Keynesian theory, a practical triumph for Keynesian economics that was to lead to an increasingly bold experiment with low-measured rates of unemployment. This has led to a situation in which brother Greenspan stands within just a few decimal points of becoming the first Federal Reserve chairman actually to achieve the interim targets for full employment and reasonably stable prices that (forgive me for boasting) I helped to write into the Full Employment and Balanced Growth Act, the Humphrey–Hawkins Act of 1978.

What now? We still face a political and theoretical task ahead. On the political or the policy front there is today the risk, the grave risk, that the achievement of full employment may not be sustained. Vickrey in his final article, published by the *Journal of Post Keynesian Economics*, "A Trans-Keynesian Manifesto" (1997), warned of the danger. It lies in part, perhaps essentially, in the failure of Keynesian ideas to penetrate below the surface and into the structure of policy. The danger shows up most particularly in the fetishes of free markets, deregulation, unregulated capital flows, and balanced budgets—the latter risk especially leading, as Vickrey argued, to an unbalanced reliance on monetary policy to sustain full employment with ancillary risks, indeed virtual certainty at some point, of financial instability, bubbles, and the chance, now obviously being realized in large parts of the world, of a major debt deflation. This is an acute risk that is already in operation today. Just travel outside the United States, and it is clear that here we live in a bubble. Debt deflation is happening in Asia and Russia, and is spreading in Latin America. The challenge is whether we can adjust our thinking and our policies rapidly enough, and radically enough, to regain control of the world economy before we lose control of the American economy. And on this front, I would argue, we have urgent work to do.

There are points of entry into policy-making processes. Greenspan, having lowered the interest rate by a quarter of a point between meetings, sent an important psychological signal that he plans to be in control. The importance of this should not be minimized, as the urgent task is, in fact, financial stabilization, and Greenspan has signaled his commitment to that objective.

But for every one step forward, we have two steps back. There is Greenspan's speech on transparency, delivered November 4, 1998. In it, he repeats all the old shibboleths that had been prescribed to the Asians for years and that are in fact at the root of the Asian crisis. Greenspan's notions of free-market liberalization are not the cure for this crisis but indeed part of the cause. Yet, I regard this argument as almost epiphenomenal. Greenspan, when he strays from his core responsibilities, is obliged to restate prevailing orthodoxies. Nobody should take such rituals seriously, and I hope nobody does. But if, on the other hand, reality creeps into our consciousness from other sources, its progress can be advanced by persistent argument. This is our job. We need to address ourselves to some of the questions about the stabilization of the global economy. We need to address these and related issues in a way that I think Vickrey would have insisted upon: with a practical concern for effective policy design. This should not be an afterthought, not something that we toss in at the end. Rather, it should be at the center of many of our discussions. It is clear that there is some way to go before proposals concerning employment programs, wage subsidies, and market anti-inflation plans are brought into contact in a useful and effective way with the policy-making process.

There needs to be something that can be taken to Capitol Hill. Nobody expressed this more effectively, I think, than Vickrey in that "Trans-Keynesian Manifesto." He said—I use the paragraph as the chapter head for one of the later chapters in my book, *Created Unequal*— that "While with a sufficient dihedral, one can fly a plane in good weather and make gentle turns with a rudder and elevator, it was the Wright brothers' invention of wing warp, later realized as ailerons, that allows landing in a cross-wind without disaster" (Vickrey 1997). He also said that if market anti-inflation plans are not sufficient to do this job, then we as economists have the task of coming up with something else. To say we might pursue one thing or another does not minimize the centrality of that part of our responsibility.

Concerning the other theoretical issues that we face, it seems to me that the new classical economists are right on one essential point: Our subject, economics, is unitary; it cannot be divided effectively in some grand ideological compromise into separable domains of micro and macro. You cannot have a system where a microeconomics based on the interaction of an infinity of rational individuals and minuscule competitive firms exists side by side with a macroeconomics that is an ad hoc construction interpreting the movement of somewhat arbitrarily defined aggregated variables. The problem is simply that having defined an important issue, the new classical project attacked it in precisely the wrong way. It is very clear, once you think of it, that the Brownian motion of competitive micro actors—that is to say, of representative agents whose expectations are drawn from a common distribution—cannot possibly account for the extent or the pattern of the observed variability of macro measures.

The economy therefore, on that evidence alone, must necessarily have structure, just as the universe has geometry and shape. One of my little epiphanies some years ago was realizing exactly wherefrom Keynes drew those three words, "the general theory," that he tacked onto the front of the title of his book. He got them from Einstein, and he got them from the idea that the universe has structure and shape.

In analyzing that structure, I think we can discern the macro foundations of our market outcomes. I thus assert the continuity of Keynesian macroeconomics and the theory, in particular, of the distribution of pay, of income, but especially of pay. Macro forces affect distribution through the mechanisms of imperfect competition. The evolution of inequality is largely an evolution in the distribution of Ricardian rents. It is worth remembering that the economics of imperfect competition was part of the Keynesian revolution. One can argue about other ideas that are also part of the Keynesian revolution, but what cannot be done is to marry Keynesian macroeconomics to the Walrasian microeconomics. The economics of imperfect competition, it turns out, is an extremely useful way of thinking about the way in which macro variables affect the distribution of income.

To the economics of Keynes, we need to add, through an understanding of imperfect competition, the concepts of technological change that come to us most elegantly from Joseph Schumpeter. I would argue that inserting Schumpeter's theory into models of imperfect competition creates a way of integrating coherently and intuitively the structure of markets, the forces of change, and the role of policy. The integration of Keynes and Schumpeter is the project of my book, *Created Unequal*. It involves the application of systematic theory-driven tools of numerical taxonomy, that is, techniques to assist with category-finding or a search for patterns in data.

I began that exercise not clearly anticipating what would be found, and I was therefore surprised to discover that basic Keynesian forces, namely investment, consumption, the exchange rate, and also the military budget, defined, with a very high degree of precision, the movements of the interindustrial wage structure. These variables also discriminated quite cleanly between effects on what might be called machine-builders, or knowledge-producers—industries that are strongly involved in the processes of technological change—and machine users, those industries whose basic function is the production of consumer goods. In another quite new approach, in which I am now engaged with a group of very talented students at the University of Texas, a very similar method, but at a different level, involves comparing the movements of the internal distribution of pay, in a wide range of countries, through time.

I am a great believer in searching under street lamps for the car keys. And it turns out that ministries of labor produce quite bright street lamps, but some filters must be applied in order to see the spectrum of colors that the lights are producing. Industrial statistics constitute one such filter. From them, it is possible to arrive at a relatively clear idea of whether inequality is rising or falling in the structure of manufacturing pay in a great many countries for which more traditional sorts of distributional data, that is to say, data drawn from household surveys, simply are not available because surveys have not been taken but once every five or ten years and may not be comparable in what they show from one survey date to the next. Having seen the street lamps under which no one else was looking for the car keys, we have calculated now for over seventy countries, with various starting and ending dates, but generally for periods of thirty to forty years, annual data on the movement of the distribution of industrial pay.

One of the things that you can see in these data is that the United States, in relative terms, was already increasing its pay inequality quite early, that is, through the 1970s. The data we have show that during the same period, there were numerous countries that decreased their inequality—Iran being one, the 1979 revolution having a dramatic effect. And there were also increases in inequality in Europe in this period of the oil shocks, although less so in Scandinavia. But the increases in southern and central Europe were not as great as they were in the United States.

The next time period, the 1980s, is really quite different. This is the period of recessions, financial crisis, and falling oil prices, which reverse the picture for at least some of the oil-exporting countries. In the 1980s, the United States is no longer the most rapidly increasing-in-inequality region. That dubious distinction shifts to parts of Latin America. But, nevertheless, increases in inequality in the United States continue during this time. On the other hand, China and India show declines in inequality in the 1980s. India, showing big increases in the 1970s, actually shows stabilization through the 1980s, reflecting the fact that India and China, which were never exposed to free capital flows, had much more successful growth experiences through this decade than much of the rest of the world.

Finally, we have 1989 to 1995, during which time the United States actually demonstrates improvement. China, by contrast, shows a very great increase in inequality in the present decade. The mechanisms of the Asian boom, it could be argued on a priori grounds, would reduce inequality and, indeed, through this period in Malaysia and Indonesia, you do see declining inequality, although from very high levels.

I am not prepared to lean too heavily on this evidence. I use these data only to argue that this kind of analysis of the macro movements of inequality across countries and through time gives us a way of launching a research program into the macro dynamics of inequality. In particular, questions naturally arise, such as, what is the relationship between unemployment and inequality through time? There is data available, in fine detail, for countries where unemployment is measured. It is very consistent, through time, with the Blanchflower and Oswald wage-curve phenomenon. That is to say, the data reflect the positive association between unemployment and inequality that they find through space as it affects particular groups. The relationship between growth and inequality could also be explored for countries where unemployment data are not so well defined. We have rather good data drawn from monthly series of wages and employment going back to the late 1960s in the case of Mexico; to the 1970s for Brazil. These detailed data show a very stable relationship between growth and inequality. The higher the growth rate, the greater the decline in inequality, and vice versa.

I do expect that these relative effects will tell us something about the role of trade and financial liberalization, and about export-promoting strategies versus import-substituting strategies in the evolution of inequality inside countries. And I expect that we will be able to say something about the movement of the oil price, particularly across those cases, which are spread out over the globe, of countries that are heavily dependent on the export of oil. But that is not the point. The point is only to suggest that the dynamics of the movement of income distribution, of changes in inequality, is not a neoclassical research program but is properly a Keynesian research program, a research program of which I think Vickrey would have approved.

References

Galbraith, James K. 1998. *Created Unequal: The Crisis in American Pay*. New York: Free Press.
Stiglitz, Joseph. 1993. Keynote address, symposium titled "Perspectives on the Natural Rate of Unemployment," organized by the *Journal of Economic Perspectives*, Georgetown University Conference Center, September 13.
Vickrey, William. 1997. "A Trans-Keynesian Manifesto." *Journal of Post Keynesian Economics* 19, no. 4 (fall): 495–510.

15

WILLIAM S. VICKREY

We Need a Bigger "Deficit"

The So-Called "Deficit"

We are not going to get out of the economic doldrums as long as we continue to be obsessed with the unreasoned ideological goal of reducing the so-called deficit.

The "deficit" is not an economic sin but an economic necessity.

Its most important function is to be the means whereby purchasing power not spent on consumption, or recycled into income by the private creation of net capital, is recycled into purchasing power by government borrowing and spending. Purchasing power not so recycled becomes nonpurchase, nonsales, nonproduction, and unemployment.

A Private-Capital Approach to Full Employment

We have not had a satisfactory approach to full employment, except in wartime, since 1926. Over much of this century, trends in the ratio of profitable private capital to national product have been downward, as a result of capital-saving innovation such as fiber optics, the trend to light industry away from steel mills and other heavy industry, and the increasing importance of services. Prospects are that for the foreseeable future the capacity of private industry to find profitable use for private capital will be not much greater than two years of gross domestic product.

On the other hand, aspirations of individuals to acquire assets to provide for retirement and other purposes have been growing, due to longer life expectancy, higher retirement aspiration levels, the loosening of family ties, the development of expensive medical technologies, and other factors. Current aspirations appear to be moving toward three years or more of gross domestic product. This leaves a gap to be filled by government debt of about one year of gross domestic product.

The author last worked on this chapter in August 1993. It is being published posthumously and reflects the incomplete nature of the original manuscript.

Government Debt to Fill the Gap the Private Sector Cannot Fill

If we aspire to a satisfactory level of full employment by 1998, whereby anyone not too finicky about the type of work could find a job at a living wage within 48 hours, this will, if we assume inflation to average about 3 percent, call for a gross domestic product of about 10 trillion dollars. To fill the gap between the asset aspirations of individuals at this level of income and the ability of the private sector to provide assets, the supply of government securities would have to rise to 10 trillion dollars, implying a level of income recycling by governments of about 1 trillion a year on the average over the next five years.

Paying for the Debt that Fills the Gap

Once this level is reached, to continue in equilibrium, the supply of government securities will need to grow pari passu with the gross domestic product, to correspond to the gap between the demand of the population for assets and the provision of assets by the private sector. Whatever interest charges on the debt are not financed out of this growth in the debt can more than be met out of savings in unemployment insurance payments, and the increased tax revenues derived from the larger national product at rates no greater than at present. A 10 trillion debt with a full-employment economy will be far easier to deal with than a 5 trillion debt with an economy in the doldrums.

What if the Gap Is Not Filled?

If governments fail to fill the gap and meet the demand for assets by issuing an adequate volume of securities, the attempt by individuals to acquire assets by nonspending will cause a reduction in sales, temporary investment in excess inventories, cutbacks in orders, unemployment, and reduced national income and product. This may be partially offset by the bidding up of asset values, leading to a certain amount of additional spending out of capital gains, but the "saving" imbedded in these capital gains does not involve the creation of new capital or the employment of individuals in construction. The reduction in interest rates could in principle increase "deepening" types of investment in labor-saving technology, but after the initial stimulus, the effect on employment tends to be negative. Little "widening" investment is likely to take place regardless of reduced interest rates if the market for the product is not there. There is a serious danger that the bidding up of asset prices could create a bubble of unsustainable values that is likely to collapse disastrously, as occurred in 1929 after the budget surpluses of the preceding years. Sooner or later a reduction in production and national income will set in until the reduction in income reduces the demand for assets to conform to the supply.

Tangible Real Effects

Reducing the "deficit" may reduce the debt of the government, but it also reduces the supply of assets people want to acquire to take care of their security needs. Reducing the "deficit" does not improve the real heritage left for the future, rather it impairs that heritage by leaving a legacy of inexperienced workers, impaired infrastructure, and reduced investment in plants because of reduced demand for the products, to say nothing of the impact of unemployment on health, delinquency, crime, and broken homes.

The "deficit" is not even calculated on a businesslike basis. It makes no distinction between current account and capital account items. If GM, AT&T, and the nation's households had been compelled to "balance their budget" calculated in the way the federal budget is calculated, we would now have many fewer automobiles, telephones, and houses.

Individual Saving (Absent Strong Demand) Is Counterproductive

Urging individuals to save more is counterproductive. Individual saving does not mean that funds are created out of thin air to put into savings accounts or the capital market. For most individuals, savings is nonspending, which becomes the nonincome and reduced savings of the vendor. Funds are transferred from the bank account of the vendor to the account of the saver, there is no increase in total money in the bank, and no facilitation of investment, while reduced market demand will actually discourage investment. Savings are neither a prerequisite nor an inducement for investment. Rather, nonspending by reducing market demand lowers incentives to invest.

Profitable Investment and Saving

On the other hand, if a businessman can show good prospects for profitable investment, he can nearly always get credit and proceed with the investment, which will constitute an increase in someone's wealth, which is ipso facto savings. Supply does not create its own demand as soon as some of the income generated is saved, but investment does create its own savings, and more.

Inflation and Full Employment

Eventually, in all likelihood, we will have to find some way of dealing with the threat of an unacceptably high rate of inflation that does not involve the maintenance of what Marxists used to call "the reserve army of the unemployed." For the moment, however, that threat seems sufficiently remote that we could proceed with the first steps toward full employment and deal with that bridge when we come to it. There has been no dearth of plans for controlling inflation in ways that preserve the essence of free markets.

We Have the Resources but Refrain from Using Them

The administration is trying to bring the Titanic into harbor with a canoe paddle, while Congress is arguing over whether to use an oar or a paddle, and the Perots and budget balancers seem eager to lash the helm hard-a-starboard toward the iceberg. Some of the argument seems to be over which foot is the better one to shoot ourselves in. We have the resources, in terms of idle manpower and idle plants, to do so much, while the preachers of austerity, most of whom are in little danger of themselves suffering any serious consequences, keep telling us to tighten our belts and refrain from using the resources that lie idle all around us.

Alexander Hamilton, William Jennings Bryan

Alexander Hamilton once wrote "A national debt, if it be not excessive, would be for us a national treasure." William Jennings Bryan used to declaim, "You shall not crucify mankind upon a cross of gold." Today's cross is not made of gold, but is concocted of a web of obfuscatory financial rectitude from which human values have been expunged.

16

WILLIAM S. VICKREY

Fifteen Fatal Fallacies
of Financial Fundamentalism

A Disquisition on Demand Side Economics

Much of the conventional economic wisdom prevailing in financial circles, largely subscribed to as a basis for governmental policy, and widely accepted by the media and the public, is based on incomplete analysis, contrafactual assumptions, and false analogy. For instance, encouragement to saving is advocated without attention to the fact that for most people encouraging saving is equivalent to discouraging consumption and reducing market demand, and a purchase by a consumer or a government is also income to vendors and suppliers, and government debt is also an asset. Equally fallacious are implications that what is possible or desirable for individuals one at a time will be equally possible or desirable for all who might wish to do so or for the economy as a whole.

And often analysis seems to be based on the assumption that future economic output is almost entirely determined by inexorable economic forces independent of government policy so that devoting more resources to one use inevitably detracts from availability for another. This might be justifiable in an economy at chock-full employment, or it might be validated in a sense by postulating that the Federal Reserve Board will pursue and succeed in a policy of holding unemployment strictly to a fixed "non-accelerating inflation" or "natural" rate. But under current conditions such success is neither likely nor desirable.

Some of the fallacies that result from such modes of thought are as follows. Taken together their acceptance is leading to policies that at best are keeping us in the economic doldrums with overall unemployment rates stuck in the 5 to 6 percent range. This is bad enough merely in terms of the loss of

---

The author last worked on this chapter in October 1996. It is being published posthumously and reflects the incomplete nature of the original manuscript.

10 to 15 percent of our potential production, even if shared equitably, but when it translates into unemployment of 10, 20, and 40 percent among disadvantaged groups, the further damages in terms of poverty, family breakup, school truancy and dropout, illegitimacy, drug use, and crime become serious indeed. And should the implied policies be fully carried out in terms of a "balanced budget," we could well be in for a serious depression.

Fallacy 1

Deficits are considered to represent sinful profligate spending at the expense of future generations who will be left with a smaller endowment of invested capital. This fallacy seems to stem from a false analogy to borrowing by individuals.

Current reality is almost the exact opposite. Deficits add to the net disposable income of individuals, to the extent that government disbursements that constitute income to recipients exceed that abstracted from disposable income in taxes, fees, and other charges. This added purchasing power, when spent, provides markets for private production, inducing producers to invest in additional plant capacity, which will form part of the real heritage left to the future. This is in addition to whatever public investment takes place in infrastructure, education, research, and the like. Larger deficits, sufficient to recycle savings out of a growing gross domestic product (GDP) in excess of what can be recycled by profit-seeking private investment, are not an economic sin but an economic necessity. Deficits in excess of a gap growing as a result of the maximum feasible growth in real output might indeed cause problems, but we are nowhere near that level.

Even the analogy itself is faulty. If General Motors, AT&T, and individual households had been required to balance their budgets in the manner being applied to the federal government, there would be no corporate bonds, no mortgages, no bank loans, and many fewer automobiles, telephones, and houses.

Fallacy 2

Urging or providing incentives for individuals to try to save more is said to stimulate investment and economic growth. This seems to derive from an assumption of an unchanged aggregate output so that what is not used for consumption will necessarily and automatically be devoted to capital formation.

Again, actually the exact reverse is true. In a money economy, for most individuals, a decision to try to save more means a decision to spend less; less spending by a saver means less income and less saving for the vendors and producers, and aggregate saving is not increased, but diminished as vendors in turn reduce their purchases, national income is reduced, and with it national saving. A given individual may indeed succeed in increasing his own saving, but only at the expense of reducing the income and saving of others by even more.

Where the saving consists of reduced spending on nonstorable services, such as a haircut, the effect on the vendor's income and saving is immediate and obvious. Where a storable commodity is involved, there may be an immediate temporary investment in inventory, but this will soon disappear as the vendor cuts back on orders from his suppliers to return the inventory to a normal level, eventually leading to a cutback of production, employment, and income.

Saving does not create "loanable funds" out of thin air. There is no presumption that the additional bank balance of the saver will increase the ability of his bank to extend credit by more than the credit-supplying ability of the vendor's bank will be reduced. If anything, the vendor is more likely to be active in equities markets, or to use credit enhanced by the sale to invest in his business, than a saver responding to inducements such as IRAs, exemption or deferral of taxes on pension fund accruals, and the like, so that the net effect of the saving inducement is to reduce the overall extension of bank loans. Attempted saving, with corresponding reduction in spending, does nothing to enhance the willingness of banks and other lenders to finance adequately promising investment projects. With unemployed resources available, saving is neither a prerequisite nor a stimulus to, but a consequence of, capital formation, as the income generated by capital formation provides a source of additional savings.

Fallacy 3

Government borrowing is supposed to "crowd out" private investment.

The current reality is that, on the contrary, the expenditure of the borrowed funds (unlike the expenditure of tax revenues) will generate added disposable income, enhance the demand for the products of private industry, and make private investment more profitable. As long as there are plenty of idle resources lying around, and monetary authorities behave sensibly (instead of trying to counter the supposedly inflationary effect of the deficit), those with a prospect for profitable investment can be enabled to obtain financing. Under these circumstances, each additional dollar of deficit will in the medium-long run induce two or more additional dollars of private investment. The capital created is an increment to someone's wealth and ipso facto someone's saving. "Supply creates its own demand" fails as soon as some of the income generated by the supply is saved, but investment does create its own saving, and more. Any crowding out that may occur is the result, not of underlying economic reality, but of inappropriate restrictive reactions on the part of a monetary authority in response to the deficit.

Fallacy 4

Inflation is called the "cruelest tax." The perception seems to be that if only prices would stop rising, one's income would go further, disregarding the consequences for income.

Current reality: The tax element in anticipated inflation in terms of gain to the government and loss to the holders of currency and government securities is limited to the reduction in the value in real terms of non-interest-bearing currency (equivalent to the increase in the interest rate saving on the no-interest loan, as compared to what it would have been with no inflation), plus the gain from the increment of inflation over what was anticipated at the time the interest rate on the outstanding debt was established. On the other hand, a reduction in the rate of inflation below that previously anticipated would result in a windfall subsidy to holders of long-term government debt and a corresponding increase in the real impact of the debt on the fisc.

In previous regimes where regulations forbade the crediting of interest on demand deposits, the seigniorage profit on these balances, reflecting the loss to depositors in purchasing power, that would be enhanced by inflation would accrue to banks, with competition inducing some pass-through to customers in terms of uncharged-for services. In an economy where most transactions are in terms of credit card and bank accounts with respect to which interest may be charged or credited, the burden will be trivial for most individuals, limited to loss of interest on currency outstanding. Most of the gain to the government will be derived from those using large quantities of currency for tax evasion or the carrying on of illicit activity, plus burdens on those few who keep cash under the mattress or in cookie jars.

The main difficulty with inflation, indeed, is not with the effects of inflation itself, but with the unemployment produced by inappropriate attempts to control the inflation. Actually, unanticipated acceleration of inflation can reduce the real deficit relative to the nominal deficit by reducing the real value of the outstanding long-term debt. If a policy of limiting the nominal deficit is persisted in, this is likely to result in continued excessive unemployment due to reduction in effective demand. The answer is not to decrease the nominal deficit to check inflation by increased unemployment, but rather to increase the nominal deficit to maintain the real deficit, controlling inflation, if necessary, by direct means that do not involve increased unemployment.

Fallacy 5

"A chronic trend toward inflation is a reflection of living beyond our means." Alfred Kahn, quoted in *Cornell*, summer 1993 issue.

Reality: The only time we could be said to have been really living beyond our means was in wartime when capital was being destroyed and undermaintained. We have not lived even up to our means in peacetime since 1926, when it is now estimated that unemployment according to today's definition went down to around 1.5 percent. This level has not been approached since, except at the height of World War II.

Inflation occurs when sellers raise prices; they can do this profitably when the forces of competition are weakened by the differentiation of products, real and factitious, misleading advertising, obfuscating sales gimmicks and package deals, mergers and takeovers, and the increasing importance of ancillary services, trade secrets, patents, copyrights, economies of scale, overheads, and start-up costs. Inflation can and does occur in the midst of underutilized resources, and need not occur even if we were to consume our capital by failure to maintain and replace it, consuming more than we produce.

Fallacy 6

It is thought necessary to keep unemployment at a "non-accelerating inflation" level (NAIRU) in the range of 4 to 6 percent if inflation is to be kept from increasing unacceptably.

Currently the unemployment rate as officially measured has fallen to 5.1 percent, while the Congressional Budget Office (CBO) has put the NAIRU for 1964 at 6 percent, having ranged between 5.5 and 6.3 since 1958. Recent CBO projections were for unemployment to remain steady at 6 percent through the year 2005, with inflation in the urban consumer price index fairly steady at about 3 percent (*Economic and Budget Outlook*, May 1996, xv, xvi, 2, 3).

This may be a fairly optimistic forecast of the results to be expected from current tendencies, but as a goal it is simply intolerable. While even 5 percent unemployment might be barely acceptable if it meant a compulsory extra two weeks of unpaid furlough annually for everyone, it is totally unacceptable when it means 10 percent, 20 percent, and 40 percent unemployment among disadvantaged groups, with serious consequences for poverty, homelessness, family breakups, drug addiction, and crime. The malaise that pervades our cities may be attributable in no small measure to the fact that for the first time in our history, an entire generation and more has grown up without experiencing reasonably full employment, even briefly. In contrast, while most other industrialized countries are currently experiencing higher rates of unemployment than the United States, they have nearly all had relatively recent periods of close to full employment. Unemployment insurance and other welfare programs have also been much more generous so that the sociological impacts have been much less demoralizing.

The underlying assumption that there is an exogenous NAIRU imposing an unavoidable constraint on macroeconomic possibilities is open to serious question on both historical and analytical grounds. Historically, the United States enjoyed an unemployment rate of 1.8 percent for 1926 as a whole, with the price level falling, if anything. West Germany enjoyed an unemployment rate of around 0.6 percent over the several years around 1960, and most developed countries have enjoyed episodes of unemployment under 2 percent without serious inflation. Thus a NAIRU, if it exists at all, must be regarded as highly variable over time and place. It is not clear that estimates of the NAIRU have not been contaminated by failure to allow for a possible impact of inflation on employment as well as the impact of unemployment on inflation. A Marxist interpretation of the insistence on a NAIRU might be as a stalking horse to enlist the fear of inflation to justify the maintenance of a "reserve army of the unemployed," allegedly to keep wages from initiating a "wage-price spiral." One never hears of a "rent-price spiral," or an "interest-price spiral," though these costs are also to be considered in the setting of prices. Indeed, when the FRB raises interest rates in an attempt to ward off inflation, the increase in interest costs to merchants may well trigger a small price increase.

Analytically, it would be more rational to expect that there could be a maximum non-accelerating inflation rate of reduction of unemployment (NAIRU), such that if an attempt were made to proceed more rapidly by a greater recycling of excess savings into purchasing power through government deficits, prices would start to rise more rapidly than had been generally anticipated. This would occur as a result of a failure of supply to keep up with the increased demand, giving rise to shortages and the dissipation of part of the increased demand into more rapidly rising prices. This NAIRU may be determined by limits to the rates at which labor can be hired and put to work to meet anticipated increases in demand, and perhaps lags in the realization that demand will be increased, and even new productive facilities created, installed, and brought up to speed. The ultimate technological constraint to putting unemployed to work more rapidly in the private sector may reside in a limited capacity in the capital goods industries such as construction, cement, and machine tools.

In any case, much will depend on the degree of confidence that can be engendered in the proposed increase in demand. It might be wise to start slowly, with a reduction of unemployment by, say, 0.5 percent the first year, and increasing to, say, 1 percent per year as confidence is gained. Possibly the growth rate should subsequently be reduced somewhat as full employment is approached, allowing for the increasing difficulty of matching workers to vacancies. It is mainly at the later stages of the approach to full employment that training and improving the organization of the labor market may become needed. In the face of a policy of maintaining a fixed NAIRU, "workfare" efforts to retrain and assist welfare clients amount to assistance in the playing of a cruel game of musical chairs.

Such a NAIRU is likely to prove somewhat volatile and difficult to predict, and in any case it might prove desirable to push to full employment somewhat faster than would be permitted by an unaltered NAIRU. This would call for the introduction of some new means of inflation control that does not require unemployment for it to be effective. Indeed, if we are to control three major macroeconomic dimensions of the economy, namely the inflation rate, the unemployment rate, and the growth rate, a third control is needed that will be reasonably noncollinear in its effects to those of a fiscal policy operating through disposable-income generation on the one hand, and monetary policy operating through interest rates on the other.

What may be needed is a method of directly controlling inflation that does not interfere with free-market adjustments in relative prices or rely on unemployment to keep inflation in check. Without such a control, unanticipated changes in the rate of inflation, either up or down, will continue to plague the economy and make planning for investment difficult. Trying to control an economy in three major macroeconomic dimensions with only two instruments is like trying to fly an airplane with elevator and rudder but no ailerons. In calm weather and with sufficient dihedral, one can manage if turns are made very gingerly, but trying to land in a crosswind is likely to produce a crash.

One possible third control measure would be a system of marketable rights to value added, (or "gross markups") issued to firms enjoying limited liability, proportioned to the prime factors employed, such as labor and capital, with an aggregate face value corresponding to the overall market value of the output at a programmed overall price level. Firms encountering a specially favorable market could realize a higher than normal level of markups only by purchasing rights from firms less favorably situated. The market value of the rights would vary automatically so as to apply the correct downward pressure on markups to produce the desired overall price level. A suitable penalty tax would be levied on any firm found to have had value added in excess of the warrants held.

In any case, it is important to keep in mind that divergences in the rate of inflation either up or down, from what was previously expected, produce merely an arbitrary redistribution of a given total product, equivalent at worst to legitimized embezzlement, unless indeed these unpredictable variations are so extreme and rapid as to destroy the usefulness of currency as a means of exchange. Unemployment, on the other hand, reduces the total product to be distributed. It is at best equivalent to vandalism, and when it contributes to crime, it becomes the equivalent of homicidal arson. In the United States the widespread availability of automatic teller machines in supermarkets and elsewhere would make the "shoe-leather cost" of a high but predictable inflation rate quite negligible.

Fallacy 7

Many profess a faith that if only governments would stop meddling and balance their budgets, free capital markets would in their own good time bring about prosperity, possibly with the aid of "sound" monetary policy. It is assumed that there is a market mechanism by which interest rates adjust promptly and automatically to equate planned saving and investment in a manner analogous to the market by which the price of potatoes balances supply and demand. In reality no such market mechanism exists. If a prosperous equilibrium is to be achieved, it will require deliberate intervention on the part of monetary authorities.

In the heyday of the industrial revolution, it would probably have been possible for monetary authorities to act to adjust interest rates to equate aggregate planned saving and aggregate planned investment at levels of GDP growing in such a fashion as to produce and maintain full employment. Generally, however, monetary authorities failed to recognize the need for such action and instead pursued such goals as the maintenance of the gold standard, or the value of their currency in terms of foreign exchange, or the value of financial assets in the capital markets. The result was usually that adjustments to shocks took place slowly and painfully via unemployment and the business cycle.

Current reality: The time is long gone, however, when even the lowest interest rates manageable by capital markets can stimulate enough profit-motivated net capital formation to absorb and recycle into income over any extended period the savings that individuals will wish to put aside out of a prosperity level of disposable personal income. Trends in technology, demand patterns, and demographics have created a gap between the amounts for which the private sector can find profitable investment in productive facilities and the increasingly large amounts individuals will attempt to accumulate for retirement and other purposes. This gap has become far too large for monetary or capital market adjustments to close.

On the one hand, the prevalence of capital saving innovation—found in extreme form in the telecommunications and electronics industries—high rates of obsolescence and depreciation, causing a sharp decline in the value of old capital that must be made good out of new gross investment before any net increase in the aggregate market value of capital can be registered, together with shifts from heavy to light industry to services, have sharply limited the ability of the private sector to find profitable placement for new capital funds. Over the past fifty years the ratio of the market value of private capital to GDP has remained, in the United States, fairly constant in the neighborhood of twenty-five months.

On the other hand, aspirations for asset holdings to finance longer retirements at higher living standards have increased sharply. At the same time, the increased concentration of the distribution of income has increased the share of those with a high propensity to save for other purposes, such as the acquisition of chips with which to play high-stakes financial games, the building of industrial empires, the acquisition of managerial or political clout, the establishment of a dynasty, or the endowment of a philanthropy. This has further contributed to a rising trend in the demand of individuals for assets, relative to GDP.

The result has been that the gap between the private supply and the private demand for assets has come to constitute an increasing proportion of GDP. This gap has also been augmented by the foreign trade current account deficit, which corresponds to a diminution of the stock of domestic assets available to domestic investors. For an economy to be balanced at a given level of GDP requires the provision of additional assets in the form either of government debt or net foreign investment to fill this growing gap. The gap is now tentatively and roughly estimated for the United States to be equal to about thirteen months of GDP. There are indications that, for the foreseeable future, this ratio will tend to rise rather than fall. This is in addition to whatever role Social Security and Medicare entitlements have played in providing a minimal level of old-age security.

In the absence of change in the flow of net foreign investment, a government recycling of income through current deficits of somewhat more than the desired growth in nominal GDP will be needed to keep the economy in balance. Curtailing deficits will correspondingly stifle growth. A balanced budget, indeed, would tend to stop growth in nominal GDP altogether, and in the presence of inflation would lead to a downturn in real GDP and a corresponding increase in unemployment.

Depending in part on what may happen at the state and local levels, current programs for gradually reducing the federal deficit to zero over the next seven years would in effect put a cap on total government debt at about 9 trillion dollars, implying that GDP would, in the absence of changes in net foreign investment, converge on a level of about 8 to 9 trillion, aside from short-run cyclical fluctuations. This compares with a full-employment GDP after seven years at 3 percent inflation of about 13 trillion. The balanced budget GDP of about 65 percent of this would correspond to a reported level of unemployment of 15 percent or more, in addition to unreported under-employment. Thereafter, if the strictures of a balanced budget amendment were to be adhered to, unemployment would continue to increase. Before this could happen, however, some concession to reality would probably be accepted, though not until a great deal of needless suffering would have been endured.

Fallacy 8

If deficits continue, the debt service would eventually swamp the fisc.

Real prospect: While viewers with alarm are fond of horror-story projec-tions in which per capita debt would become intolerably burdensome, debt service would absorb the entire income tax revenue, or confidence is lost in the ability or willingness of the government to levy the required taxes so that bonds cannot be marketed on reasonable terms, reasonable scenarios protect a negligible or even favorable effect on the fisc. If full employment is main-tained so that the nominal GDP continues to grow at, say, 6 percent, consist-ing of about 3 percent inflation and 3 percent real growth, the equilibrating debt would have to grow at 6 percent or perhaps at a slightly higher rate. If the nominal interest rate were 8 percent, 6 percent of this would be financed out of the needed growth in the debt, leaving only 2 percent to be met out of the current budget. Income tax on the increased interest payments would offset much of this, and savings from reduced unemployment, insurance ben-efits, and welfare costs would more than cover the remainder, even aside from substantial increases in tax revenues from the more prosperous economy. Though much of these gains would accrue to state and local governments rather than to the federal government, this could be adjusted to through changes in intergovernmental grants. A 15-trillion-dollar debt will be far easier to deal with out of a full employment economy with greatly reduced needs for unemploy-ment benefits and welfare payments than a 5-trillion debt from an economy in the doldrums with its equipment in disrepair. There is simply no problem.

Fallacy 9

The negative effect of considering the overhanging burden of the increased debt would, it is claimed, cancel the stimulative effect of the deficit. This sweeping claim depends on a failure to analyze the situation in detail.

Analytical reality: This "Ricardian equivalence" thesis, while referred to by Ricardo, may not in the end have been subscribed to by him. In any case, its validity depends crucially on the system of taxation expected to be used to finance the debt service.

At one extreme, in a Georgist economy making exclusive use of a "single tax" on land values, and where land values are expected to evolve proportionally over time, any debt becomes in effect a collective mortgage on the land parcels. Any increase in government debt to offset current tax reduction depresses the market value of land by an equal amount, aggregate wealth of individuals is unaffected, Ricardian equivalence is complete, and pure fiscal policy is impotent. A larger debt may still be desirable in terms of taking advantage of possibly lower interest rates available on government debt than on individual mortgages, and in effectively endowing property with a built-in assumable mortgage that facilitates the financing of transfers. And there may still be a possibility for stimulating the economy by tax-financed expenditures that redistribute income toward those with a higher propensity to spend.

In another scenario, if the main tax is one on all real estate, such as is common in American local finance, the effect is drastically different. In this case, any investor erecting a building thereby assumes, for the time being at least, a share in the government debt, subject to some of this burden possibly being eventually taken over by further construction. Not only does this discourage construction, but if the debt overhang gets too great, this expectation of others taking up part of the burden may vanish rather suddenly and all construction come to a grinding halt. Debt becomes a strong inhibitor of growth. While this result may resemble that claimed by the "crowding out" theory, the mechanism is not one of displacement but of disincentive.

With a sales or value-added tax as the mainstay, a deficit involving a reduction in tax rates today will have no depressing effect on capital values and will have a fully stimulating effect, through the increase in the aggregate supply of assets, possibly reinforced by anticipatory spending motivated by expectations that taxes may have to be higher at a later date to finance the debt service. There will be no Ricardian equivalence effect. If anything, anticipation of higher future taxes will encourage current spending, adding to the stimulus of the increased supply of securities.

The U.S. federal tax system is dominated by the income tax, for which the effect will be somewhat intermediate between taxes on savings and taxes on expenditure. In practice, few individuals will have any clear idea of the taxes likely to be imposed in the future as a result of the existence of a larger debt, and it can be safely said that no reasoned Ricardian equivalence phenomenon will occur, though there may be some generalized malaise among the viewers with alarm, involving a kind of partially self-fulfilling prophecy.

Fallacy 10

The value of the national currency in terms of foreign exchange (or gold) is held to be a measure of economic health, and steps to maintain that value are thought to contribute to this health. In some quarters, a kind of jingoistic pride is taken in the value of one's currency, or satisfaction may be derived from the greater purchasing power of the domestic currency in terms of foreign travel.

Reality: Freely floating exchange rates are the means whereby adaptations are made to disparate price level trends in different countries and trade imbalances are brought into line with capital flows appropriate to increasing the overall productivity of capital. Fixed exchange rates or rates confined to a narrow band can be maintained only by coordinated fiscal policies among the countries involved, by imposing efficiency-impairing tariffs or other restraints on trade, or by imposing costly disciplines involving needlessly high rates of unemployment, as is implied by the Maastricht agreements. Attempts to restrain foreign exchange rates by financial manipulation in the face of a basic disequilibrium usually break down, eventually, with large losses to the agencies making the attempt and a corresponding gain to agile speculators. Even short of breakdown, much of the volatility of foreign exchange rates can be traced to speculation over possibilities of massive central bank intervention.

Restraints on exchange rates, such as are involved in the Maastricht agreements, would make it virtually impossible for a small open economy, such as Denmark, to pursue an effective full-employment policy on its own. Much of the increase in purchasing power generated by a stimulative fiscal policy would be spent on imports, spreading the stimulating effect over the rest of the monetary union so that Denmark's borrowing capacity would be exhausted long before full employment could be achieved. With flexible exchange rates, the increased demand for imports would cause a rise in the price of foreign currency, checking the import increase and stimulating exports so that most of the effects of an expansionary policy would be kept at home. The danger of wild speculative gyrations under freely floating conditions would be greatly diminished under a well-established full-employment policy, especially if combined with a third dimension of direct control over the overall domestic price level.

Similarly, the main reason states and localities cannot pursue an independent full-employment policy is that they lack an independent currency, and are constrained to have a fixed exchange rate with the rest of the country.

Fallacy 11

It is claimed that exemption of capital gains from income tax will promote investment and growth.

Reality: Any attempt to define a special category of income entitled to differential treatment is an invitation to the sorcerer's apprentices in Congress and in the offices of the Internal Revenue Service to start casting spells that are bound to produce surprising consequences. Attempting to draw up administrable rules defining economically meaningful lines between interest credited to accounts but not drawn on, zero coupon bonds, stock appreciation from undistributed profits, inflationary gains, profits from insider trading, gains from speculation in land, gambles on derivatives, profits or losses on speculative ventures, and so on is a Sisyphean task. Taxpayers' techies can then get busy ferreting out shortcuts through the resulting labyrinth, to the detriment of the revenue and also of economic efficiency. Ten special provisions of the code can be combined with one another in over a thousand ways to produce results far beyond the capacity of a congressional committee and its staff to anticipate.

Concessions to gains must entail corresponding limitations on the deductibility of losses, lest there be intolerably large opportunities for arbitrage against the revenue. In an attempt to counter the skills of the taxpayers' techies, the rules are likely to be more severe on the deductibility of losses than liberal with respect to gains, so as to produce a number of situations where the Treasury is playing "heads I win, tails you lose" with the taxpayer. Even with effectively parallel rules, reduced effective deductibility of losses may well be more of a disincentive to speculative investment than the attractiveness of low taxes on gains in the event of success.

Most economically desirable investments take considerable time for the anticipated results to be reflected in the capital markets, and the promise of a tax concession to be effective in a remote future and subject to possible alteration by future legislatures is likely to be of little weight in the calculation of the investor. In any case, the personal income tax on gains is levied after or below the market, and has its primary effect on the disposable income of the investor and relatively little effect on the capital market from which the funds for capital formation are derived.

In practice, many capital gains arise from transactions of negligible or dubious social merit. Gains derived from speculation in land add nothing to the supply of land, and much of the gains from securities trading based on advance information, whether or not characterizable as insider trading, do no more to enhance productivity or investment than winnings from betting on basketball games. Attempts to exclude gains from speculation by limiting concessions to assets held for longer periods not only introduce new complexities in determining the holding period in cases of rollovers, reinvested dividends, and other trades, but aggravate the lock-in effect as realization is deferred to obtain the concession, an effect especially severe in the case of the total exemption from income taxation of gains on property transferred by gift or bequest.

Any increase in disposable income resulting from lower capital gains taxation is likely to accrue to individuals with a high propensity to save. If the proposal is advanced on a revenue-neutral basis, the replacement revenues are likely to have a greater impact on consumption demand, so that the net overall effect of making concessions to capital gains may be to reduce demand, sales, and investment in productive facilities. The main driving force behind the proposals may well be a pretext for providing windfalls to persons who can contribute to campaign funds as well as added commissions for brokers.

Some have argued for reductions in capital gains rates rather than full exemption, pointing to surges in revenue from the "fire sale" spate of realizations to take advantage of the new and possibly short-lived tax bargains. If this is done on a current-revenue-neutral basis, there may be some onetime stimulus to the economy and to investment, resulting from what would be an increase in the effective deficit as viewed from a longer-term perspective, but this will be small, temporary, and counterproductive in the long run.

A far more effective measure would be to reduce or eliminate the corporate income tax, which is in effect a tax above the market, constituting an additional hurdle that prospective equity-financed investments must face, as contrasted to the below- or after-market impact of capital gain concessions. In addition to this double-whammy impact on the economy whereby the tax both abstracts from disposable income and also discourages investment, the tax has numerous defects in distorting investment allocation, encouraging thin equity financing with consequent increased incidence of bankruptcies, and complicating tax laws. Unfortunately, any such elimination is likely to be opposed not only by those making a living from the complexities but by many who variously believe firmly that its burden falls on someone other than themselves. Actually, in most plausible scenarios, the chief burden will be on wage earners. If considered as a substitute for other taxes on a revenue-neutral basis, it would increase current unemployment. If current employment is assumed to be maintained by an appropriate fiscal policy, future labor productivity and wages will be depressed by labor having less capital to work with.

One excuse sometimes offered for the imposition of a corporation income tax is that undistributed profits do not bear their fair share of the individual income tax. Rather than retaining a tax on all corporate income, this consideration would call for a countervailing tax of, say, 2 percent per year on the accumulated undistributed profits, as a rough equivalent to an interest charge on the resulting deferral of the individual income tax on shareholders. This would be rough at best, since it allows neither for variations in the marginal rates payable by individual shareholders, nor for possible realization of the undistributed profits through sale of shares, but it would be far better than the inept and draconic taxes on undistributed profits enacted briefly during the 1930s.

A more thoroughgoing removal of the distorting effect of taxes on real investment could be accomplished by assessing the individual income tax on a cumulative basis, whereby a gross tax on the accumulated income to date (including interest credited with respect to past taxes paid on this income) is calculated by reference to tables that would take the period covered into account. The accumulated value, with interest, of taxes previously paid on this income is then credited against this gross tax. Provided that all income is eventually brought to account, the ultimate tax burden will be independent of the timing of realization of income; about two-thirds of the internal revenue code and regulations would become superfluous. The playing field would be effectively leveled. Equitable treatment would be afforded both to those realizing large gains in a single year and to those having to retire after a brief career of high earnings, a group not adequately dealt with under most other averaging schemes. Bias against investments yielding fluctuating or risky returns would be largely eliminated. Decisions as to when to sell assets to realize gains or losses or when to distribute dividends could be made purely on the basis of appraisal of market conditions without having to consider tax consequences. Hordes of tax techies could turn their talents to more productive activities.

Taxpayer compliance would be greatly simplified. The actual computation of the cumulative tax and tax payable requires only six additional entries on the return, three of which are items simply copied from a preceding return. As an introductory measure, cumulative assessment could be limited to those subject to rates above the initial bracket.

Fallacy 12

Debt would, it is held, eventually reach levels that cause lenders to balk, with taxpayers threatening rebellion and default.

Relevant reality: This fear arises in part from observing crises in which capital-poor countries have had difficulty in meeting obligations denominated in a foreign currency, incurred in many cases to finance imports and ultimately requiring servicing and repayment in terms of exports, the crisis often arising because of a collapse in the market for the exports. In the case at hand, the debt is intended to supply a domestic demand for assets denominated in the domestic currency, and in the absence of a norm such as a gold clause, there can be no question of the ability of the government to make payments when due, albeit possibly in a currency devalued by inflation. Nor can there be any question of balking by domestic lenders as long as the debt is limited to that needed to fill a gap created by an excess of private asset demand over private asset supply.

It is not intended that the domestic government debt should be held in any large quantity by foreigners. But should foreigners wish to liquidate holdings of this debt or any other domestic assets, they can only do so as a whole by generating an export surplus, easing the domestic unemployment problem, releasing assets to supply the domestic demand, and making it possible to get along with smaller deficits and a less rapidly growing government debt. The same thing happens if domestic investors turn to investing in foreign assets, thereby reducing their drain on the domestic asset supply.

In a panicky market, it might happen that the market price of assets would fall sufficiently rapidly so that the total market value of the assets available to meet the domestic demand would fall. In such a case, a temporary increase in government deficits rather than a decrease would be in order. Arranging this on short notice may be difficult, and the danger of overreacting or poor timing is real. Something more than mere pious declarations that the economy is fundamentally sound, however, is called for. Nevertheless, one cannot entirely rule out the possibility of this becoming a panic-generating self-fulfilling prophecy derived from concentrating attention on the financial symbols rather than on the underlying human reality. In Roosevelt's terms, the main thing to fear is fear itself.

Fallacy 13

Authorizing income-generating deficits results in larger and possibly more extravagant, wasteful, and oppressive government expenditures.

Reality: The two issues are quite independent, in spite of the fact that many anarcho-libertarians appear to have been using the ideology of budget-balancing as a way to put a straitjacket on government activity. A government could run a deficit with no activity at all other than borrowing money by issuing bonds, paying out the proceeds in old-age pensions, and levying taxes sufficient to cover any net debt service. The issue of what activities are worthwhile for the government to carry on is a totally different issue from what the government contribution to the flow of disposable income needs to be to balance the economy at full employment.

Fallacy 14

Government debt is thought of as a burden handed on from one generation to its children and grandchildren.

Reality: Quite the contrary, in generational terms (as distinct from time slices), the debt is the means whereby the present working cohorts are enabled to earn more by fuller employment and invest in the increased supply of assets, of which the debt is a part, so as to provide for their own old age. In this way the children and grandchildren are relieved of the burden of providing for the retirement of the preceding generations, whether on a personal basis or through government programs.

This fallacy is another example of zero-sum thinking that ignores the possibility of increased employment and expanded output. While it is still true that the goods consumed by retirees will have to be produced by the contemporary working population, the increased government debt will enable more of these goods to be exchanged for assets rather than transferred through the tax-benefit mechanism.

In some ways, the result of such deficit-financing is analogous to the extension of a Social Security retirement scheme to provide added benefits to middle and upper incomes beyond the existing caps to the wages and earnings subject to Social Security contributions and the corresponding benefits. There are important differences, however. The Social Security System is indeed often criticized as being in effect a kind of Ponzi scheme in which benefits to earlier cohorts are financed by taxes on later cohorts. The scheme is kept from collapsing by virtue of its being compulsory, so that there will always be succeeding cohorts to foot the bill, though possibly by higher or lower tax rates, unlike private schemes that tend to collapse when it is discovered that the emperor has no clothes and new contributors shy away.

This Ponzi element was, however, necessary to get the program off the ground during the depression. Had an attempt been made to establish the system on [. . .] fortunately any such elimination is likely to be opposed not only by those making a living from the complexities but by many who variously believe firmly that its burden falls on someone other than themselves. Actually, in most plausible scenarios, the chief burden will be on wage earners. If considered as a substitute for other taxes on a revenue-neutral basis, it would increase current unemployment. If current unemployment is assumed to be maintained by an appropriate fisliest [. . .], retirees were given pension payments far beyond what would have been financed by their contributions, and only a relatively small reserve fund was accumulated to allow for adventitious differences between receipts and outlays. Even so, the relatively brief lag between the onset of Social Security contributions out of payrolls and the beginning of substantial payments to retirees constituted a withdrawal from purchasing power, aggravated by the exclusion of the revenue in computing the formal deficit, adding to pressure to reduce governments' net addition to purchasing power, and to overall pessimism stemming from the perception of deficits as symptoms of economic ill-health. These impacts substantially aggravated the drop in industrial production in the fall of 1937, by far the sharpest ever recorded.

Currently the amount by which the present value of expected future payments to current participants exceeds that of expected future contributions by them is a real liability of the government that is probably at least as inescapable as that represented by the formal debt. While the schedules of payments are subject to alteration by an act of Congress, whether by changing the age of retirement, or subjecting more of the payments to income tax, or otherwise, political pressures are likely to require at least some degree of indexation for inflation, so that on balance the real burden is likely to prove as unavoidable a real "entitlement" obligation as that of the formal debt, which is to a much greater extent subject to possible erosion through accelerated inflation. The amounts are not small; one estimate has put the capital value of government entitlements, including military and civil service pensions, at over three years of GDP, though such estimates are necessarily subject to a wide range of uncertainty.

The situation could be formally regularized by a bookkeeping entry that would add to the assets of the Social Security System and to the explicit liabilities of the government. However, this would be a purely formal move that should in principle be of negligible practical significance, though a Congress obsessed with reducing the formal deficit might seize upon this recognition of a liability as an excuse for further inappropriate budgetary stringency. In any case, the macroeconomic impact is measured not by the magnitude of the government liability, however calculated, but by the value placed on these entitlements by the potential beneficiaries in making decisions as to saving and consumption.

Many have even complained that the investment of the small actual Social Security reserves in special government securities amounts to the diversion of Social Security contributions to government expenditure. But the situation would be no different if the Social Security Administration were to invest in private securities instead, with the private insurance industry switching its reserve funds from private to government securities. The only real impact of moving the Social Security System "off budget" would lie in the reaction of Congress to the enlargement of the nominal deficit by the disregarding of the growth in the Social Security reserve. Should the Congress react to offset this increase by budget tightening, the result would be an increase in unemployment produced as a result of a national rescuing of the Social Security reserve from being "squandered" in government expenditure.

Setting aside, as irremediable bygones, the subsidizing of the earlier co-horts, for those currently paying payroll taxes the relevant reality (as distinct from arbitrary accounting conventions) is that the relation between the taxes paid by or on behalf of any individual and the present expected value of future benefits is extremely loose. Overall, if one were to apply the rules currently on the books to a steady demographic state of a constant popula-tion with a constant expectation of life, with the relatively small Social Secu-rity reserve fund kept at a constant level, present value of benefits payable to a given cohort would fall short of the net present value of the taxes paid during its working life by the difference between the interest that would have been earned by a full actuarial reserve and the smaller amount of inter-est paid on the recorded reserve. From this viewpoint, looking only at the future, there would thus be a net contribution from the Social Security Sys-tem to the general purpose fisc, much larger, actually, than the amount in-volved in the charge that the addition to the small nominal reserve is being improperly appropriated to current government expenditures.

In terms of actual demographic changes, a growing population and a length-ening expectation of life both mean that if the reserve fund is held constant, current cohorts still gain at the expense of later cohorts. In practice this is somewhat modified by differentials between total current tax revenues and total current benefit payments, reflected in fluctuations in the reserve fund.

Within each cohort, the often arbitrary and even capricious operation of the complex formulas by which benefits are determined mean that the rela-tion between taxes paid at any given time by a given individual and the consequent increase in expected eventual benefits varies widely and often capriciously. At one extreme, many of those who accumulate less than forty quarters of covered employment over their working life will not become eligible for any benefits; their contributions are effectively a tax on their wages, whether nominally paid by themselves or their employer. Examples are women who start work at eighteen but marry and leave the labor force at twenty-five, or "empty nesters" who enter the labor force for the first time at age fifty-four or later. For such persons, squeezing in a fortieth quarter of coverage could be extremely lucrative.

Even for most of those who do become eligible, there is an arbitrary ex-clusion from the formula of the five years of lowest indexed annual covered earnings, so that for these years the contributions are again a pure tax. This is particularly unfortunate in that these lowest years are in most cases the earli-est years of employment, at ages for which unemployment rates are highest and the effects of the tax most unfortunate.

Benefits are not paid on the basis of taxes paid but on the basis of covered wages, which means that those employed during years in which tax rates were low obtain benefits as though they had paid taxes at the later higher rates. On the other hand, in computing, benefits wages are indexed, not by a price index or by a compound interest factor, but by a nationwide average. The result is that over a period of constant tax rates, taxes on earlier wages purchase fewer benefits in terms of present value than those on later wages.

Benefits are determined on a fairly steeply progressive basis, being roughly ninety percent of the first $5,000 of the individual's average indexed annual wages, 32 percent of wages between $5,000 and $30,000, 15 percent between $30,000 and $60,000, and zero above $60,000. The result is a fairly substantial transfer from high-wage earners to low-wage earners. Low-wage earners may actually receive, as a group, benefits exceeding in present value that of the payroll taxes paid on their earnings, while a relatively large part of the payroll taxes paid on higher wages would be effectively a tax rather than a premium.

Because of this low return in terms of benefits on taxes on wages in the $30,000–$60,000 bracket, the fact that no payroll taxes are levied on wages above this $60,000 cap produces a highly anomalous dip in the combined marginal effective tax rate on earnings as earnings rise above this cap. Not only is this inversion of progression inefficient in term of incentives, it even opens the door to an arrangement whereby an employer would agree with his employee to pay $20,000 and $100,000 in alternate years, instead of a constant $60,000. This would reduce the payroll taxes payable while producing only a relatively minor reduction in expected benefits. This might be partially offset by consequent increases in the individual's income tax unless some countervailing shifting of other income can be devised.

The impact of the Social Security System on the balance between the demand for and supply of assets and on employment is thus fairly complex. However, it does not depend so much on the intricate realities of the system as on the way it is perceived, both by its participants and by Congress. Many in Congress seem bemused by wildly irrelevant rhetoric concerning the supposed "diversion" of surplus Social Security revenues to government expenditure, and contentions over whether the system should be considered "off budget" or on. Most payroll taxpayers are only dimly aware of the relation of their "contributions" to eventual benefits. Most younger wage earners probably pay little attention to the prospect of benefits several decades in the future, and tend to treat their contribution as entirely a tax, though perhaps persisting under the delusion that the "employer's" share of the tax is actually borne by the employer.

Older low-wage workers are perhaps more likely to take future benefits into consideration in determining their attitude toward payroll taxes, expectations of benefits, and decisions on the level of expenditure. High-wage earners, on the other hand, may be more likely to regard payroll contributions as a tax, encouraged, in many cases, by propaganda showing how their contributions, if invested instead on an individual basis in private pensions or annuities, could yield substantially greater benefits, so that Social Security appears to be a bad bargain for them.

Another way of looking at it is to inquire what the equivalent is, in terms of individual wealth, of the interest of clients in the system. On the one hand, the level of future benefits is not guaranteed, but is subject to modification by Congress, such as by subjecting benefits to individual income tax, increasing the normal age of retirement in terms of which benefits are calculated, increasing the cap on taxable wages, or even changing the benefit formulas themselves. While there is no guaranteed minimum below which benefits cannot be reduced, the political reality seems to be that taxpayers can rely on a fairly substantial wealth-equivalence. There is even a fairly well established practice of indexing benefits by the consumer price index, so that Social Security wealth is likely to be less impaired by inflation than investment in long-term government securities.

Also, Social Security wealth is much less heavily concentrated among middle and upper classes than wealth in general, and thus tends to have a greater favorable influence on the level of consumption expenditure.

Fallacy 15

Unemployment is not due to lack of effective demand, reducible by demand-increasing deficits, but is either "structural," resulting from a mismatch between the skills of the unemployed and the requirements of jobs, or "regulatory," resulting from minimum wage laws, restrictions on the employment of classes of individuals in certain occupations, requirements for medical coverage, or burdensome dismissal constraints, or is "voluntary," in part the result of excessively generous and poorly designed social insurance and relief provisions.

Current situation: To anyone acquainted with labor market conditions, it is abundantly apparent that a large proportion of those currently officially registered as unemployed, as well as large numbers who are not, are ready and able to take most, if not all, of the kinds of jobs that would be opened up by an increase in market demand. In the absence of such an increase, at current levels of unemployment, attempts to move selected unemployed individuals or groups into jobs by training, instruction in job search techniques, threats of benefit withdrawal or denial, and the like merely move the selected individuals to the head of the queue without reducing the length of the queue. Merely because any one traveler can secure a seat on a flight by getting to the airport sufficiently early does not mean that, if everyone gets to the airport sufficiently early, 200 passengers can get on a flight with seats for 150.

Even if jobs are specifically created for selected clients—for example, by facilitating the opening of a new shop or business—there may be a temporary stimulus to the economy from whatever capital investment is involved, but ultimately in many cases this will merely draw purchasing power from other establishments, resulting in reduced sales, reduced capital value, and eventually reduced employment elsewhere. Only if some element of novelty tempts consumers to spend additional amounts, impinging on their planned savings, or if "workfare" involves producing a free public good or service enhancement that does not compete for purchasing power or replace other public employment, will there be any net reduction in unemployment. But while such public works programs can indeed convert unemployed labor into improved public amenities and facilities of various types, as long as they are financed on the basis of an unchanged deficit, any further impact on the economy as a whole will be limited to the difference between the appending rate of those deriving income from the program and the spending rate of those paying the taxes to finance it.

Aside from such a public works program, the result of attempts to push people into jobs is simply a vast game of musical chairs in which local agencies instruct their clients in the art of rapid sitting, with "workfare" curmudgeons threatening to confiscate the crutches of the unsuccessful, while Washington is busy removing the chairs by deficit slashing.

As for "voluntary" unemployment, much of this would disappear as demand and activity increases, and over-qualified workers move up out of low-skill jobs into the expanding demand for higher skills, leaving more openings for low-skilled unemployed to fill and removing the depressing effect of high unemployment levels on low-skill wages. Wages for low-skill but necessary jobs would tend to increase, raising them sufficiently above the safety-net level to mitigate the adverse incentives of the welfare state. Higher wages would raise the prices of low-skill products, increasing the measured "productivity" of such jobs and diminishing the stigma attached to them as "low-productivity" or "dead-end" jobs. Prices of high-skill products may fall to offset this, possibly as a result of technological advance or economies of scale, but if not, there may be a small one-shot increase in the cost of living. This would still be a small price to pay for the benefits of full employment. It should not be assumed that this is the beginning of an inflationary spiral.

To be sure, there are horror stories of individuals who quite rationally decline employment because of the combined impact of the resulting reductions in various means-tested welfare benefits, increases in taxes and Social Security contributions, and travel, child care, and other costs associated with employment. To a considerable extent, this is the result of designing a variety of welfare and income-dependent programs independently of each other without regard to interactions and combined effects. As each means-tested program is set up separately, the benefits tend to be phased out or capped in ways designed to keep down the direct costs attributed to the particular program or measure. These phaseouts and caps may seem quite reasonable when considered separately, but when several of them happen to overlap, the combined results create absurdly high effective marginal "tax" rates. Slower phaseouts are called for, even if that increases the budgeted cost of the programs.

In many cases there is no overall justification for any phaseout. In the case of the earned income credit, for example, eliminating the phaseout and recouping the revenue by increases in marginal rates on upper income brackets would result in a smoother pattern of effective marginal rates with smaller overall disincentive effects and a considerable simplification of tax forms and reduction in compliance costs. The existing law seems to have arisen because the earned income credit was enacted as a patch on the pre-existing law, subject to a taboo against raising nominal marginal rates, while the raising of effective marginal rates by the phaseout could get by. Political posturing and the arcane mechanics of the legislative process prevented a rational examination of the tax structure as a whole.

Ready availability of jobs at respectable wages would make it easier to deny benefits to those unduly finicky about the type of employment they will accept, and reduce the need for severance pay and other forms of featherbedding. Real full employment would also reduce the pressure for protectionism, reduce resistance to the abandonment of redundant military installations and other obsolete activities, and make job security generally less of an issue. Real full employment would also encourage employers to compete in arranging work schedules and workplace arrangements to accommodate those with family obligations or other constraints, and otherwise pay more attention to improvement of working conditions. There will be less need for minimum-wage laws and other government regulation of working conditions, and less difficulty in the enforcement of those that there are.

These fallacious notions, which seem to be widely held in various forms by those close to the seats of economic power, are leading to policies that are not only cruel but unnecessary and even self-defeating in terms of their professed objectives. In some quarters there seems even to be a move on toward "declaring prosperity" and taking steps to "prevent the economy from overheating" or bringing on a higher inflation rate. The Congressional Budget Office, indeed, echoing the prevailing mood in Washington, appears satisfied with projections that involve unemployment rates continuing at close to

6 percent indefinitely. To those with even a minimal concern with the plight of the unemployed and the homeless, such an attitude appears callous in the extreme.

We will not get out of the economic doldrums as long as we continue to be governed by fallacious notions that are based on false analogies, one-sided analysis, and an implicit, underlying counterfactual assumption of an inevitable level of unemployment. Worse, we may well be in a situation comparable to 1926 when, according to the orthodoxy of the day, the debt accumulated during World War I was something to be retired as rapidly as possible. Accordingly, purchasing power was taken from the income stream by taxes and used to retire the debt. The amounts paid out to retire bonds were not considered by the recipients as income to be spent, so that consumer demand grew insufficiently to maintain the level of employment, and unemployment increased considerably from 1926 to 1928 to 1929. Instead, the proceeds were used to bid up asset prices. For a time, this slowing of growth was moderated by the euphoria created by the corresponding accrual of capital gains and the resulting enhanced rate of spending. But even the easier financing afforded by the higher price/earnings ratios of stocks could not induce much capacity expansion beyond the ability of demand to provide profitable sales, and when it was realized that further increases in asset prices could not be justified by the slower increases in the demand for products, capital gains ceased to accrue and the system collapsed into the depression of the 1930s.

The parallel of today is that although we are not actually retiring debt, in relation to current conditions, deficit cutting is a comparable reduction in the net contribution of the government to disposable income. In its projections, the CBO appears to discount almost entirely the effect of a diminution of this recycling on the level of activity. On the contrary, the CBO assumes that if this recycling is further reduced by a budget-balancing program, the result will be a slight increase in the growth rate of GDP by 0.1 percent per year, rather than a decrease (*Economic and Budget Outlook*, May 1996, 1–3).

Apparently it was assumed that the reduction in the deficit will induce the Federal Reserve Board to lower interest rates, and that this will lead to an increase in investment activity. But it seems unlikely that there is anything the FRB would or could do that would overcome over any extended period the discouragement to investment inherent in the reduction of market demand resulting from the reduction in government recycling of income. There is, indeed, a tendency to overstate the long-run effect of interest rate changes on rates of investment as a result of observing the short-to-medium-run responses of investment flows to changes in interest rates. Once installed stocks of capital have reached a level corresponding to the lower interest rate, further investment will fall to near its former rate. This is similar to the flow in the millrace that, while increased for a time by lowering the top of the weir, will fall back to its former level as soon as the surface of the millpond has been lowered correspondingly. Action by the Federal Reserve Board may be able to postpone, but not overcome, the consequences of inadequate government recycling of savings into income.

If a budget-balancing program should actually be carried through, the above analysis indicates that sooner or later a crash comparable to that of 1929 would almost certainly result. To be sure, it would probably be less severe than the depression of the 1930s by reason of the many cushioning factors that have been introduced since, and enthusiasm for the quest of the Holy Grail of a balanced budget may wane in the face of a deepening recession, but the consequences of the aborted attempt would still be serious. To ensure against such a disaster and start on the road to real prosperity, it is necessary to relinquish our unreasoned ideological obsession with reducing government deficits, recognize that it is the economy and not the government budget that needs balancing in terms of the demand for and supply of assets, and proceed to recycle attempted savings into the income stream at an adequate rate, so that they will not simply vanish in reduced income, sales, output, and employment. There is too a free lunch out there, indeed a very substantial one. But it will require getting free from the dogmas of the apostles of austerity, most of whom would not share in the sacrifices they recommend for others. Failing this, we will all be skating on very thin ice.

About the Contributors

Heather Boushey is a postdoctoral research fellow at the New York City Housing Authority, where she is conducting research on welfare reform and low-wage labor markets.

David Colander is the Christian A. Johnson Distinguished Professor of Economics at Middlebury College. His extensive written works include *Principles of Economics, History of Economic Thought* (with Harry Landreth), *Why Aren't Economists as Important as Garbagemen?* And *A Market Anti-Inflation Plan* (with Abba Lerner). He has been president of the Eastern Economic Association and the History of Economic Thought Society and has served on the editorial boards of several economics publications. His latest work focuses on economic education and complexity, and the methodology appropriate to applied policy economics.

Paul Davidson holds the Holly Chair of Excellence in Political Economy at the University of Tennessee. He is the author, coauthor, or editor of eighteen books, including *Post Keynesian Macroeconomic Theory: A Foundation for Successful Economic Policies for the Twenty-first Century.* Professor Davidson has written over 250 professional articles.

Mathew Forstater is assistant professor of economics and director of the Center for Full Employment and Price Stability at the University of Missouri–Kansas City. His research on full-employment policy, the history of economic thought, and economic methodology has appeared in numerous books and journals, including *Journal of Post Keynesian Economics, Journal of Economic Issues, Review of Social Economy, Economie Appliquée, Advances in Austrian Economics,* and *Review of Political Economy.* Forstater received his Ph.D. from the New School for Social Research in 1996. He is a research associate with the Jerome Levy Economics Institute of Bard College.

James K. Galbraith is a professor at the Lyndon B. Johnson School of Public Affairs and in the Department of Government, the University of Texas at Austin, and senior scholar at the Jerome Levy Economics Institute. He is author of *Created Unequal: The Crisis in American Pay* (New York: Free Press, 1998).

Helen Lachs Ginsburg is professor of economics emerita at Brooklyn College of the City University of New York, a member of the Executive Committee of the National Jobs for All Coalition, and current chair of the Columbia University Seminar on Full Employment. She is coeditor of a special issue of *Economic and Industrial Democracy,* "The Challenge of Full Employment and the Global Economy" (1997); coauthor of *Jobs for All: A Plan for the Revitalization of America* (1994); and author of *Full Employment in the United States and Sweden* (1983).

Gertrude Schaffner Goldberg is professor of social policy, Adelphi University School of Social Work; chair of the National Jobs for All Coalition; and coauthor of *The Feminization of Poverty: Only in America?* (1990); *Jobs for All: A Plan for the Revitalization of America* (1994); *Washington's New Poor Law: Welfare "Reform" and the Roads Not Taken, 1935–1999* (2000); and *Diminishing Welfare: A Cross-National Study of Social Provision* (2000).

Professor Emeritus **C. Lowell Harriss** taught economics at Columbia University from 1938 to 1981. During this period, he also served in the United States Army and, for an extended time, as economic consultant to the Tax Foundation and as associate of the Lincoln Institute of Land Policy. As a visiting professor, he has taught at several other universities in the United States and abroad. After 1981, he was executive director of the Academy of Political Science.

Philip Harvey is associate professor of law at Rutgers School of Law, Camden, New Jersey. He is the author of *Securing the Right to Employment* and coauthor, with Theodore Marmor and Jerry Mashaw, of *America's Misunderstood Welfare State.*

Robert Heilbroner is the author of some twenty books—perhaps the best known is *The Worldly Philosophers,* just out in its seventh edition. He has taught for many years at the Graduate Faculty of the New School for Social Research.

John Langmore is director of the Division for Social Policy and Development in the Secretariat of the United Nations. He was previously economic advisor to the Australian Treasurer and member of the Australian House of Representatives. He is coauthor of *Work for All,* published in 1994.

Edward J. Nell, a former Rhodes scholar, is the Malcolm B. Smith Professor of Economics in the Graduate Faculty of the New School University, where he is the director of the Research Program on Transformational Growth and Full Employment. He is the author of *The General Theory of Transformational Growth* (1998) and the editor of *Transformational Growth and the Business Cycle* (1998).

Thomas I. Palley is assistant director of Public Policy at the AFL-CIO in Washington, D.C. He has written extensively on macroeconomic theory and policy. His latest book is *Plenty of Nothing: The Downsizing of the American Dream and the Case for Structural Keynesianism,* published in 1998.

Dimitri B. Papadimitriou is president of the Jerome Levy Economics Institute, executive vice president of Bard College, and Jerome Levy Professor of Economics at Bard College. His current research focuses on poverty and employment issues. He is examining the effects of demographic shifts on the labor market in an evaluation of the need to revise policies concerning employment and Social Security. Professor Papadimitriou has been appointed vice chairman of the Trade Deficit Review Commission, a bipartisan congressional panel.

Sumner M. Rosen taught social welfare policy at Columbia University until his retirement in 1993. He is vice chair of the National Jobs for All Coalition, a research and advocacy organization that has been committed since 1994 to restoring authentic full employment as a national and global policy priority.

Aaron W. Warner is Buttenweiser Professor Emeritus of human relations and dean emeritus of the School of General Studies of Columbia University where he has been director of University Seminars since 1976. For many years he was professor of economics at Columbia University, specializing in labor relations. He had previously served as regional director of the National Labor Relations Board.

Index

DATE DUE

~~JAN 08 2001~~			
			Printed in USA

HIGHSMITH #45230